This book should be read in its original Japanese right-to-left format.
Please turn it around to begin!

Original story and screenplay written and directed by
Hayao Miyazaki

MIYAZAKI'S
SPIRITED AWAY

1 of 5

Unedited English-Language Adaptation/Cindy Davis Hewitt & Donald H. Hewitt
Original Japanese Script Translation/Linda Hoaglund & Jim Hubbert

Film Comic Adaptation/Yuji Oniki
Lettering/Susan Daigle-Leach
Design & Layout/tee graphics
Editors/Alvin Lu, Carl Gustav Horn

Sen to Chihiro no Kamikakushi (Spirited Away)
Copyright © 2001 Studio Ghibli – NDDTM. All rights reserved. First published in Japan by Tokuma Shoten Co., Ltd.

Printed in China

Published by
VIZ Media, LLC
P.O. Box 77010
San Francisco, CA 94107

First printing, August 2002
Seventh printing, October 2018

W9-BIP-984

ViZ mEDIA

RATED
PARENTAL ADVISORY
SPIRITED AWAY is
suitable for all ages.
FOR ALL AGES
ratings.viz.com

124.2	FX:	SU [fsh]
125.3	FX:	SUUUU [hhhhhh]
126.3	FX:	KOTO
		[sound of walking on wood]
126.4	FX:	KOTO KOTO
		[walking on wood]
126.5	FX:	KOTO KOTO KOTO...
		[walking on wood]
127.1	FX:	KOTO KOTO KOTO...
		[walking on wood]
127.4.1	FX:	YURAAAA [fwomm]
127.4.2	FX:	KOTO KOTO...
		[walking on wood]
128.1	FX:	KOTO KOTO
		[walking on wood]
128.2	FX:	KOTO KOTO
		[walking on wood]
129.4-5	FX:	PIYOOON [hop]
129.5-6	FX:	PIYOOON [hop]
129.6	FX:	KYAHAHAHA...
		[hee hee hee]
130.4	FX:	GU [tuk]
130.5-6	FX:	PIYOOON [hop]
131.1	FX:	GU [fup]
131.2	FX:	BA [fwoosh]
131.4	FX:	SA [fsh]
131.5	FX:	DA [tugg]
131.6	FX:	BA [fwish]
132.1	FX:	TA TA TA [tmp tmp tmp]
132.2	FX:	TA [tmp]
132.3	FX:	SA [fsh]
132.4	FX:	BUWA [fwoosh]
133.2	FX:	SU [fsh]
133.4	FX:	BATA BATA [tup tup]
133.5	FX:	SA [fsh]
133.8	FX:	KOTO... [tok]
134.3	FX:	FU [fup]
134.4	FX:	BECHA [plipp]
134.5	FX:	KYOTON... [hmmm..]
135.1.1	FX:	TA TA TA... [tmp tmp tmp]
135.1.2	FX:	DOYA DOYA DOYA
		[thwud thwud thwud]
135.2	FX:	DOYA DOYA [thwud thwud]
138.1	FX:	SU... [fsh]
138.2	FX:	PO... [zing]
142.2	FX:	SU... [fsh]
145.3	FX:	KOKU... [nod]
147.3	FX:	GYU [clench]
147.4	FX:	SU... [fsh]

148.1	FX:	SUKKU [fsh]
148.5	FX:	DOYA DOYA... [wump wump]
148.6	FX:	GARA GARA [zhoop zhoop]
149.4	FX:	GARA GARA... [zhoop zhoop]
149.5	FX:	PISHA [klak]
152.1	FX:	ZORO ZORO [foom foom]
152.2	FX:	KOTO... [tok]
152.4	FX:	KOTO... [tok]
153.1-2	FX:	HYUUUU... [fweeeee]
153.2	FX:	GOOOO... [whrrrrrrr]
154.1	FX:	HYUUUU... [fweeeee]
154.2	FX:	GOKU... [gulp]
154.3	FX:	SOOO [fmmm]
155.2	FX:	SU [fip]
155.8	FX:	DOTE DOTE [thud thud]
156.4	FX:	HYUUUU... [fweeeee]
157.5	FX:	HAA HAA... [huff huff]
158.1	FX:	TON [tup]
158.2	FX:	GUGU... [krrrpp]
158.3-4	FX:	BARI [krakk]
158.4	FX:	DADA [fwuwump]
159.1-3	FX:	DADADADADADADADA...
		[wpwpwpwpwpwpwpwp]
159.4-5	FX:	DA...DAADADADADA...
		[wp...wmp...wpwpwpwp]
160.1-4	FX:	
		DADADADADADADADADADA
		[wpwpwpwpwpwpwpwpwpwp]
160.2-4	FX:	KYAAAAAA... [aieeeeee]
161.1-2	FX:	DA DA DA... [tmp tmp tmp]
162.1-4	FX:	DADADADADADADADADA
		[tmptmptmptmptmptmptmptmptmp]
162.4	FX:	BECHA [fwump]
163.2	FX:	GARA... [zhoop]
163.4.1	FX:	TAN TAN [clatter clatter]
163.4.2	FX:	GARA GARA [zhoop zhoop]
164.1.1	FX:	JYAAA JYAAA [water tap]
164.1.2	FX:	GARA GARA [zhoop zhoop]
164.2	FX:	KOTO KOTO KOTO
		[tok tok tok]
164.3.1	FX:	PUHAAAAA [exhale smoke]
164.3.2	FX:	JYUUU [sound of frying]
164.3.3	FX:	TON TON [tmp tmp]
166.1	FX:	GOOOO... [whrrrrrr]
166.2	FX:	TA TA TA... [tmp tmp tmp]
167.2	FX:	KIII... [creak]
167.4	FX:	PATAN [chnk]

Written and Directed by

HAYAO MIYAZAKI

MIYAZAKI'S SPIRITED AWAY

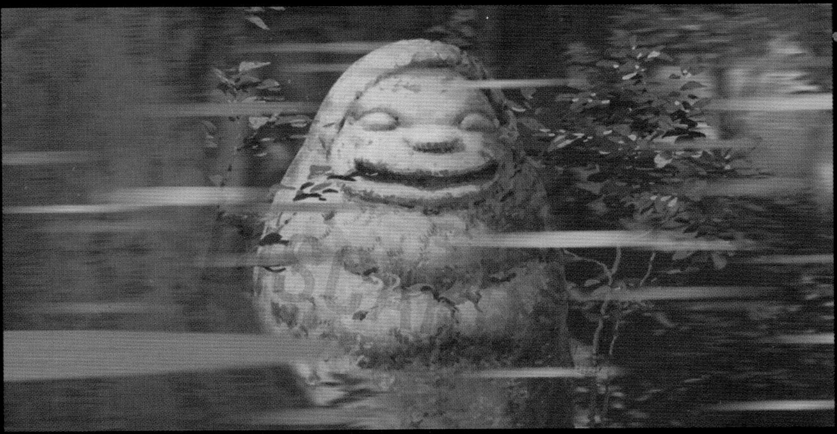

1 of 5

STUDIO GHIBLI LIBRARY

MAIN CHARACTERS

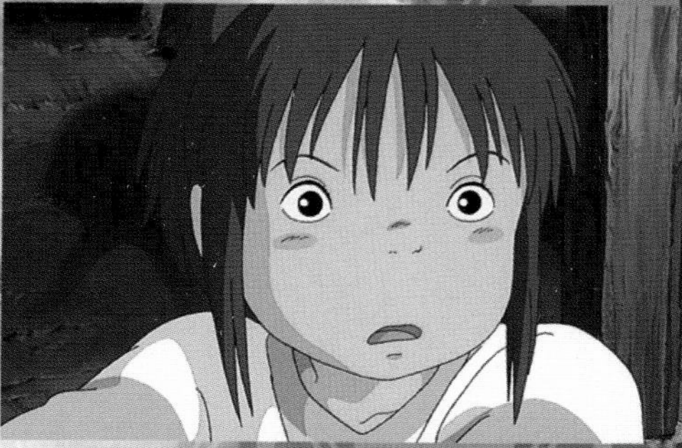

Chihiro Ogino

An average ten year old girl. She's disappointed her family's moving away from her hometown and her friends.

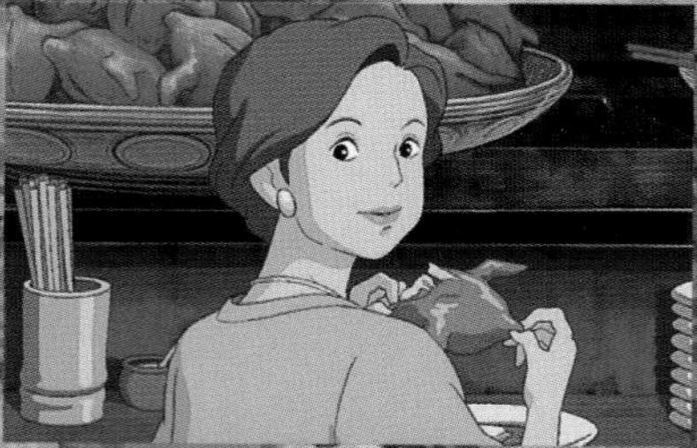

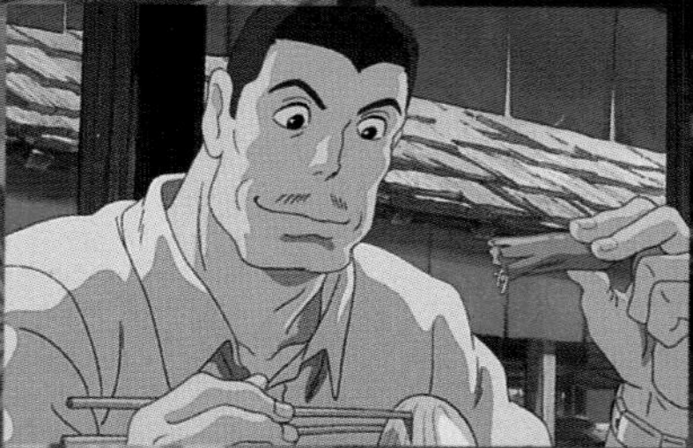

Mother

Chihiro's mother. 35 years old. Practical. Her husband's equal, she is a very direct kind of person.

Father

Chihiro's father. 38 years old. Employee at an architectural firm. An easygoing optimist. He tends to be overly confident everything will work out.

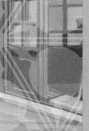

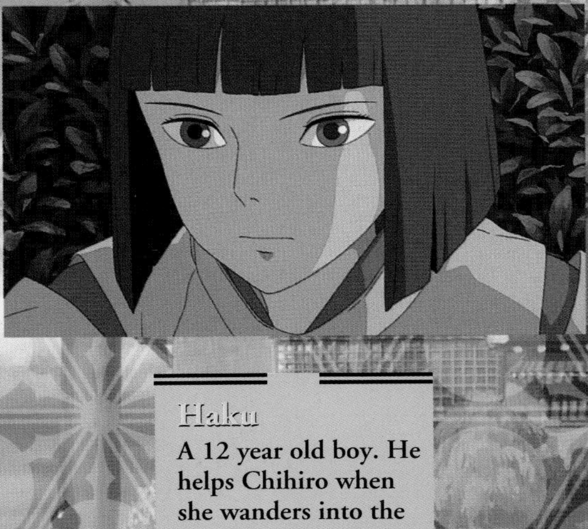

Haku

A 12 year old boy. He helps Chihiro when she wanders into the Abura-ya bath house. He seems to have known Chihiro for a long time.

スタジオジブリ作品
STUDIO GHIBLI

徳間書店・スタジオジブリ・日本テレビ
電通・ディズニー・東北新社・三菱商事

提携作品

©2001 二馬力・TGNDDTM

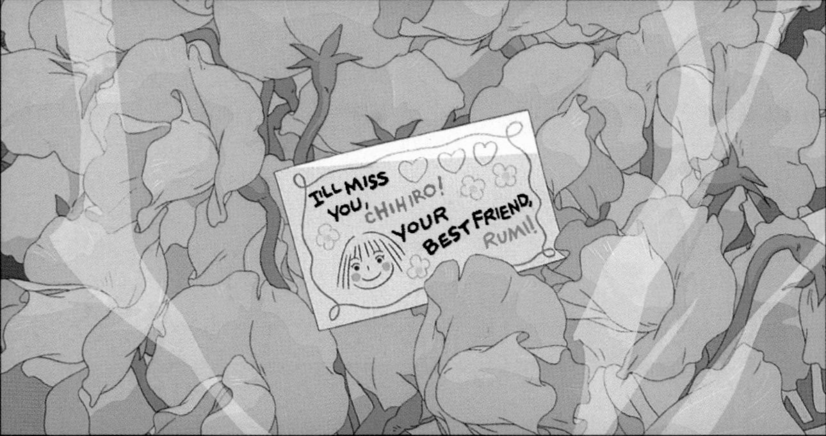
I'LL MISS YOU, CHIHIRO!
YOUR BEST FRIEND, RUMI!
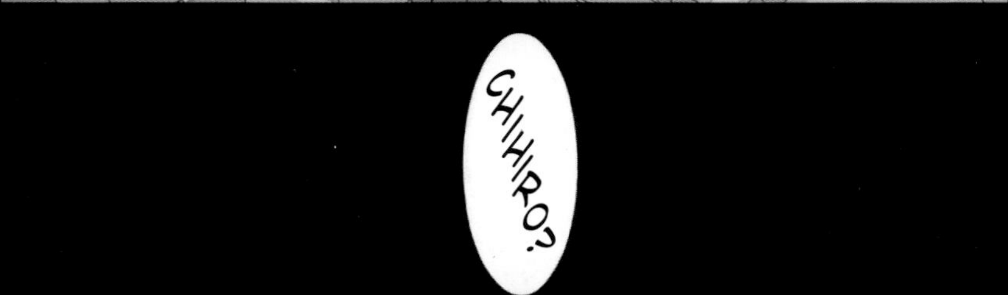
CHIHIRO?

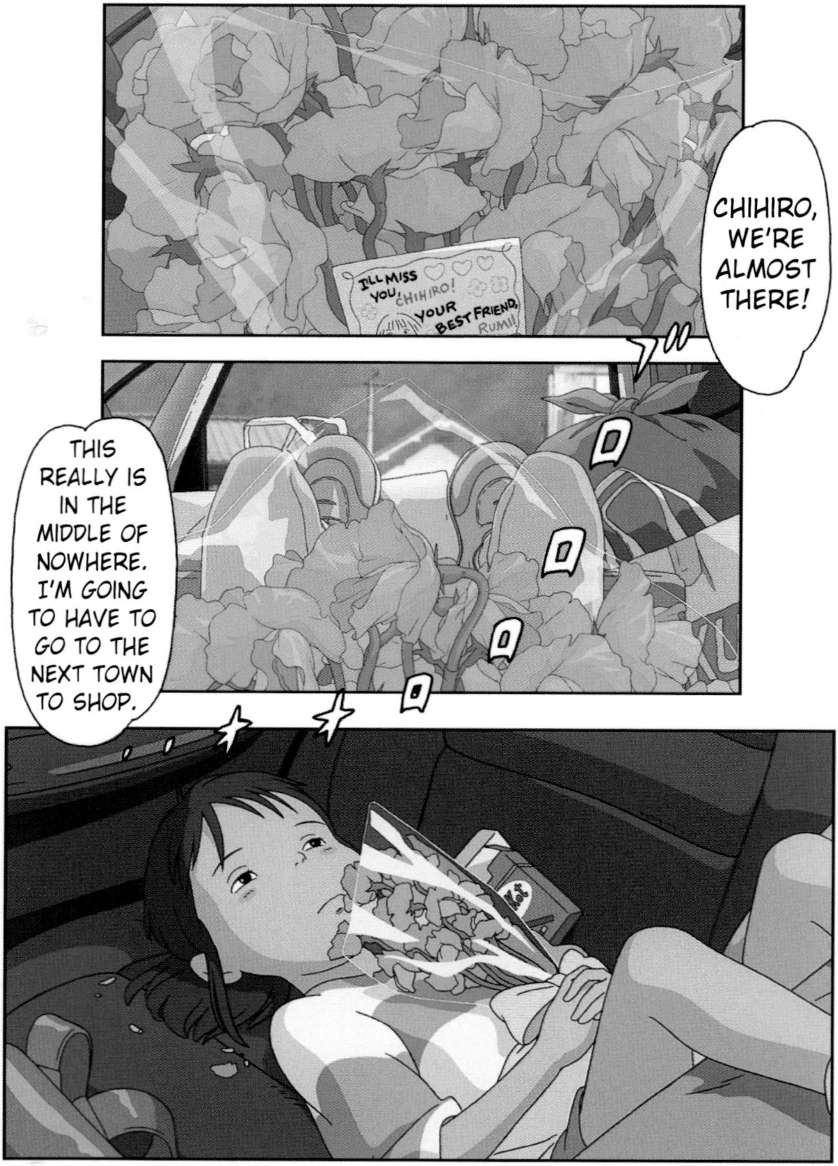
ILL MISS YOU, CHIHIRO! YOUR BEST FRIEND, RUMI!
CHIHIRO, WE'RE ALMOST THERE!
THIS REALLY IS IN THE MIDDLE OF NOWHERE. I'M GOING TO HAVE TO GO TO THE NEXT TOWN TO SHOP.

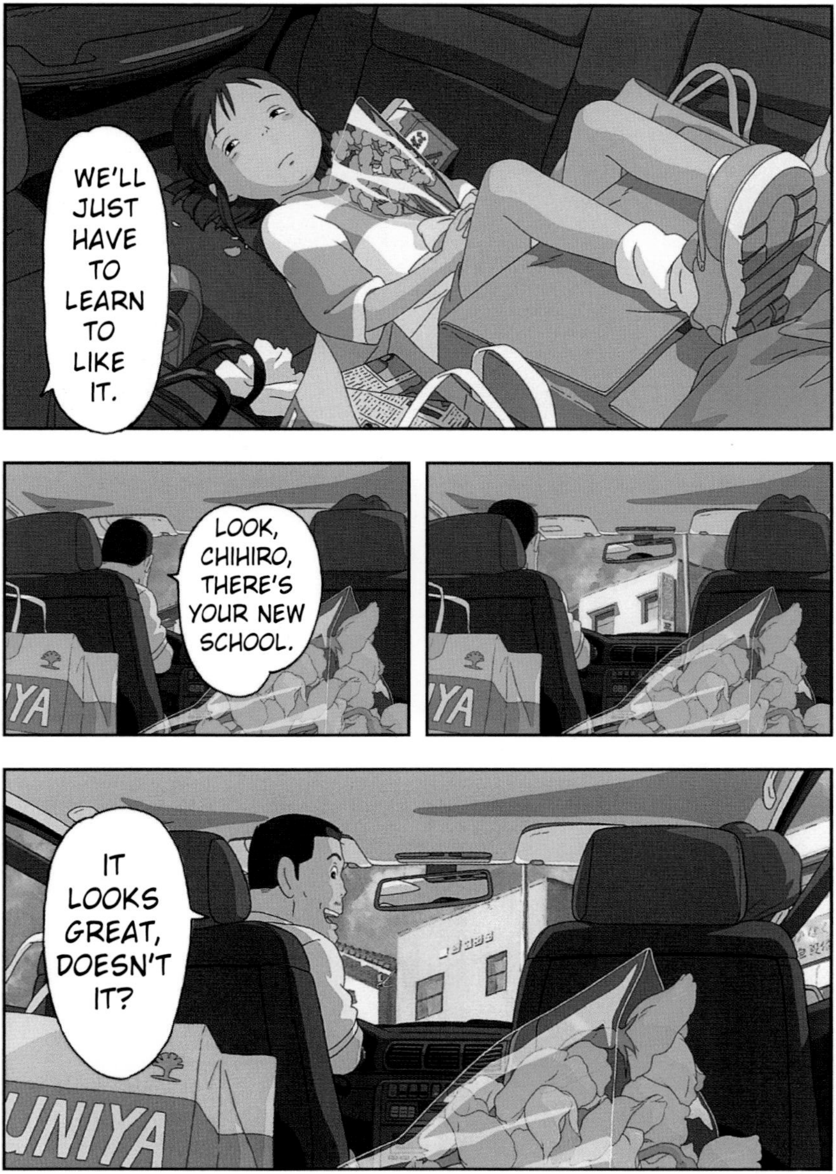
WE'LL JUST HAVE TO LEARN TO LIKE IT.
LOOK, CHIHIRO, THERE'S YOUR NEW SCHOOL.
IT LOOKS GREAT, DOESN'T IT?

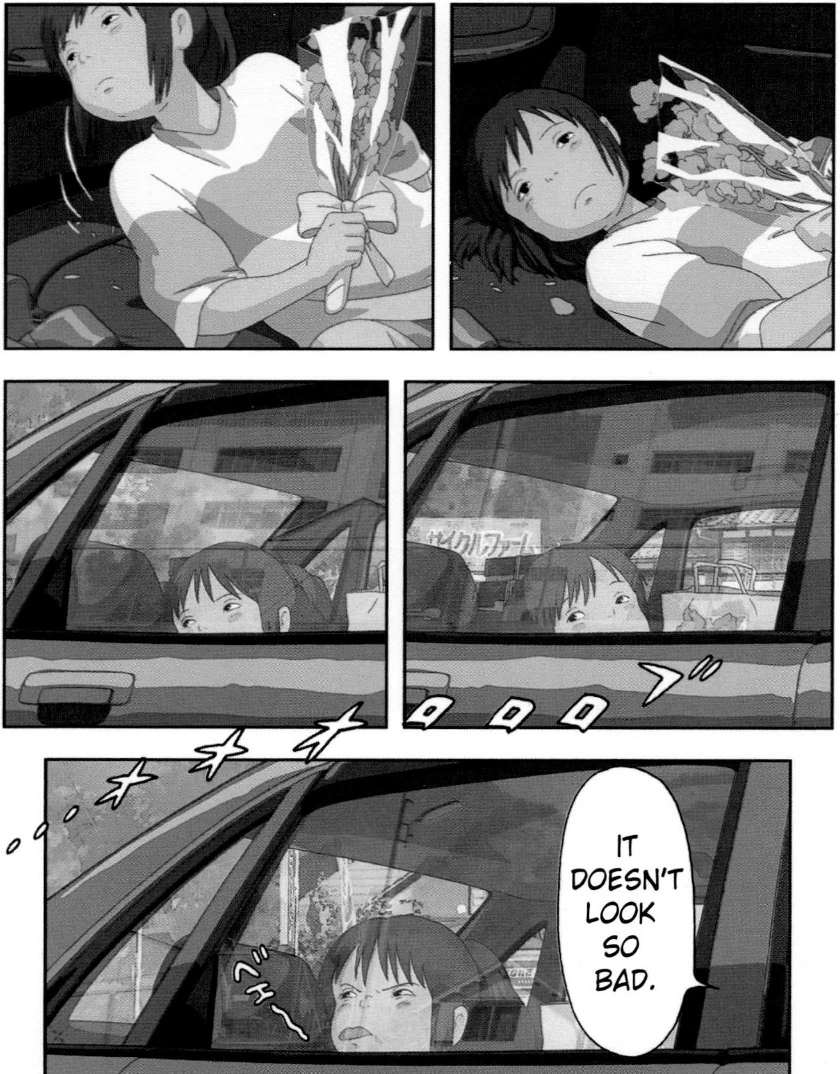
サイクルファーム
ブロロロオオオ…
IT DOESN'T LOOK SO BAD.
ベー〜

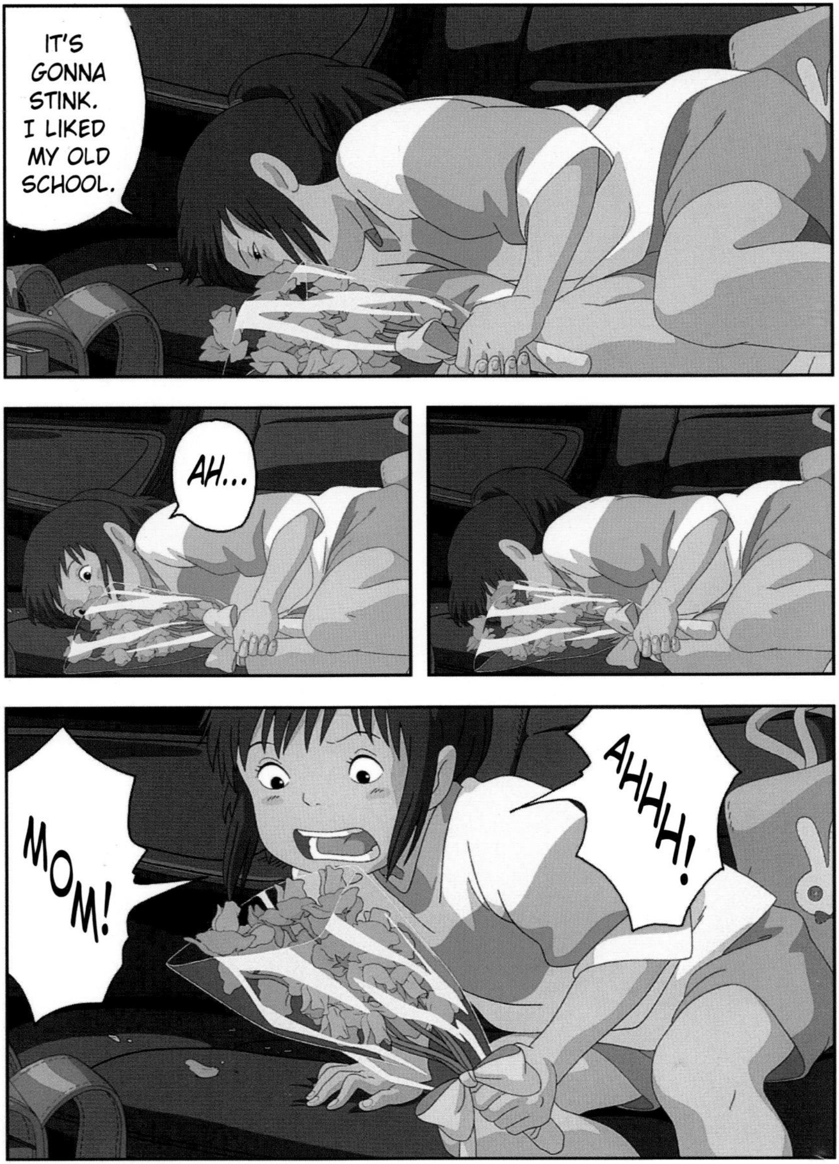
IT'S GONNA STINK. I LIKED MY OLD SCHOOL.
AH...
AHHHH!
MOM!

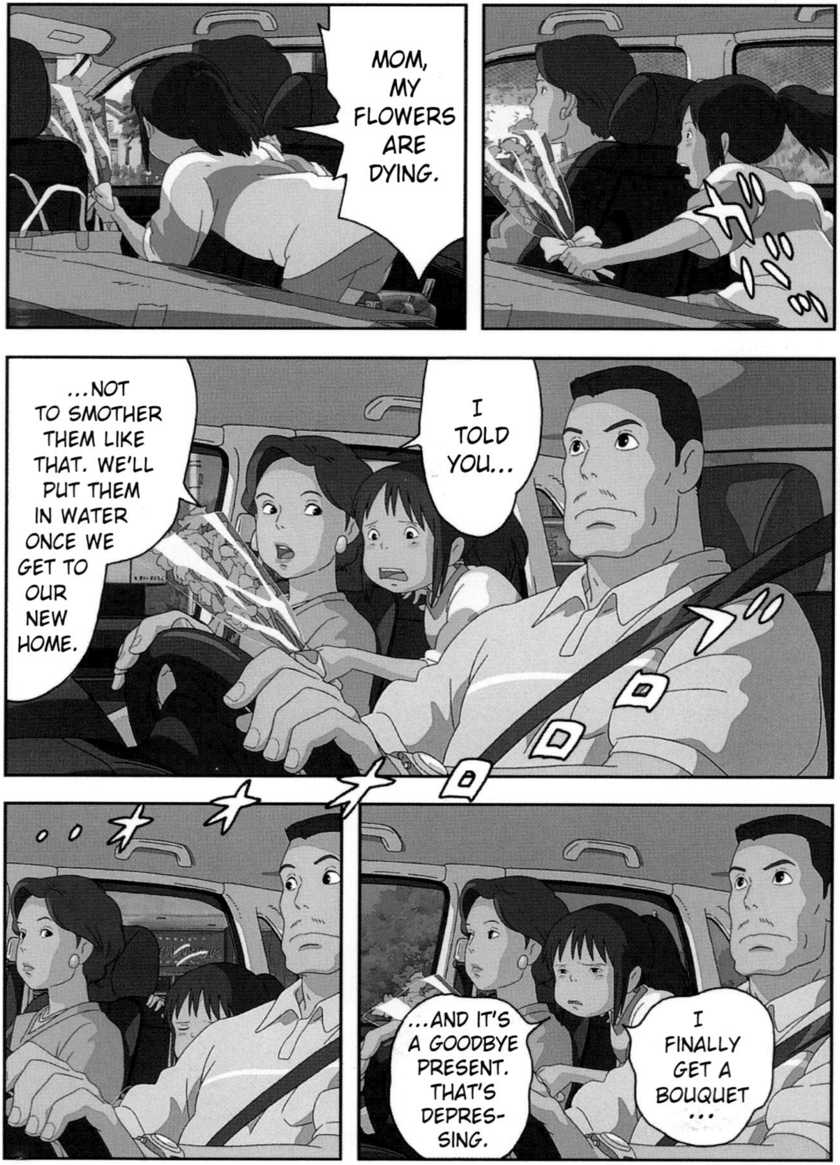
MOM, MY FLOWERS ARE DYING.
I TOLD YOU...
...NOT TO SMOTHER THEM LIKE THAT. WE'LL PUT THEM IN WATER ONCE WE GET TO OUR NEW HOME.
I FINALLY GET A BOUQUET...
...AND IT'S A GOODBYE PRESENT. THAT'S DEPRES-SING.

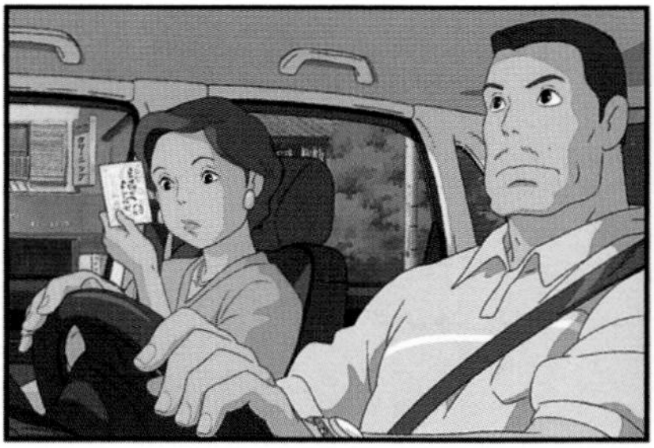

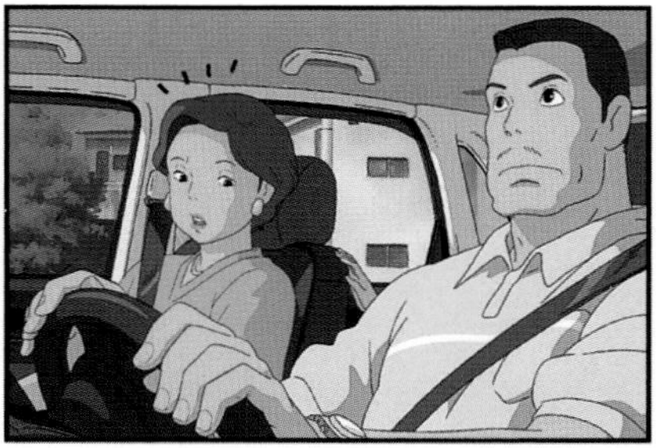

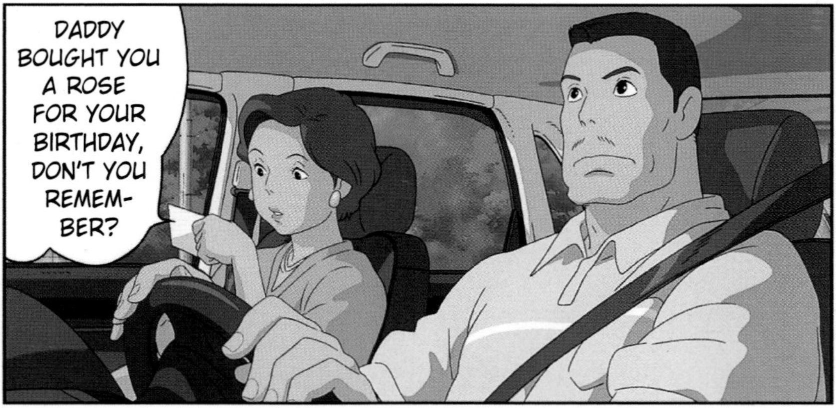
DADDY BOUGHT YOU A ROSE FOR YOUR BIRTHDAY, DON'T YOU REMEMBER?

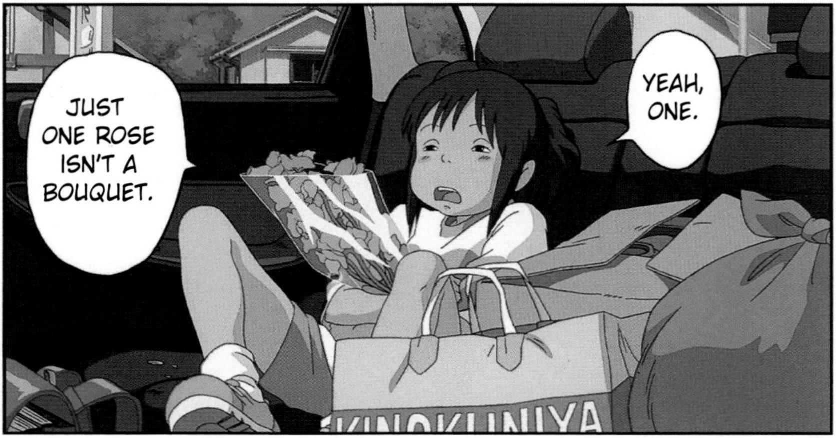
JUST ONE ROSE ISN'T A BOUQUET.
YEAH, ONE.
KINOKUNIYA

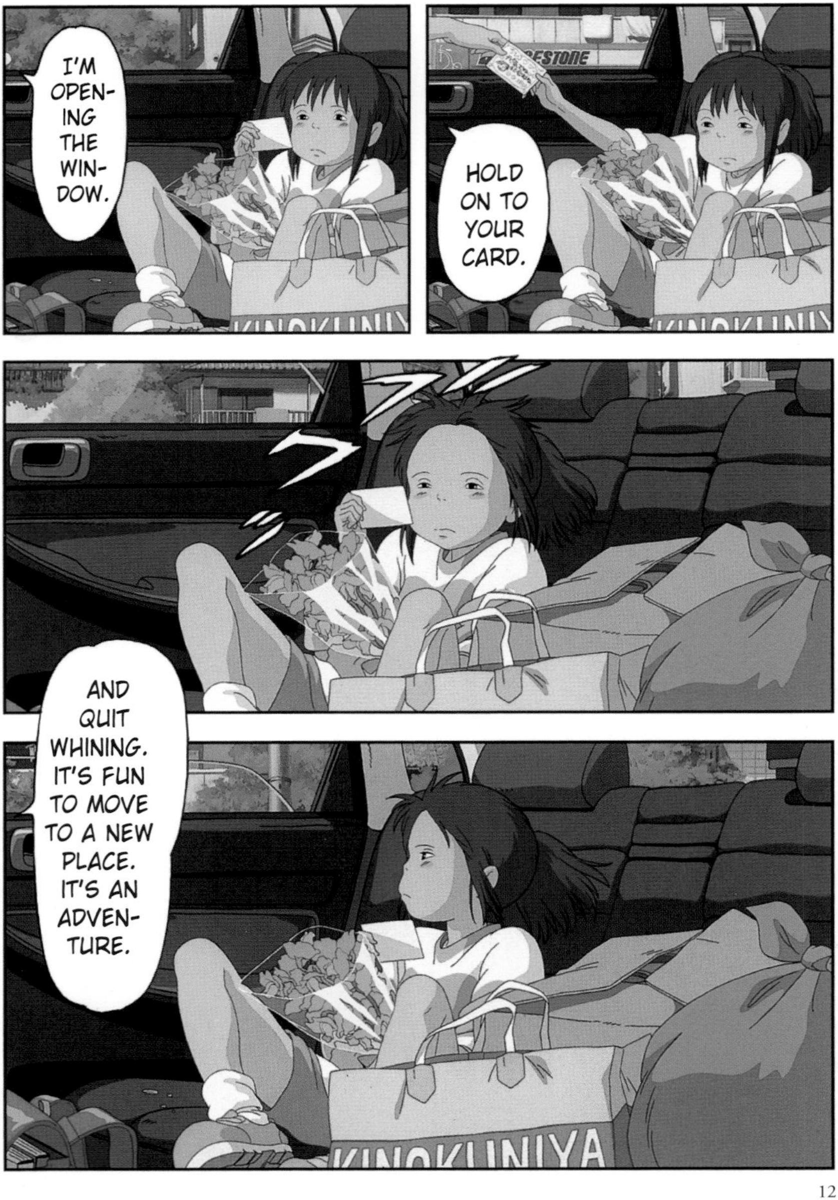
I'M OPENING THE WINDOW.
HOLD ON TO YOUR CARD.
AND QUIT WHINING. IT'S FUN TO MOVE TO A NEW PLACE. IT'S AN ADVENTURE.
KINOKUNIYA

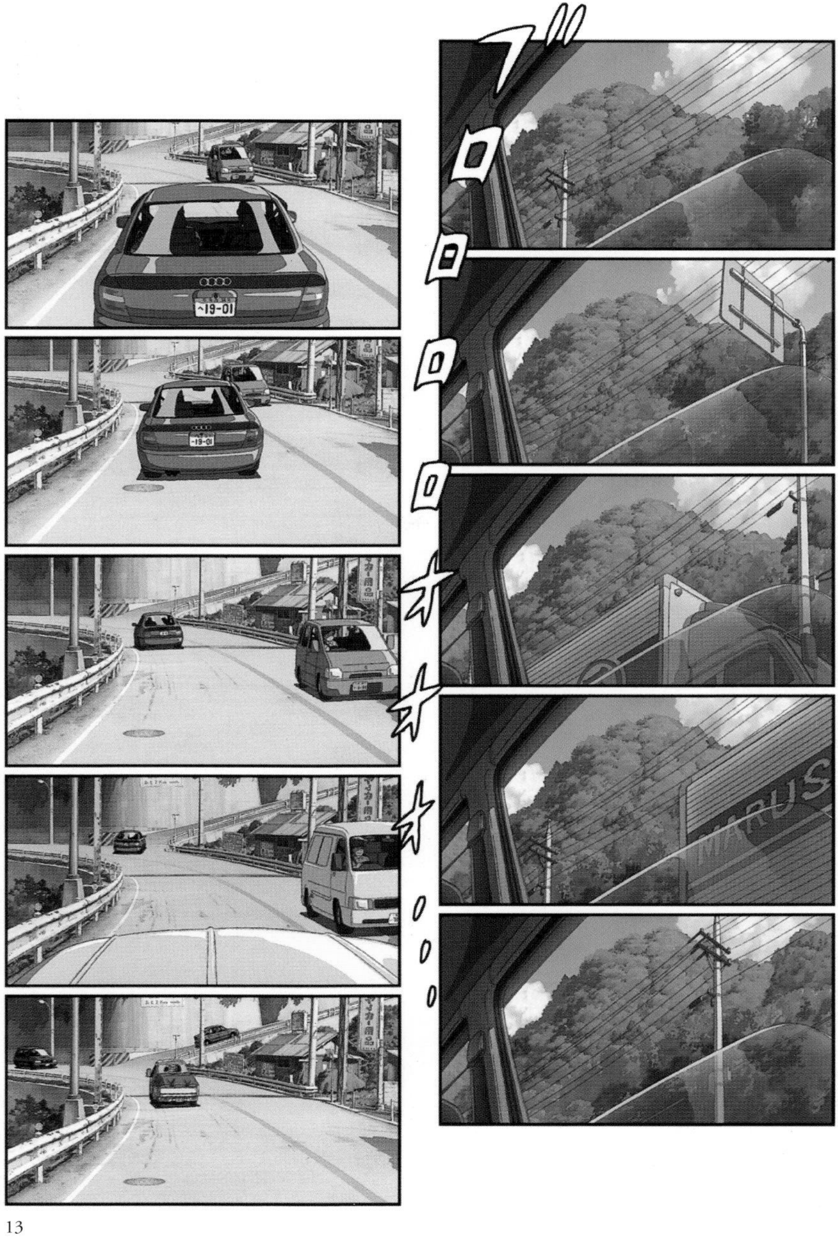
ブロロロロオオオ
MARUS
ヘ19-01

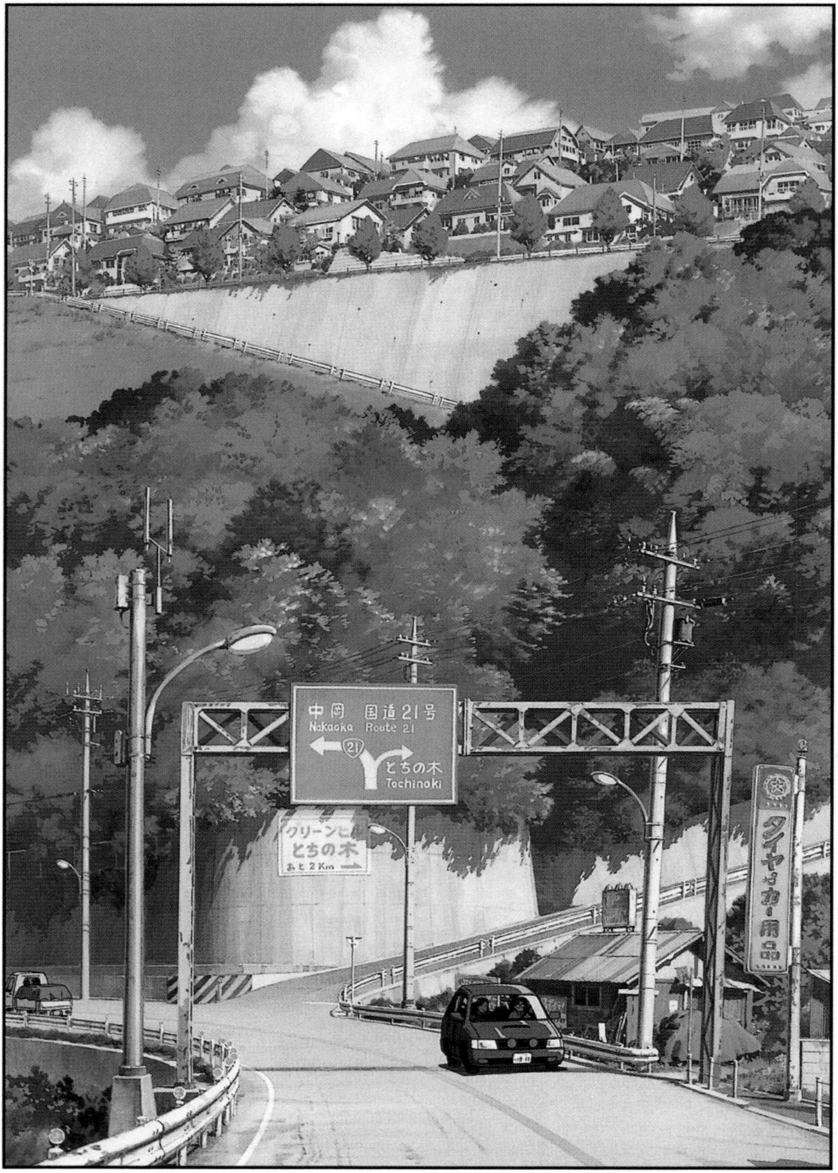
中岡　国道21号
Nakaoka　Route 21
21
とちの木
Tochinoki
クリーンヒ
とちの木
あと2Km
タイヤ・カー用品

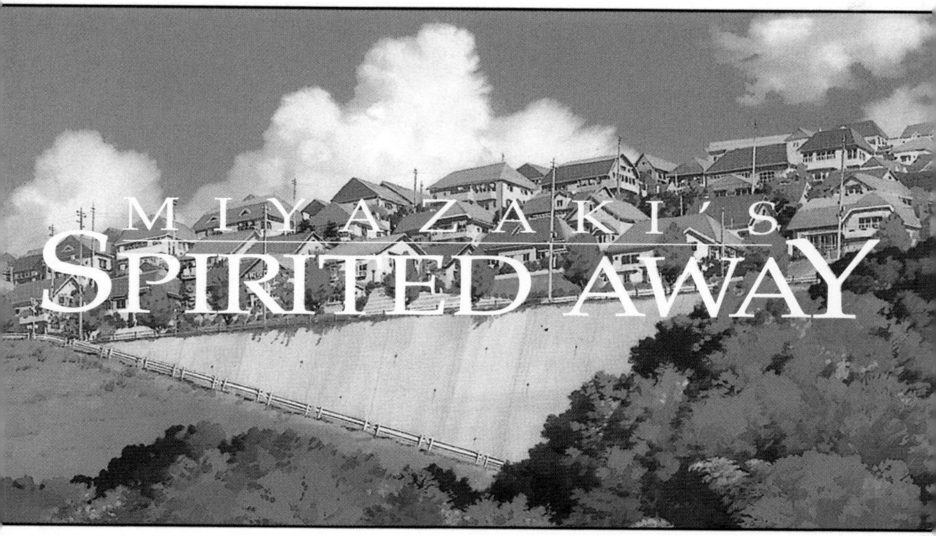
MIYAZAKI'S
SPIRITED AWAY

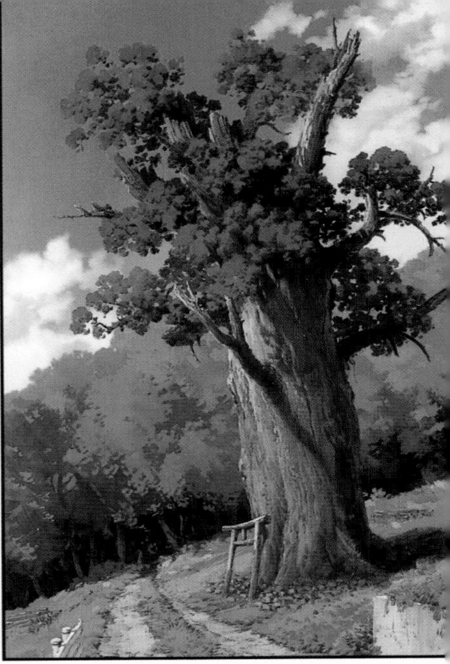

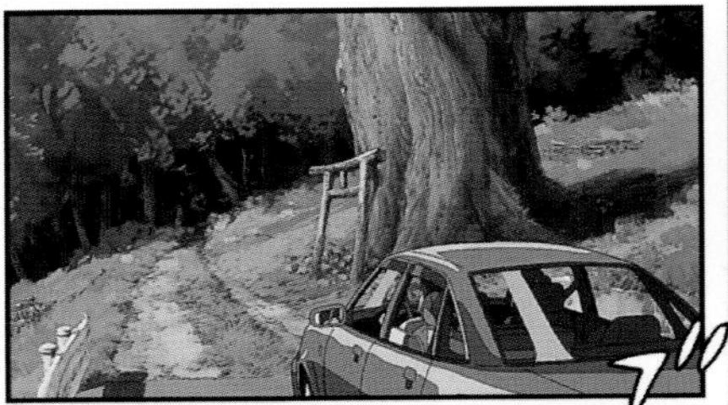

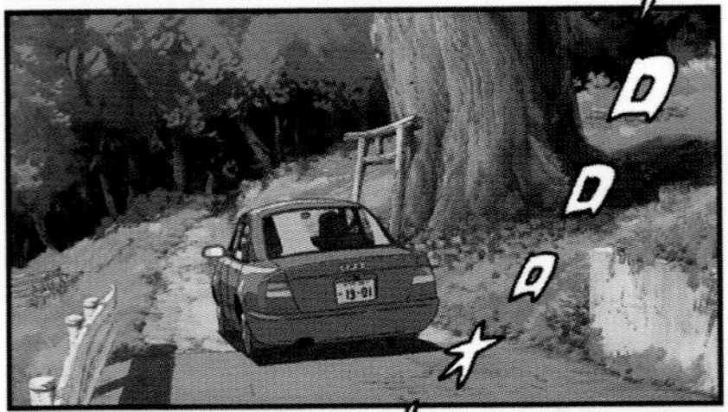

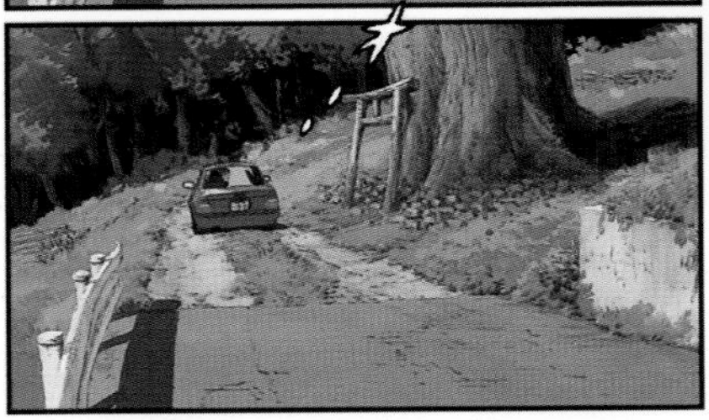

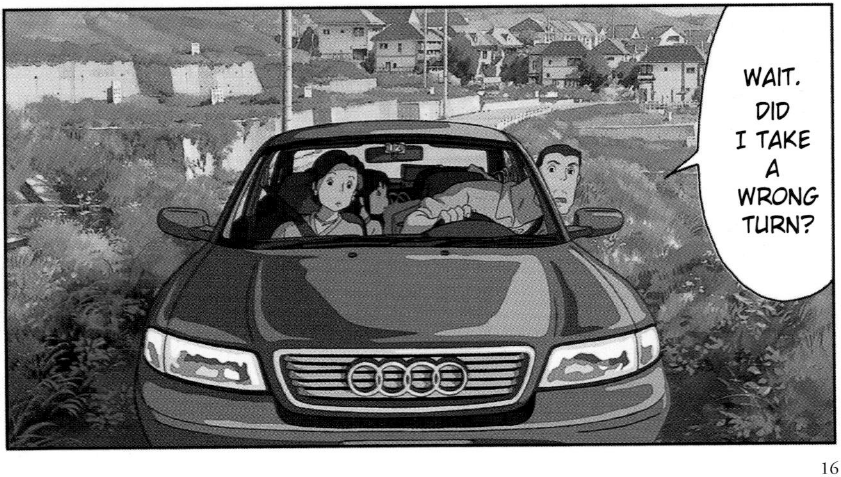
WAIT. DID I TAKE A WRONG TURN?

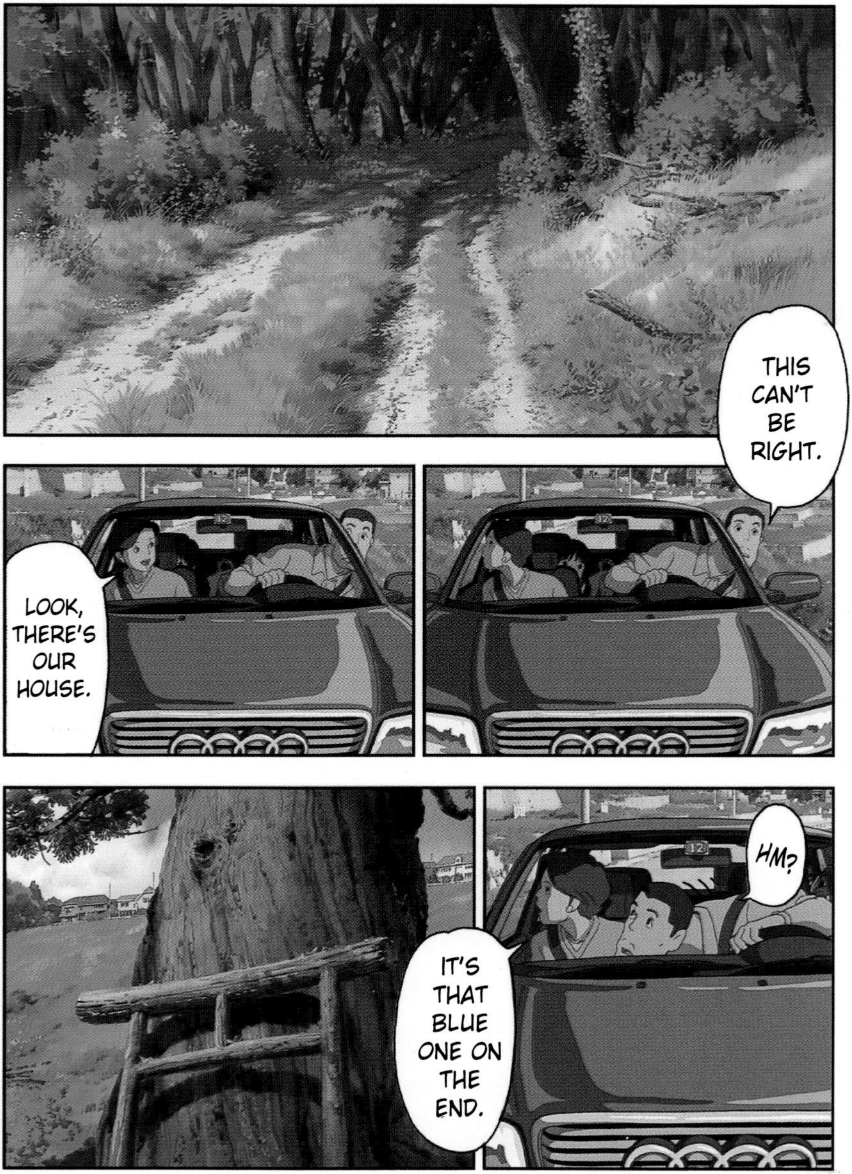
THIS CAN'T BE RIGHT.
LOOK, THERE'S OUR HOUSE.
HM?
IT'S THAT BLUE ONE ON THE END.

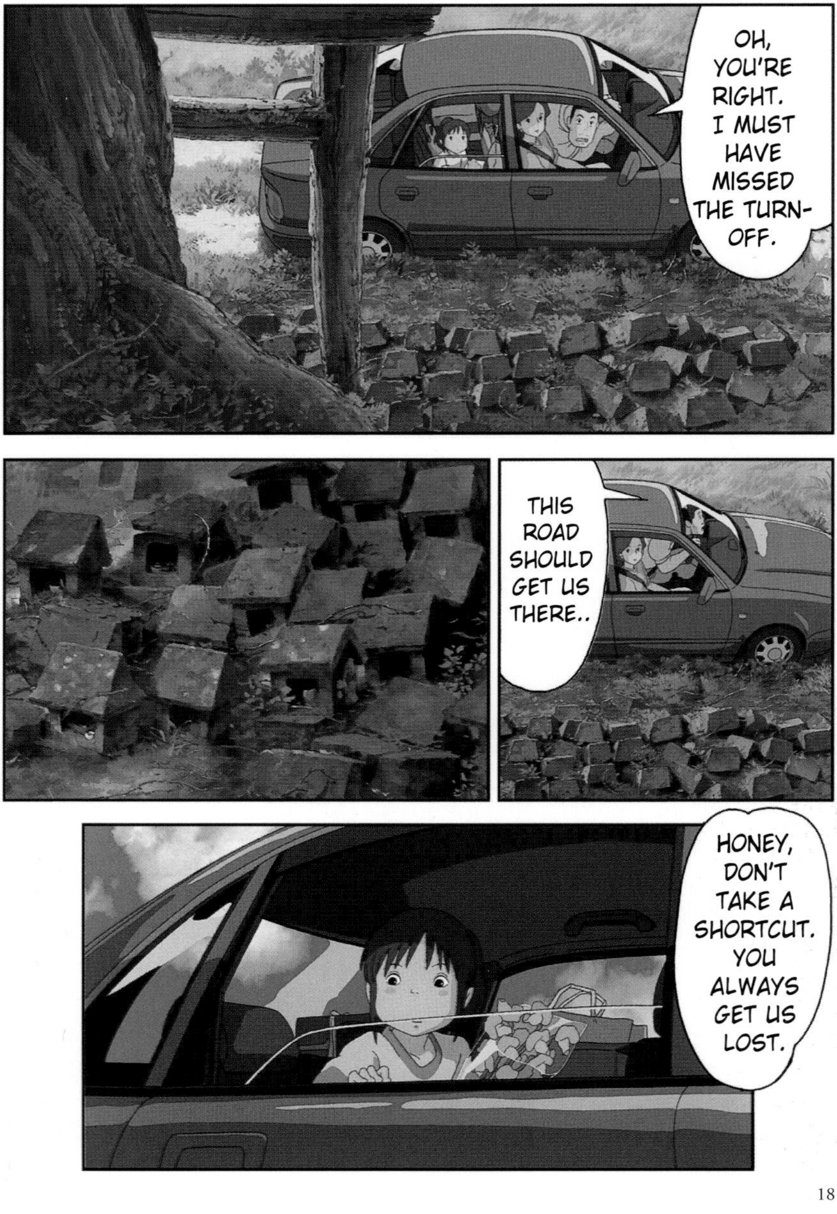
OH, YOU'RE RIGHT. I MUST HAVE MISSED THE TURN-OFF.
THIS ROAD SHOULD GET US THERE..
HONEY, DON'T TAKE A SHORTCUT. YOU ALWAYS GET US LOST.

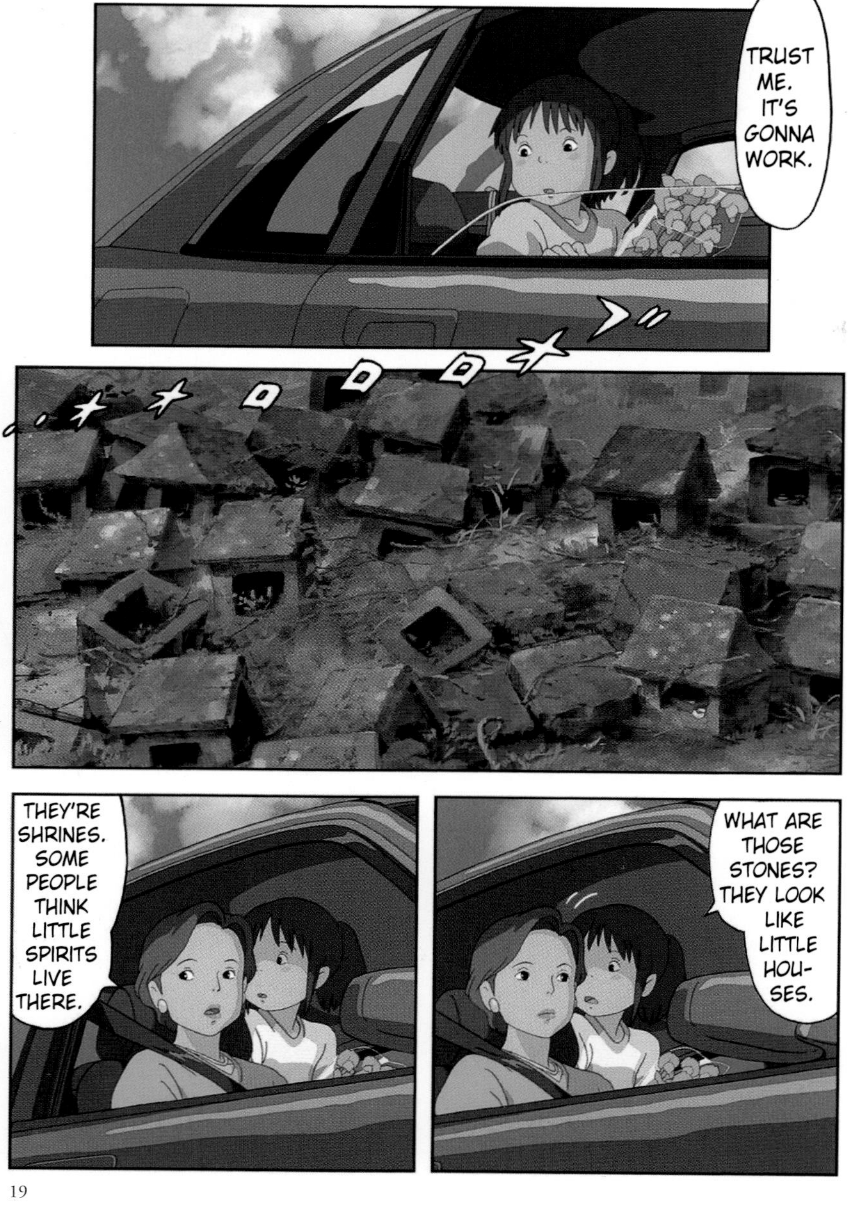
TRUST ME. IT'S GONNA WORK.
WHAT ARE THOSE STONES? THEY LOOK LIKE LITTLE HOU-SES.
THEY'RE SHRINES. SOME PEOPLE THINK LITTLE SPIRITS LIVE THERE.

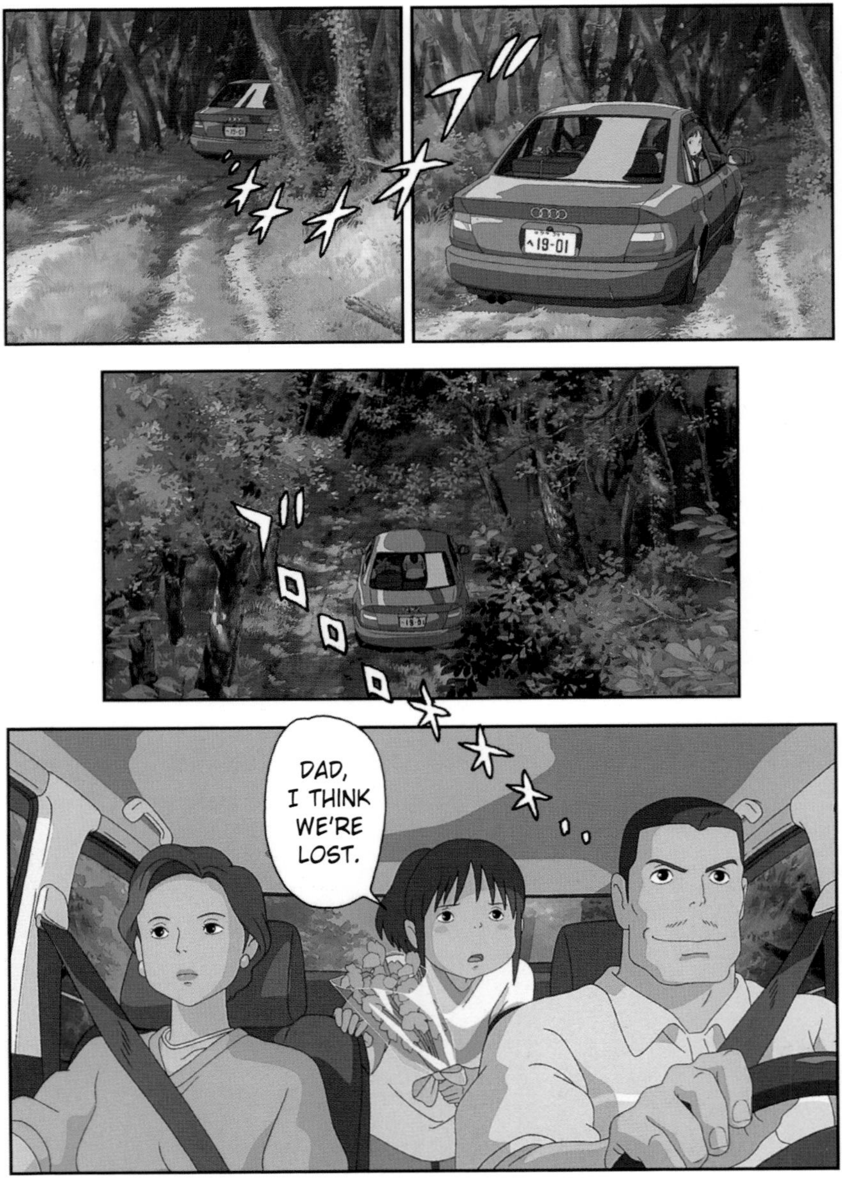
DAD, I THINK WE'RE LOST.

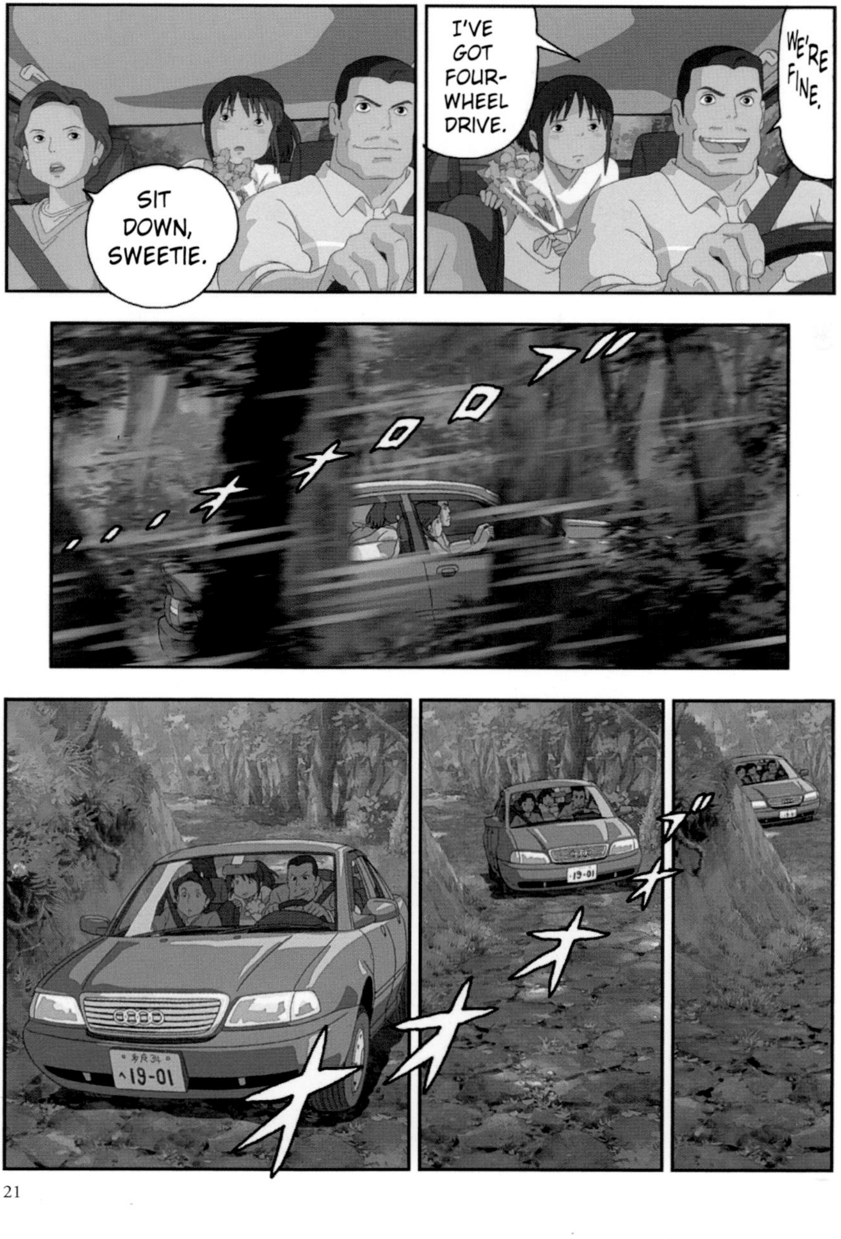
SIT DOWN, SWEETIE.
I'VE GOT FOUR-WHEEL DRIVE.
WE'RE FINE.

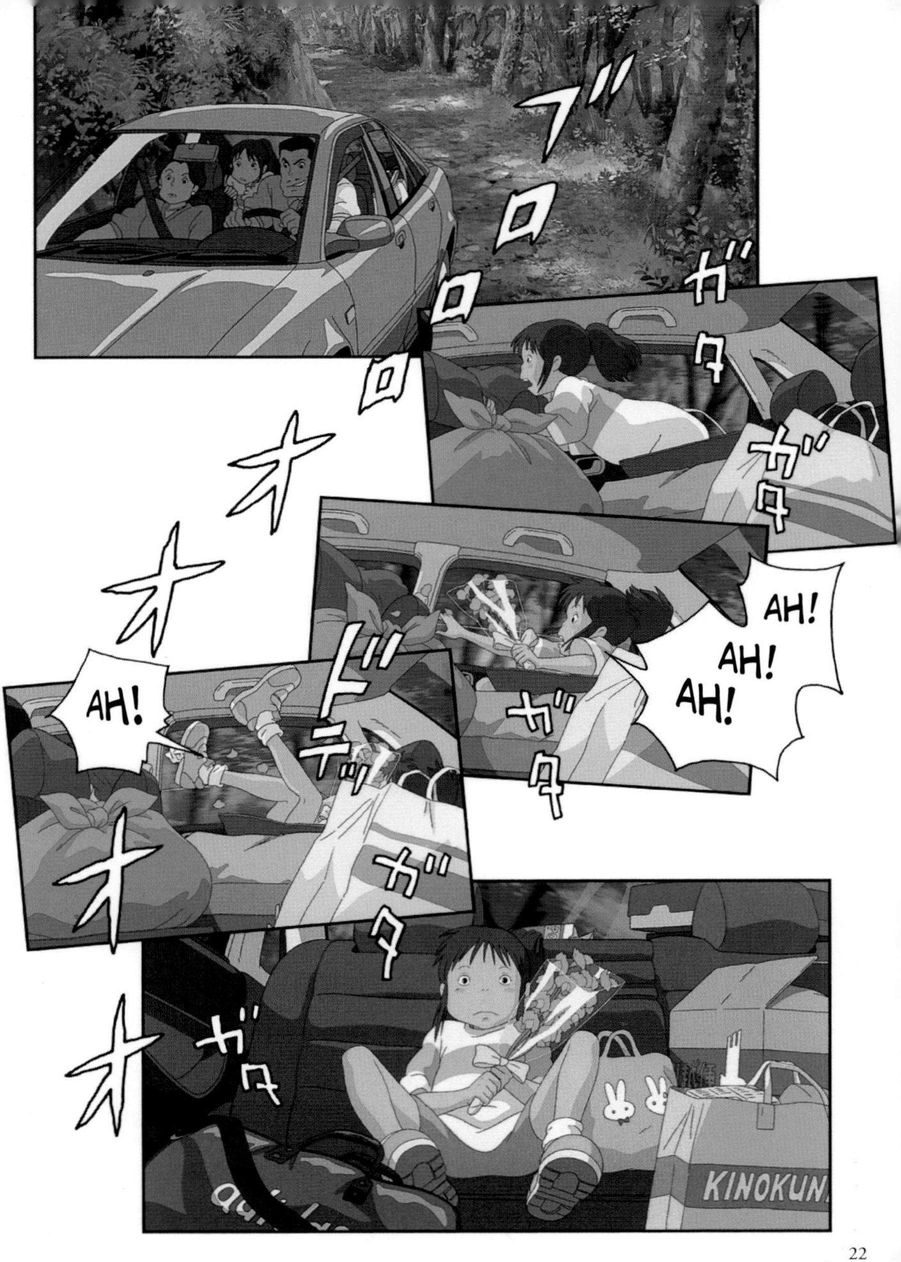
ブロロロオオオオ
ガタ
ガタ
AH! AH! AH!
ガタ
AH!
ドテッ
ガタ
ガタ

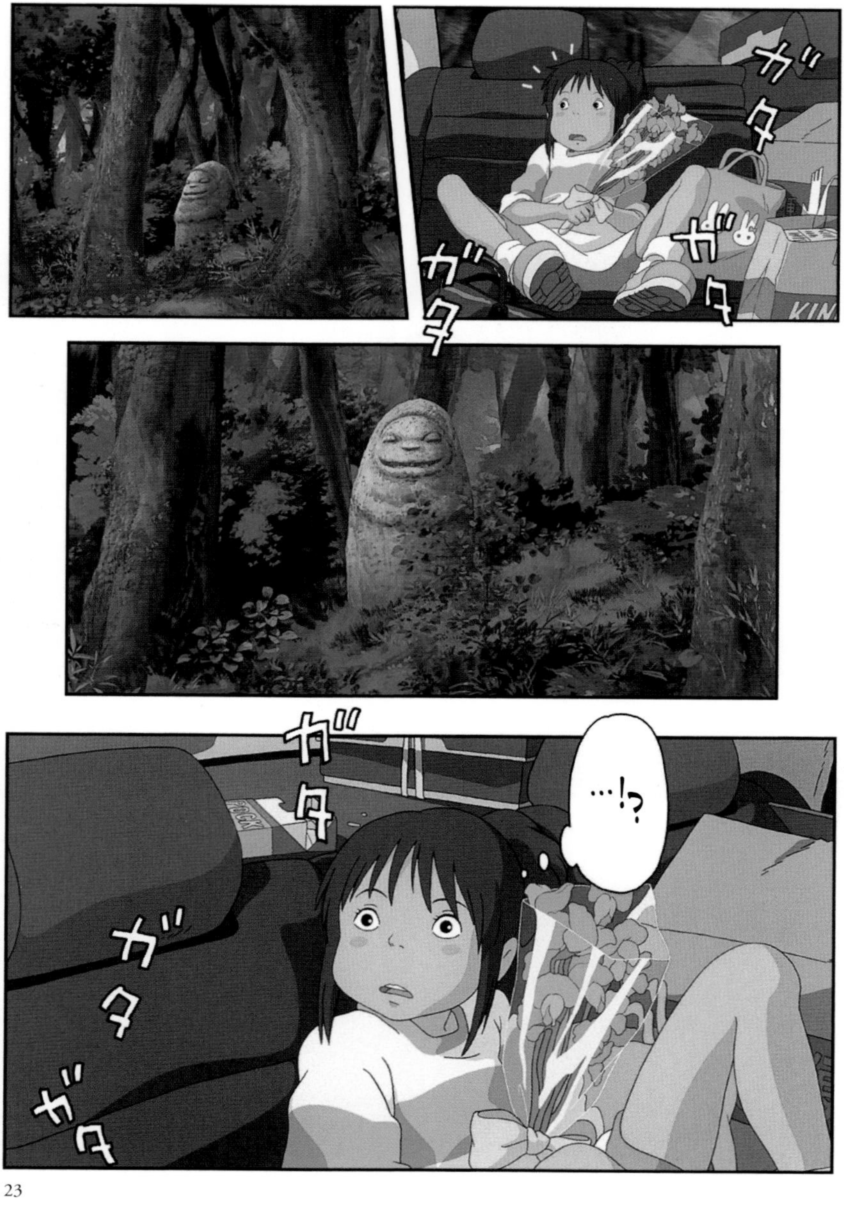
ガタ
ガタ
ガタ
ガタ
…!?
ガタ
ガタ

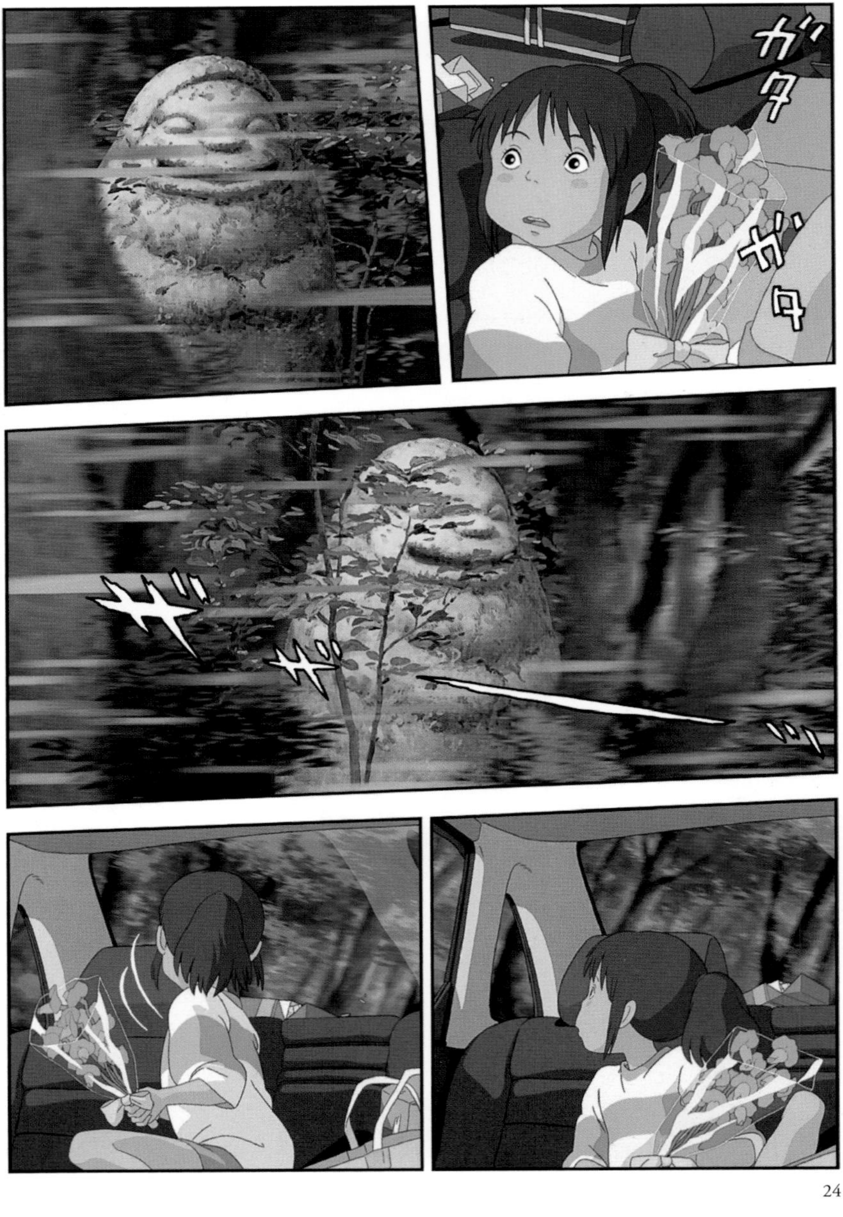
ガタ
ガタ
ザザ
ザザーッ

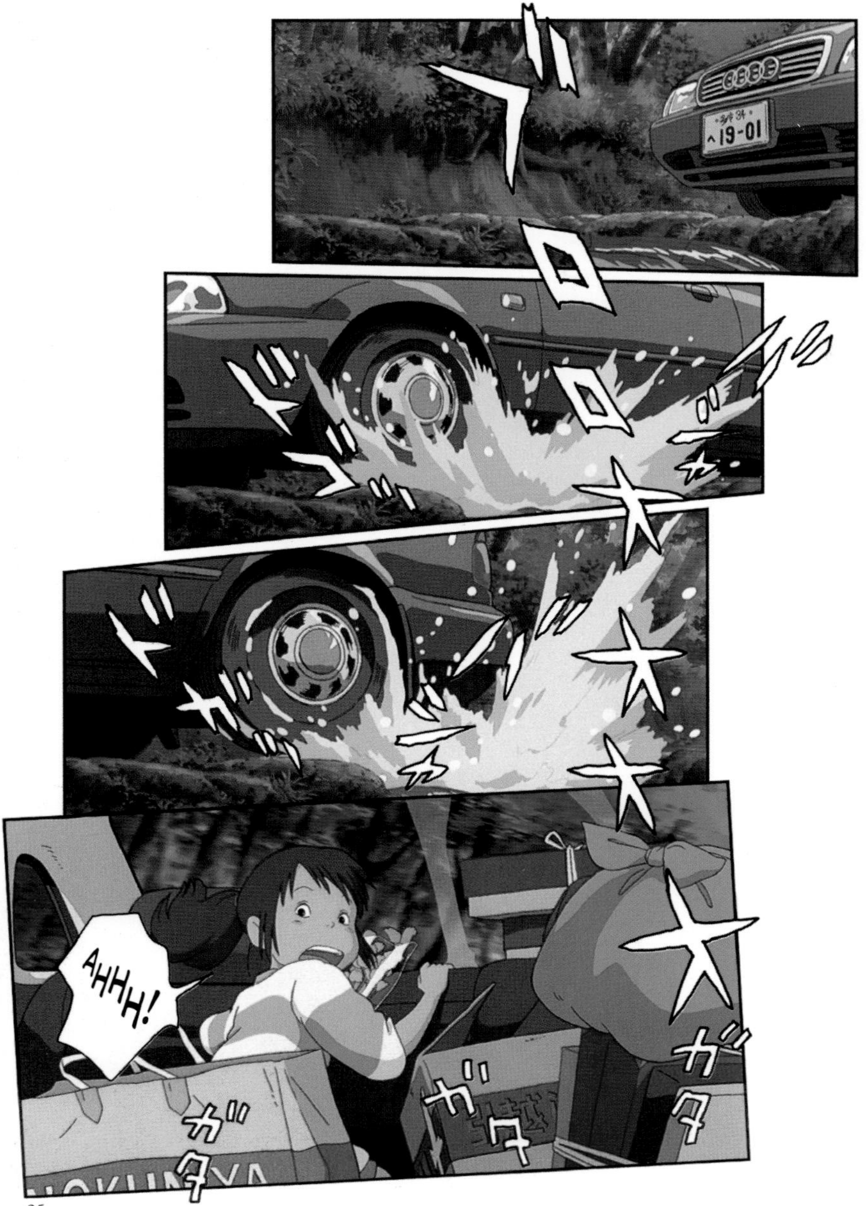
AHHH!

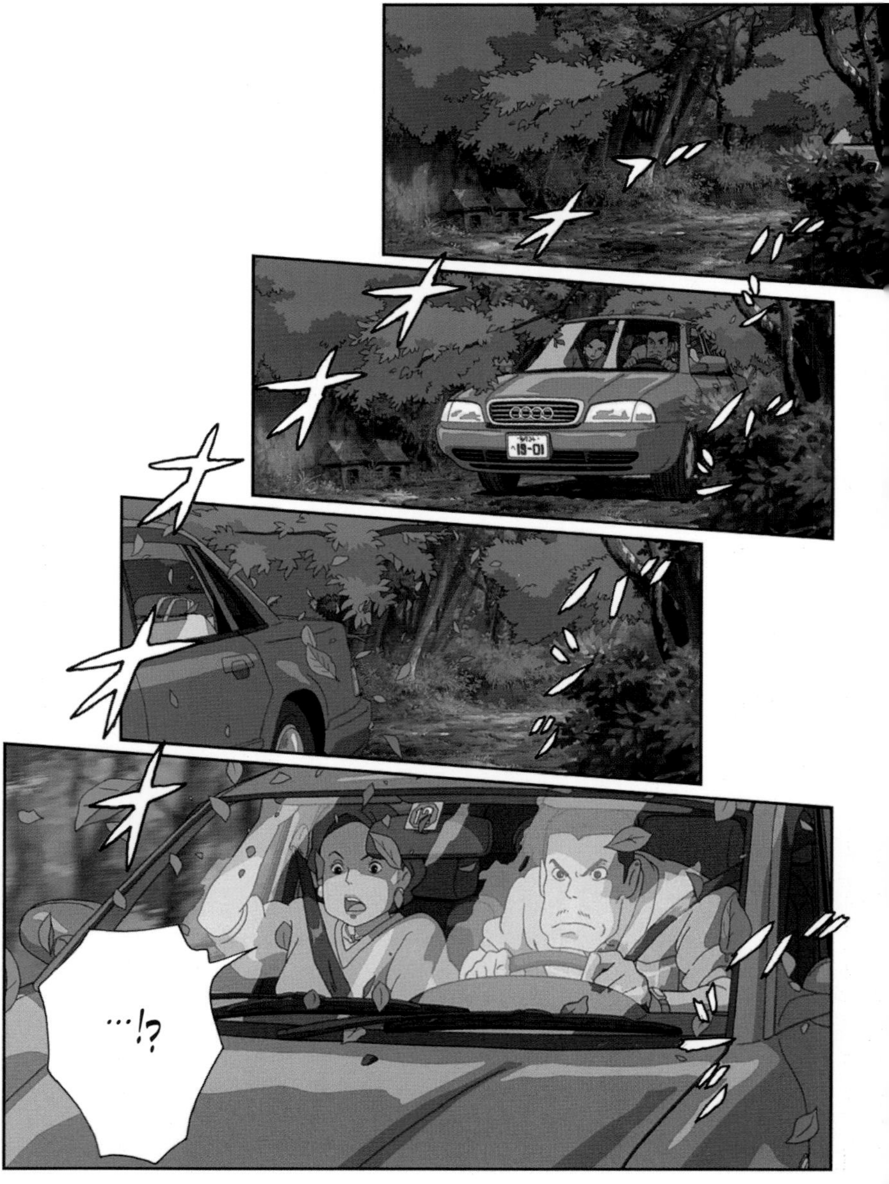
...!?

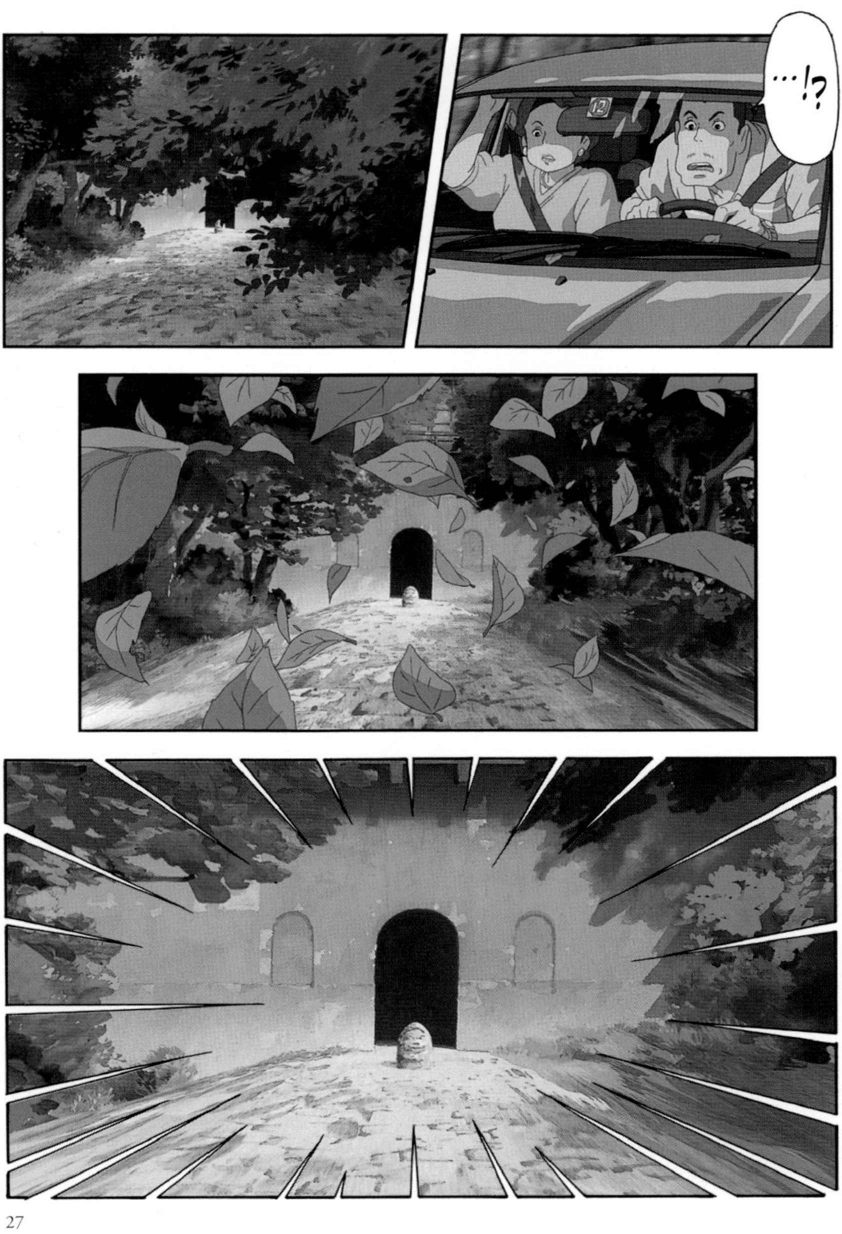
...!?

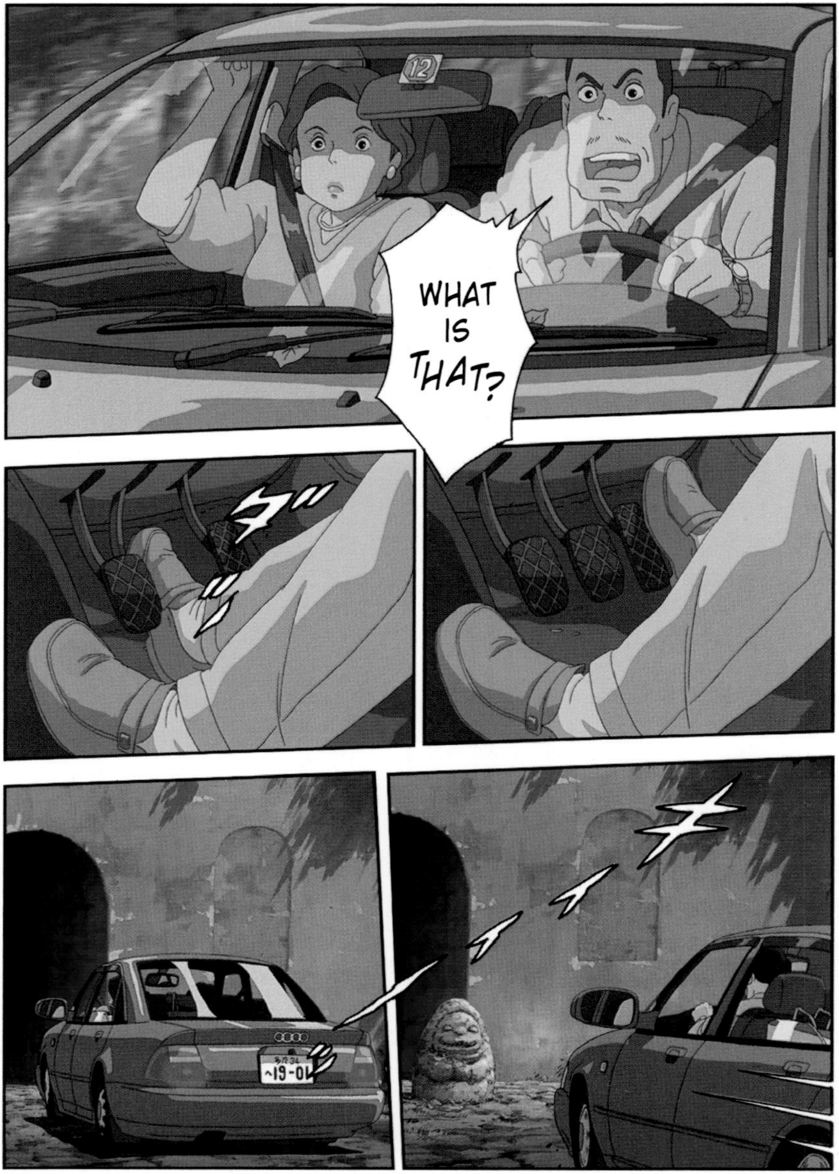
WHAT IS THAT?

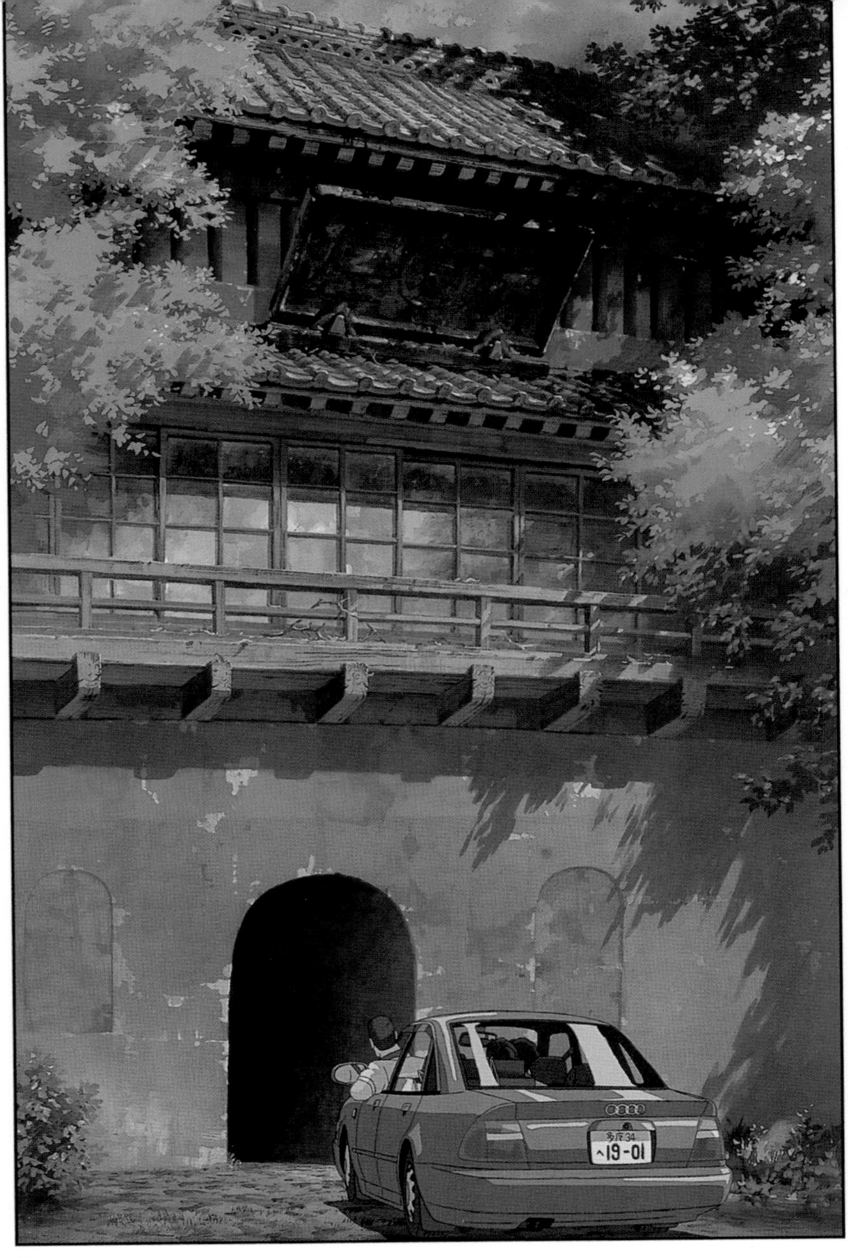
へ19-01

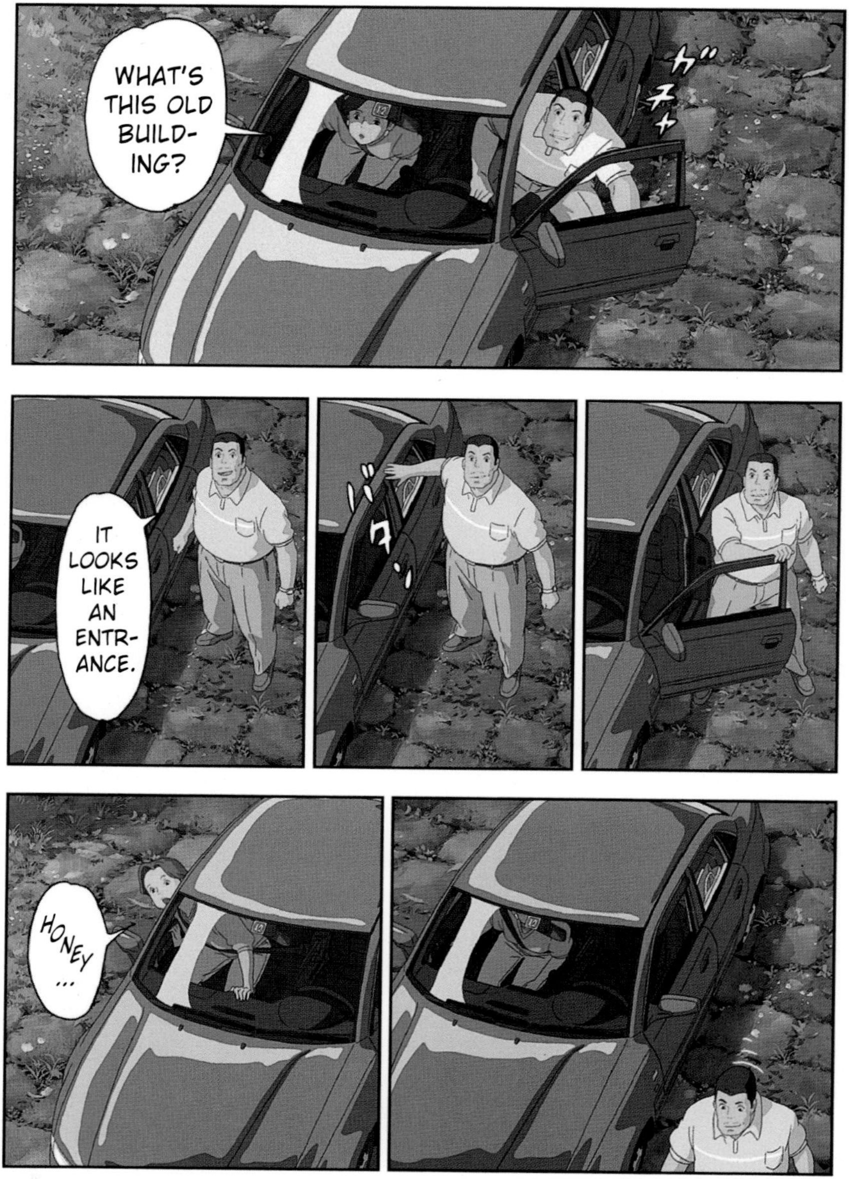
WHAT'S THIS OLD BUILD-ING?
IT LOOKS LIKE AN ENTR-ANCE.
HONEY ...

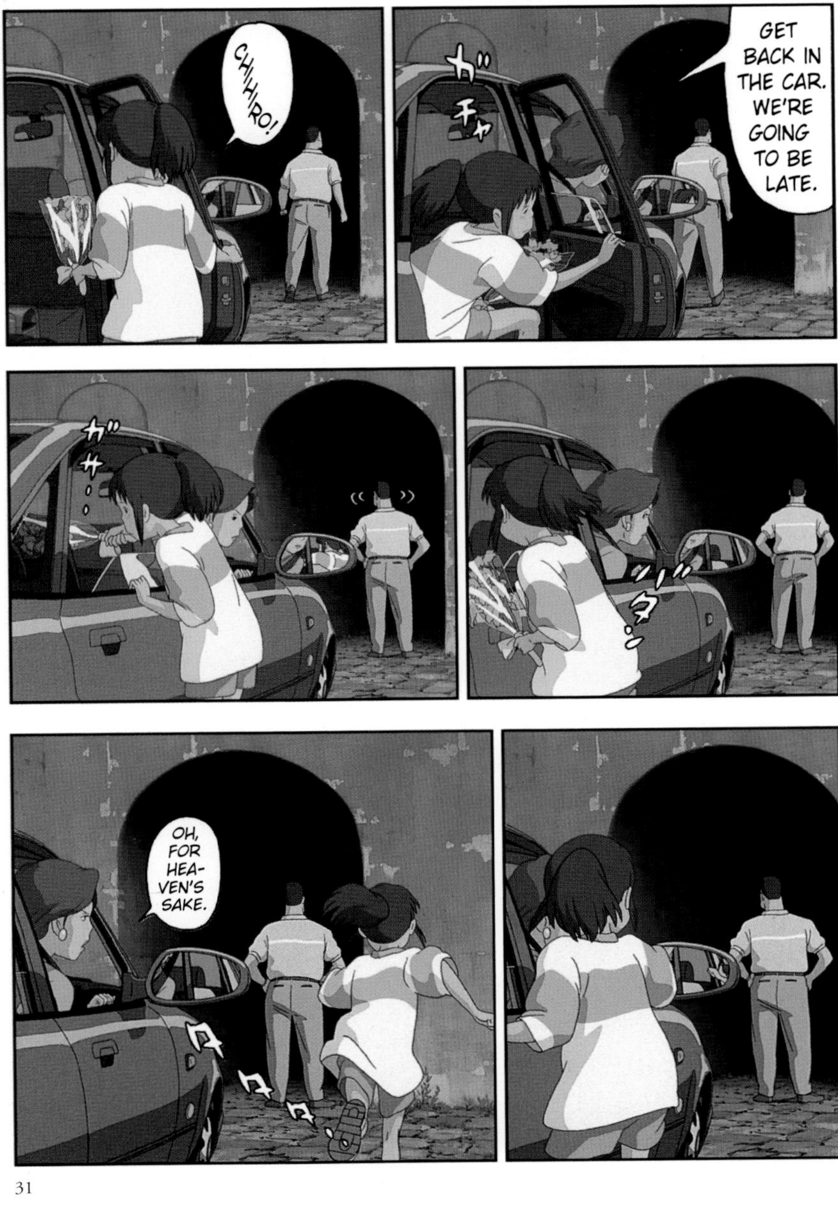
CHIHIRO!
ガチャ
GET BACK IN THE CAR. WE'RE GOING TO BE LATE.
OH, FOR HEAVEN'S SAKE.

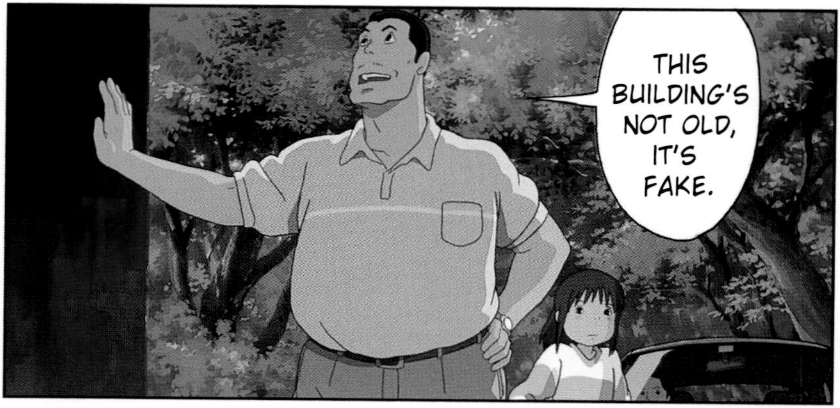
THIS BUILDING'S NOT OLD, IT'S FAKE.
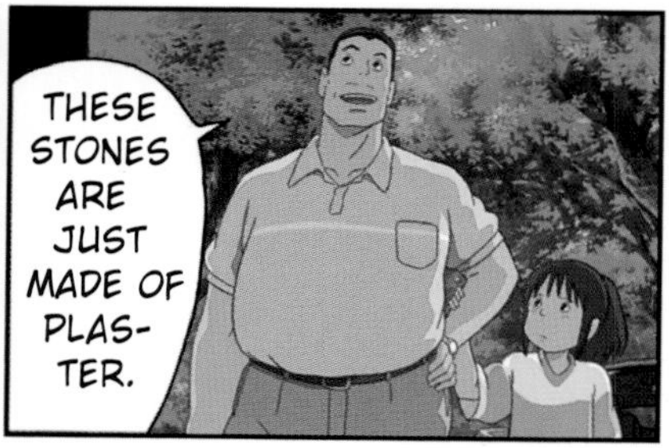
THESE STONES ARE JUST MADE OF PLAS- TER.
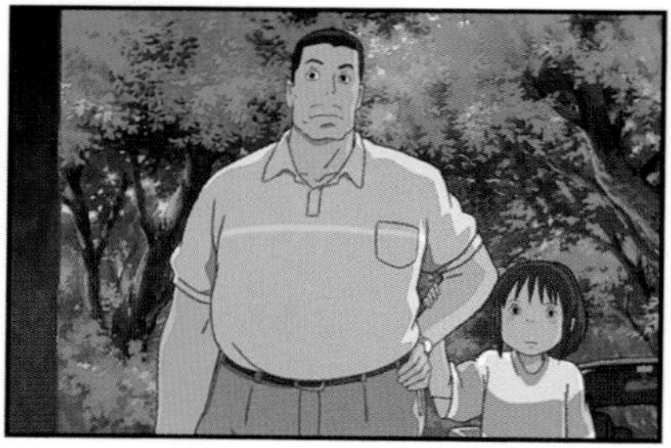
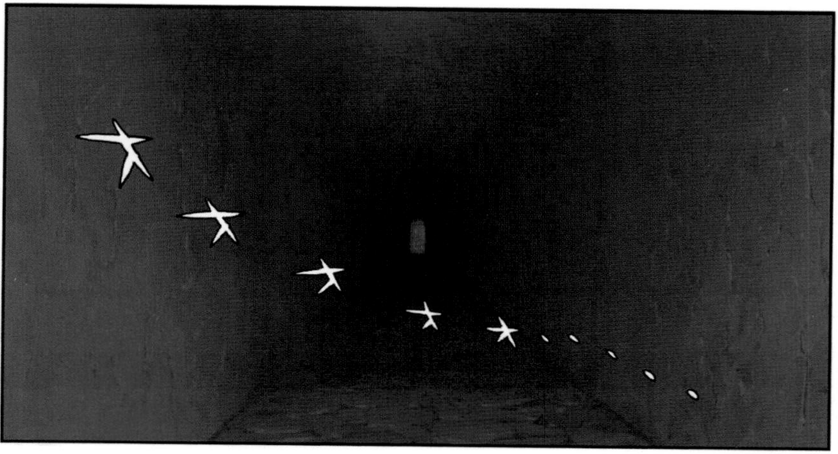

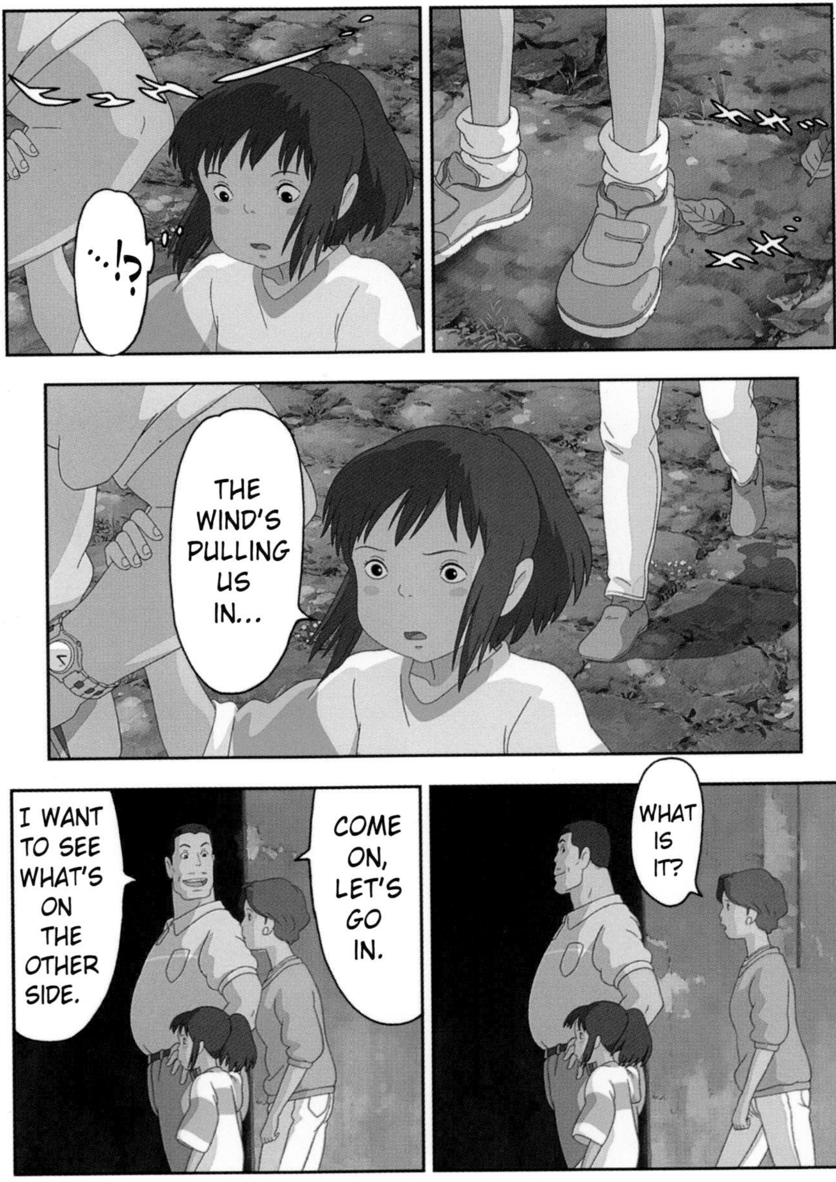
...!?
THE WIND'S PULLING US IN...
WHAT IS IT?
COME ON, LET'S GO IN.
I WANT TO SEE WHAT'S ON THE OTHER SIDE.

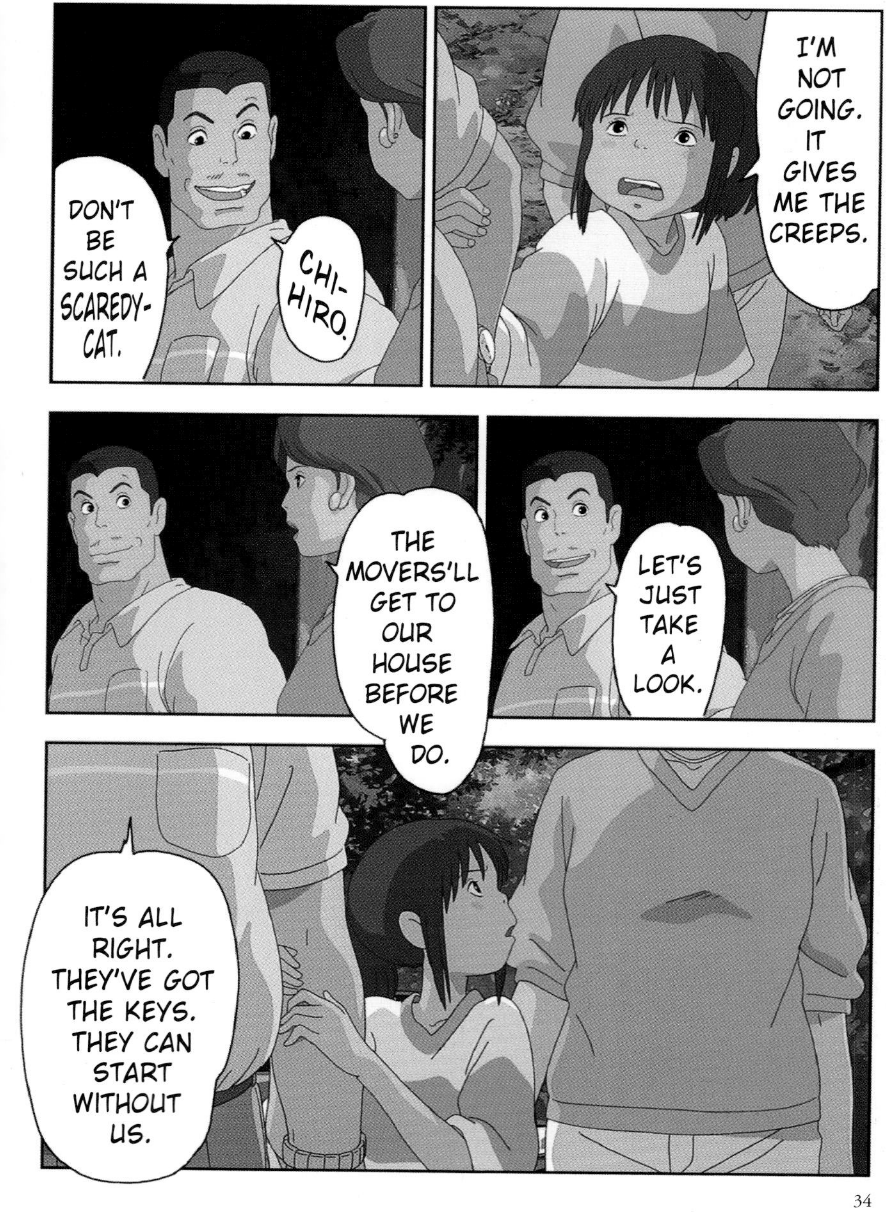
I'M NOT GOING. IT GIVES ME THE CREEPS.
CHI-HIRO.
DON'T BE SUCH A SCAREDY-CAT.
LET'S JUST TAKE A LOOK.
THE MOVERS'LL GET TO OUR HOUSE BEFORE WE DO.
IT'S ALL RIGHT. THEY'VE GOT THE KEYS. THEY CAN START WITHOUT US.

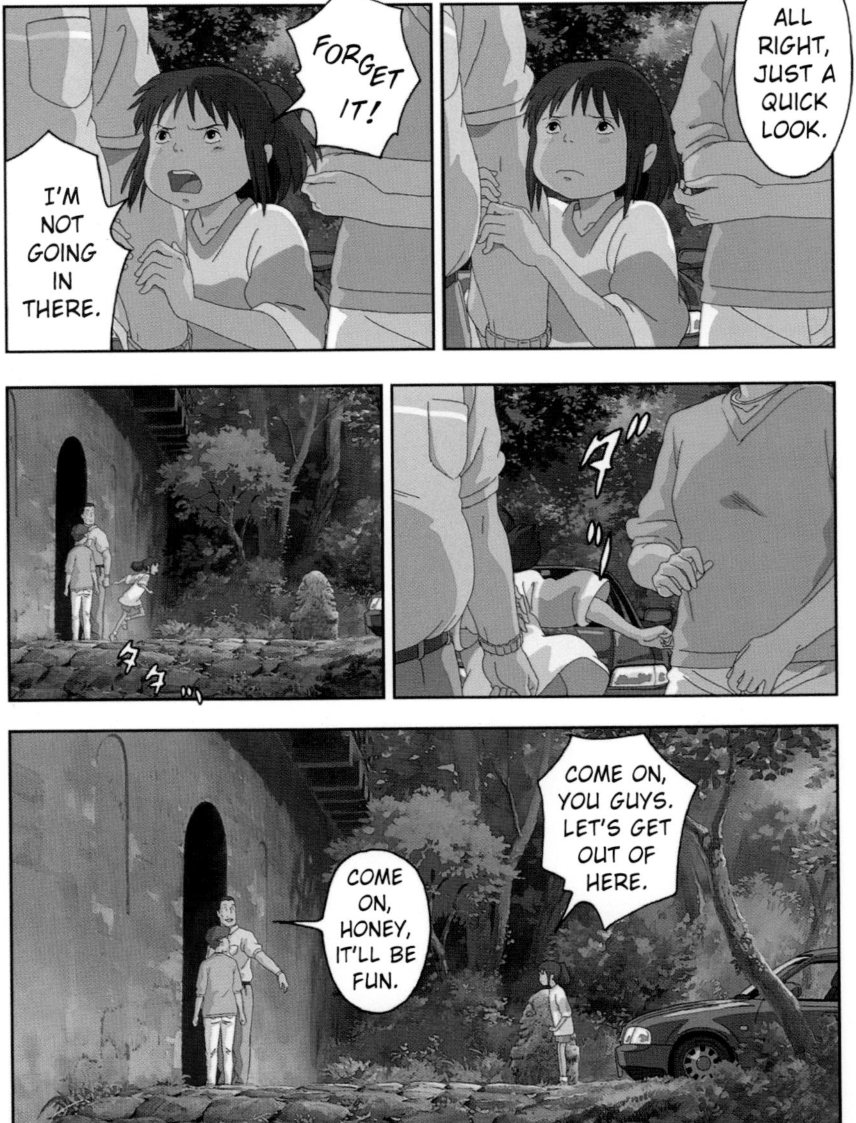
FORGET IT!
I'M NOT GOING IN THERE.
ALL RIGHT, JUST A QUICK LOOK.
COME ON, HONEY, IT'LL BE FUN.
COME ON, YOU GUYS. LET'S GET OUT OF HERE.

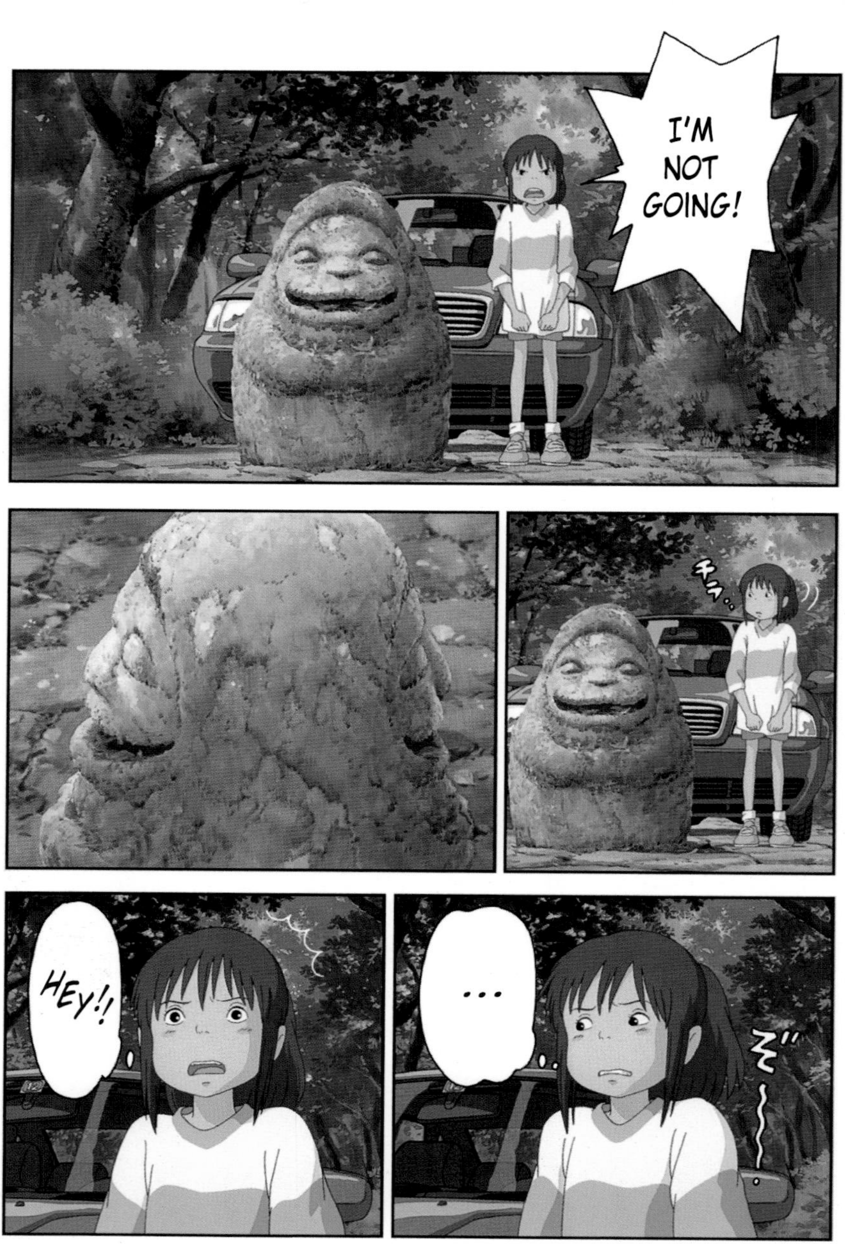
I'M NOT GOING!
...
HEY!!

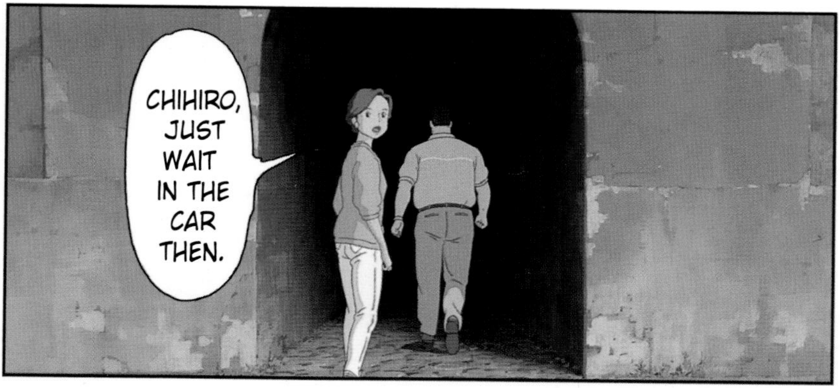
CHIHIRO, JUST WAIT IN THE CAR THEN.
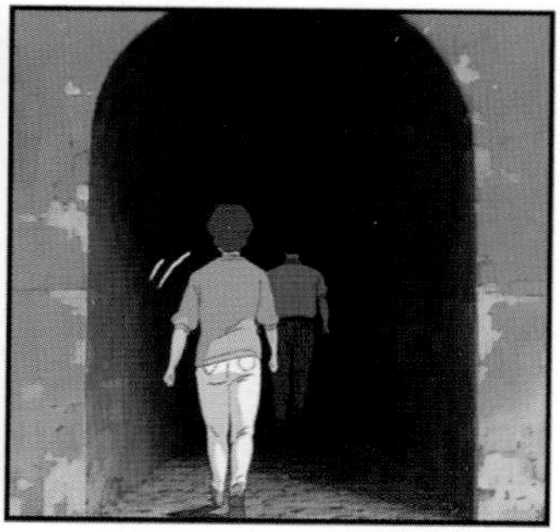
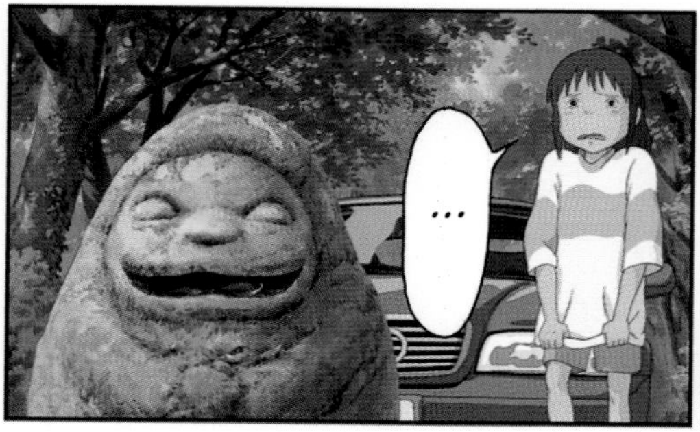
...
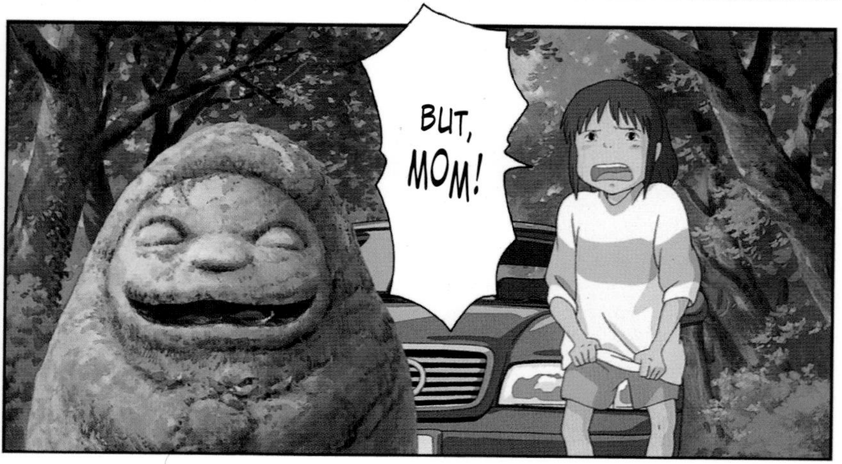
BUT, MOM!

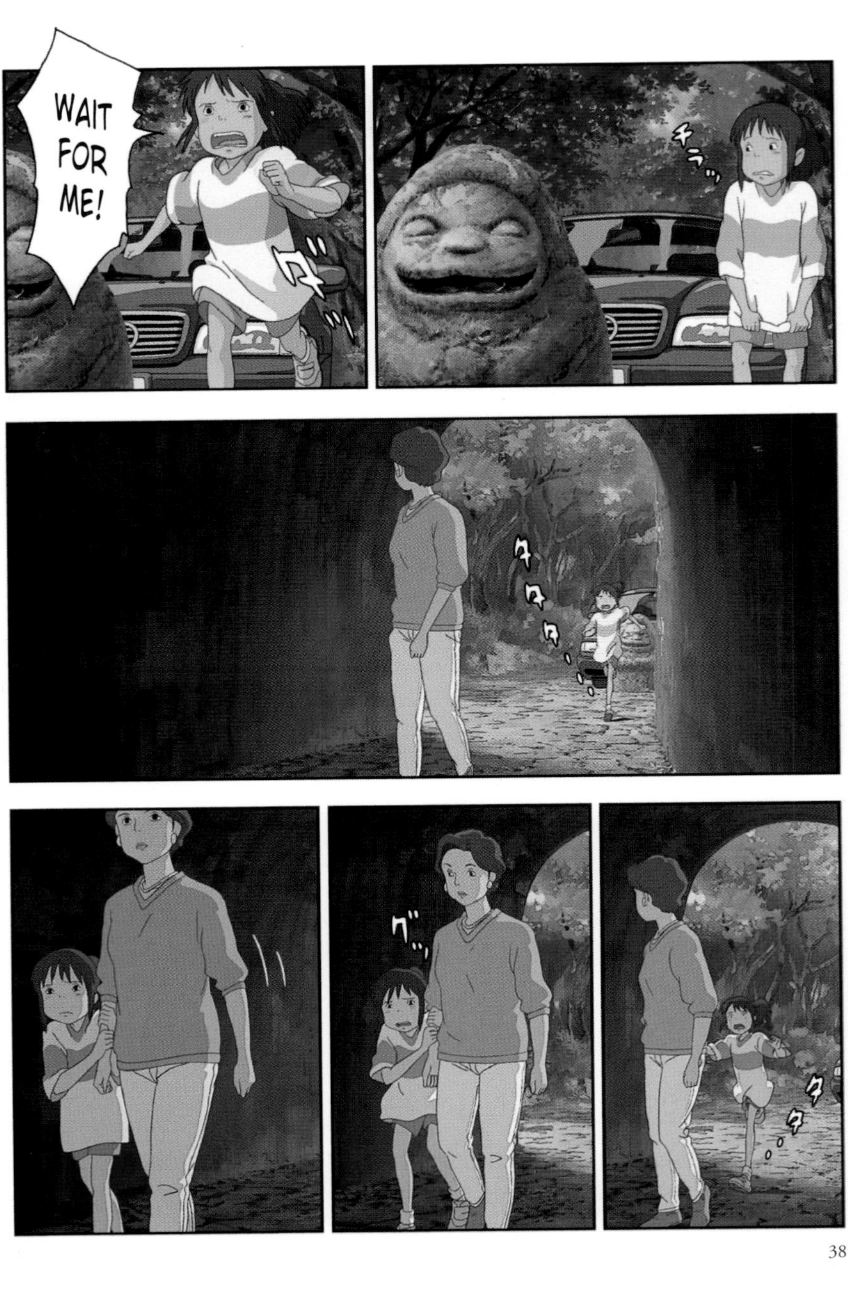
WAIT FOR ME!

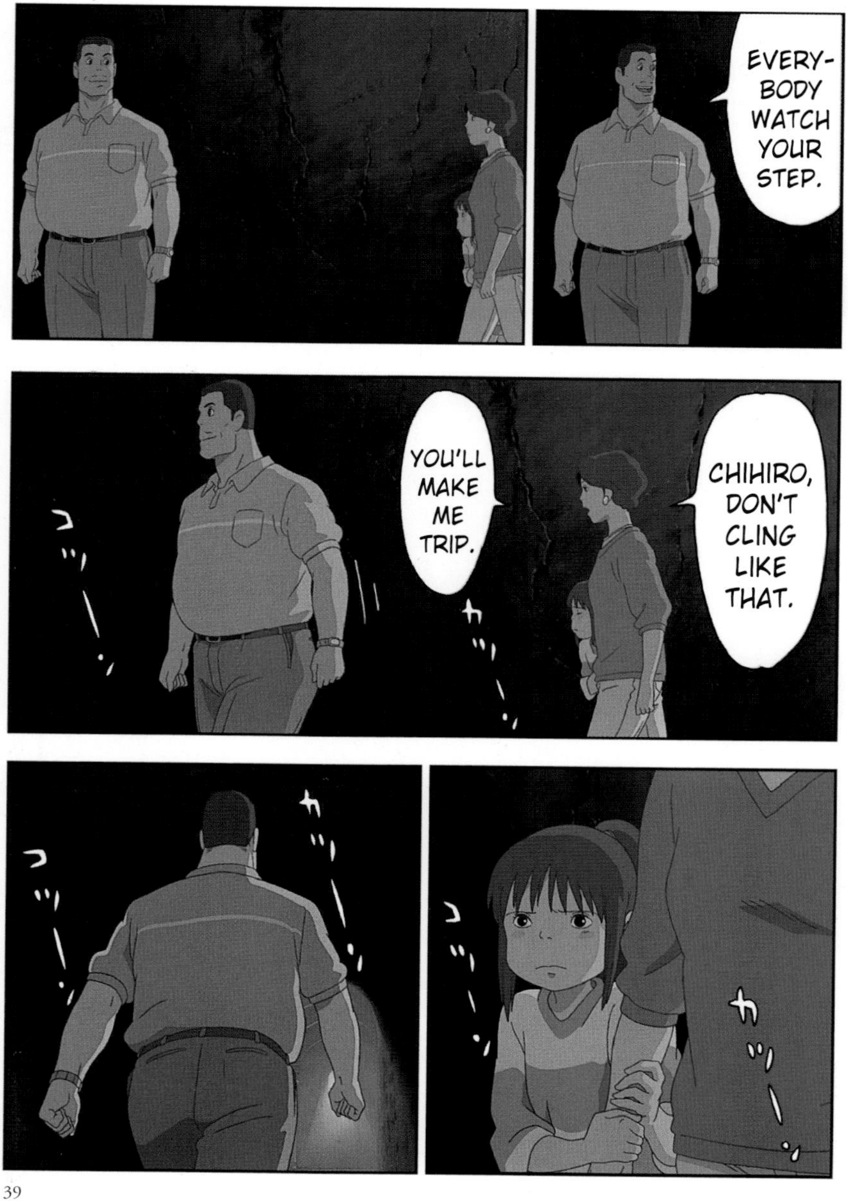
EVERY-BODY WATCH YOUR STEP.
CHIHIRO, DON'T CLING LIKE THAT.
YOU'LL MAKE ME TRIP.

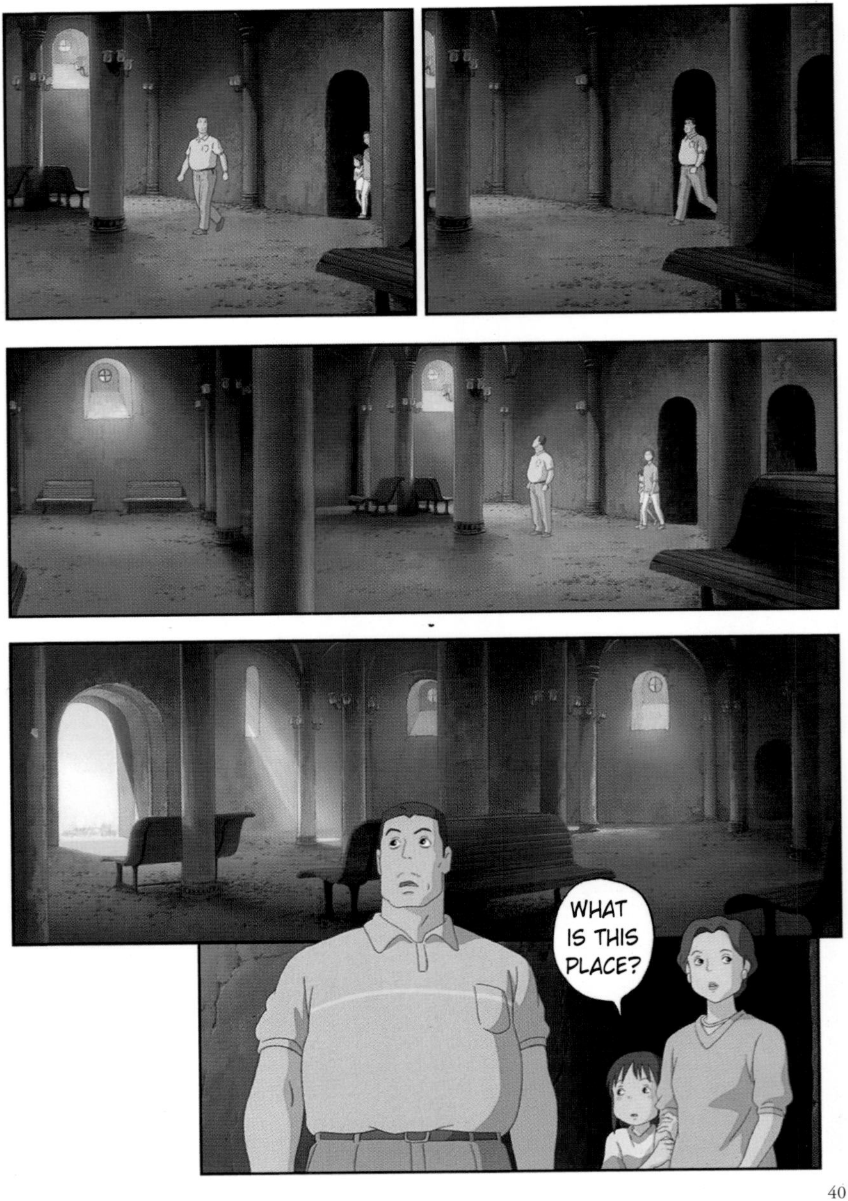
WHAT IS THIS PLACE?

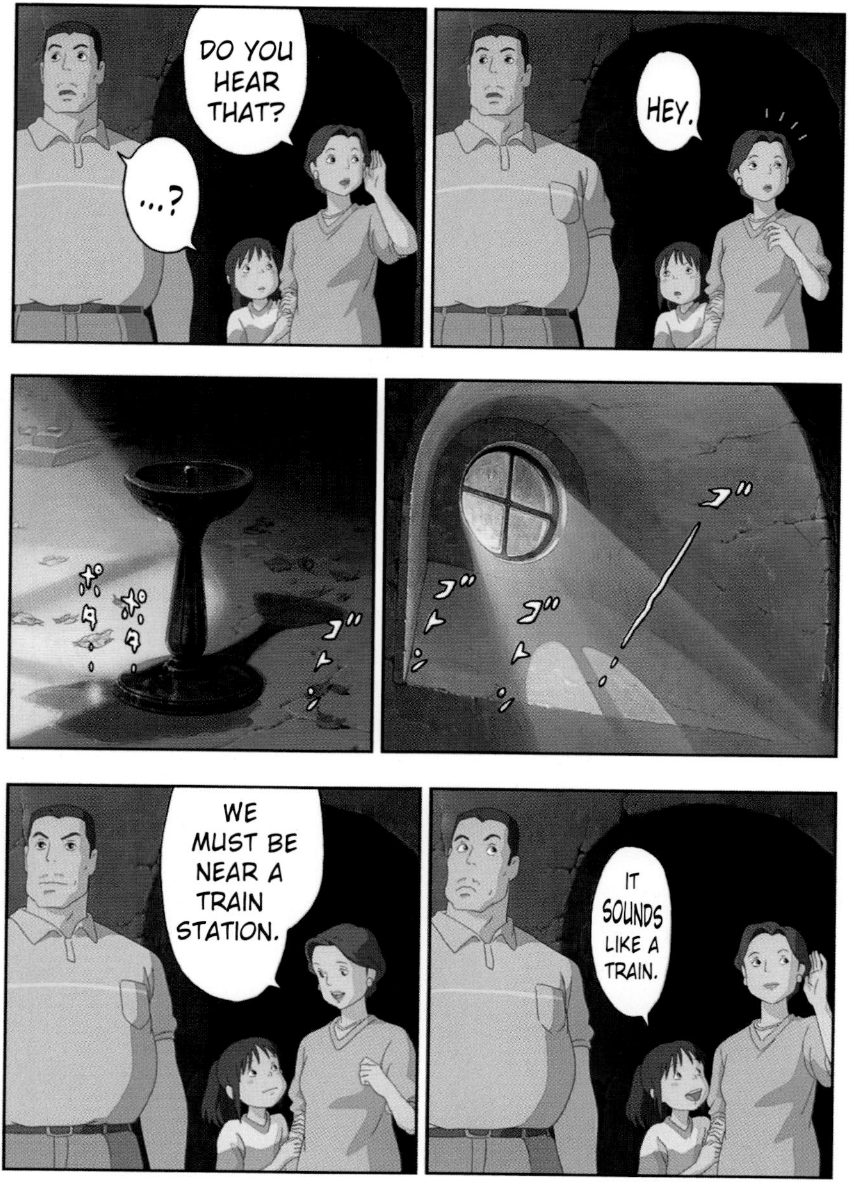
HEY.
DO YOU HEAR THAT?
...?
ゴトン
ゴトン
ゴ
ポタ
ポタ
ゴトン
IT SOUNDS LIKE A TRAIN.
WE MUST BE NEAR A TRAIN STATION.

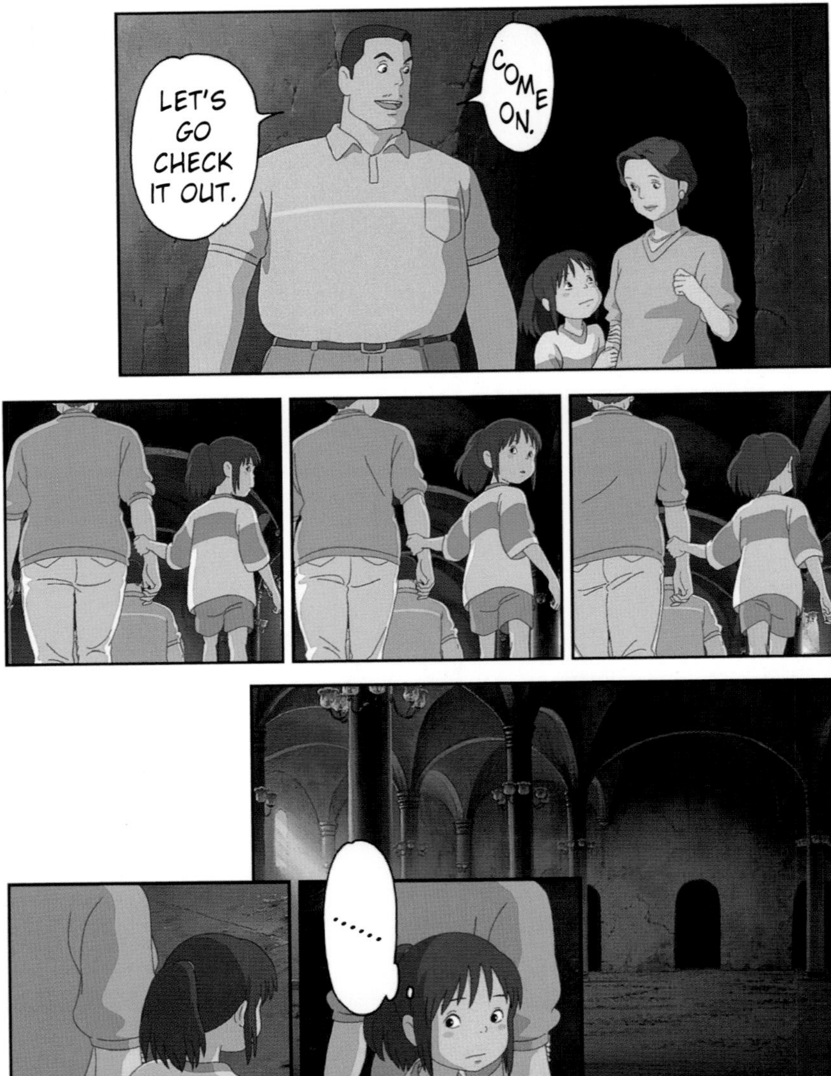
COME ON.
LET'S GO CHECK IT OUT.
......

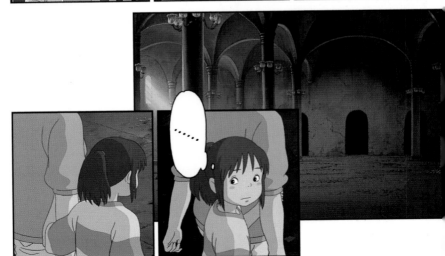

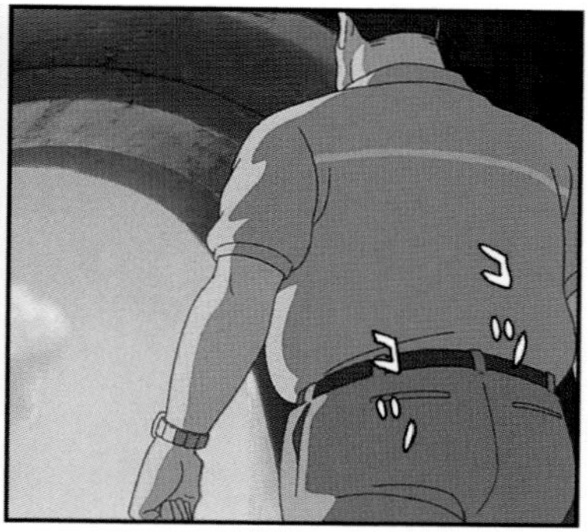
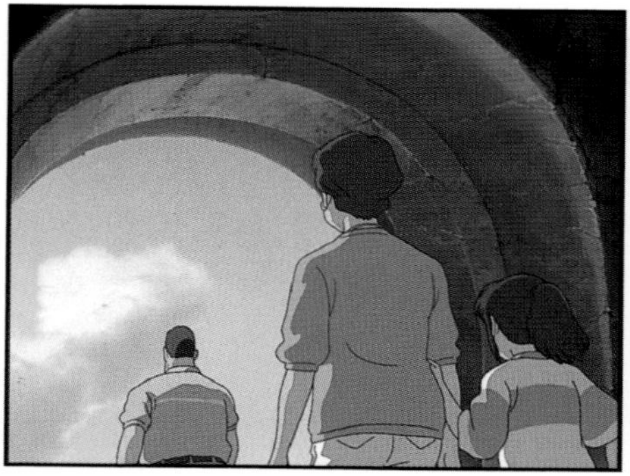
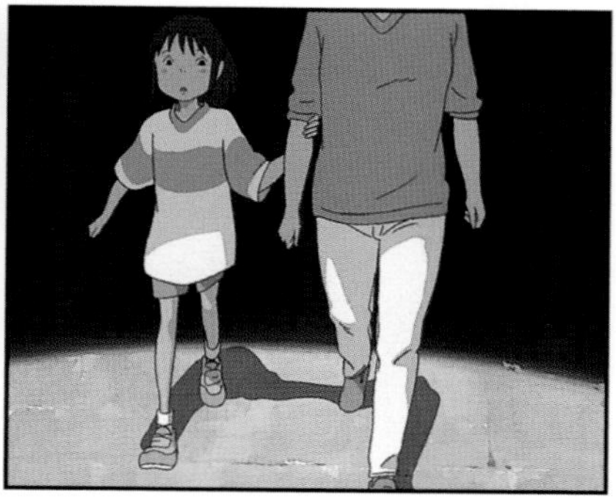
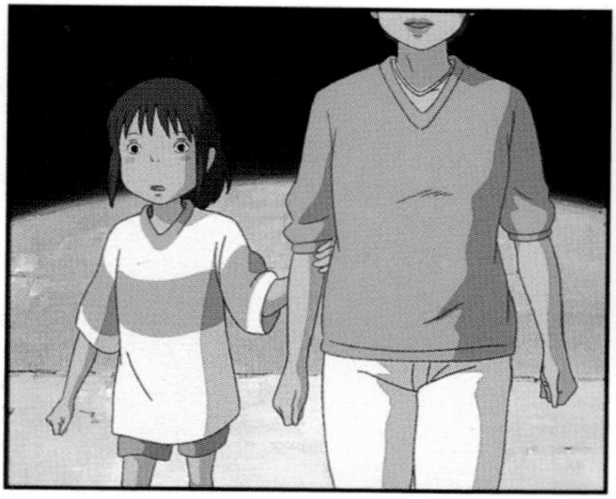
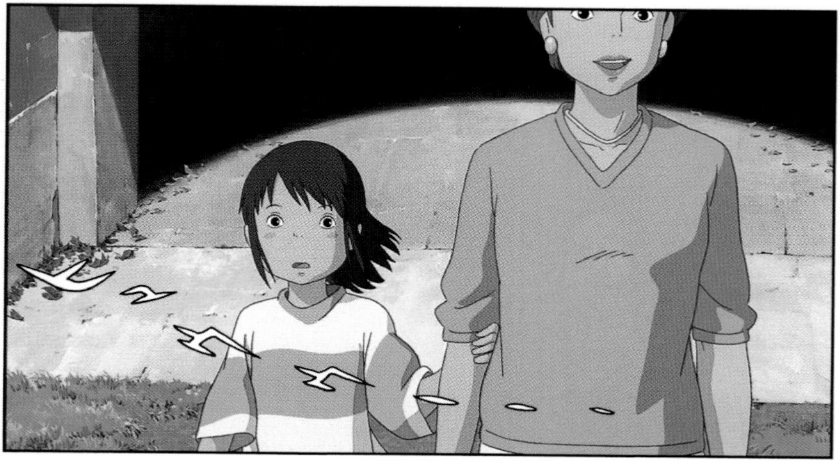

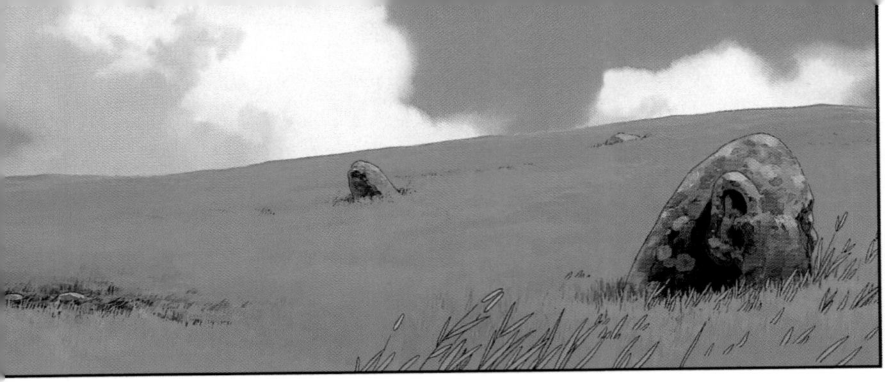

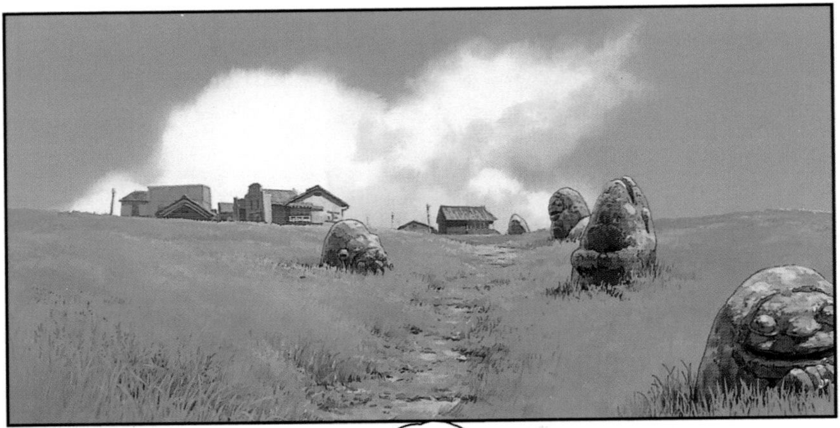

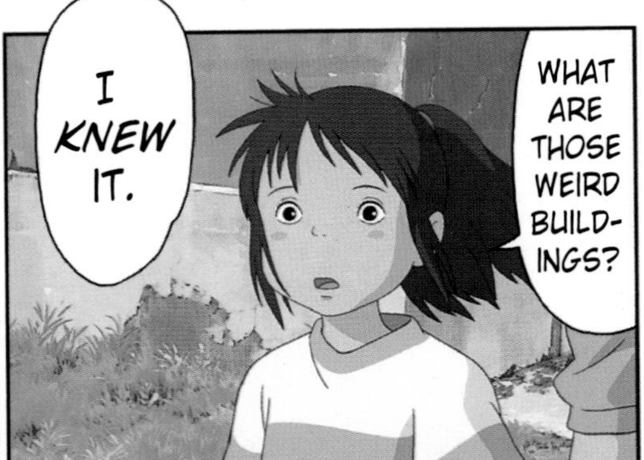
WHAT ARE THOSE WEIRD BUILD-INGS?
I KNEW IT.

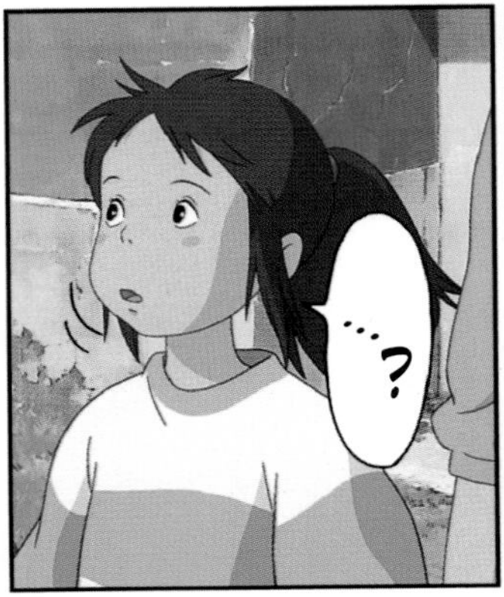
...?

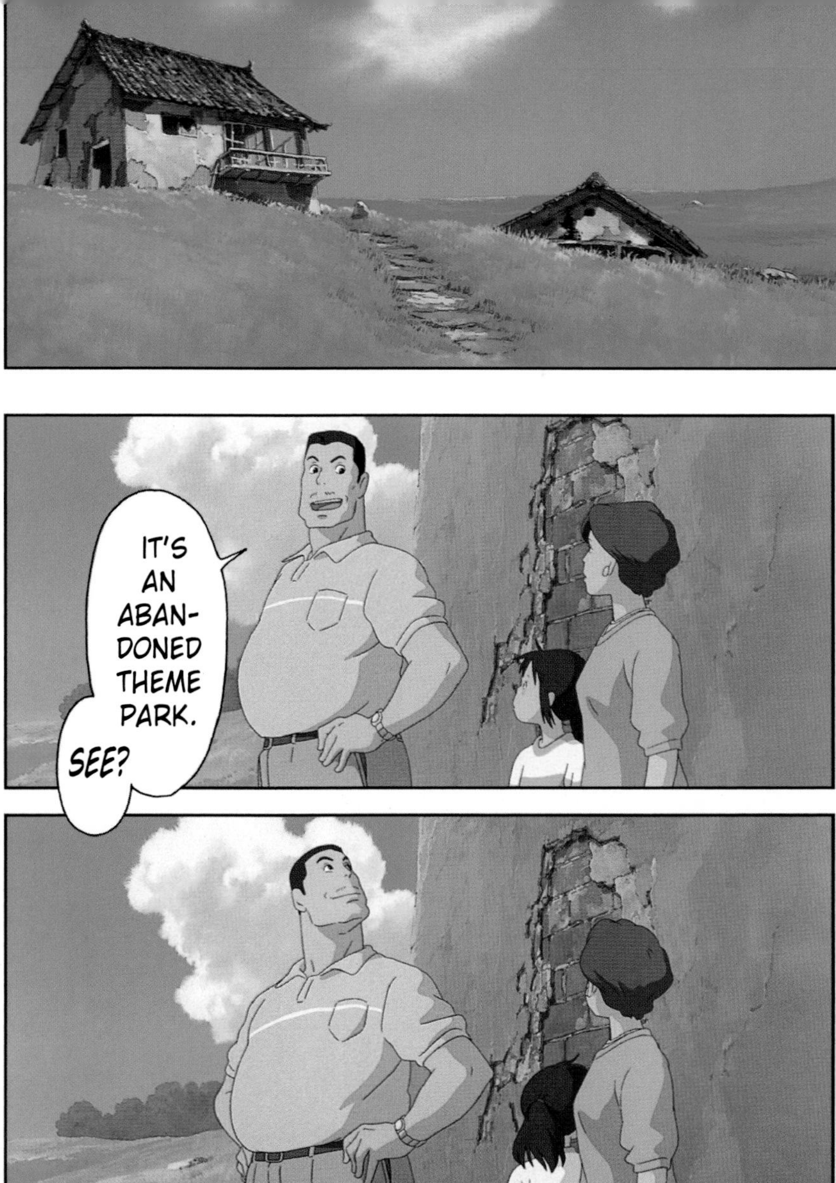
IT'S AN ABANDONED THEME PARK.
SEE?

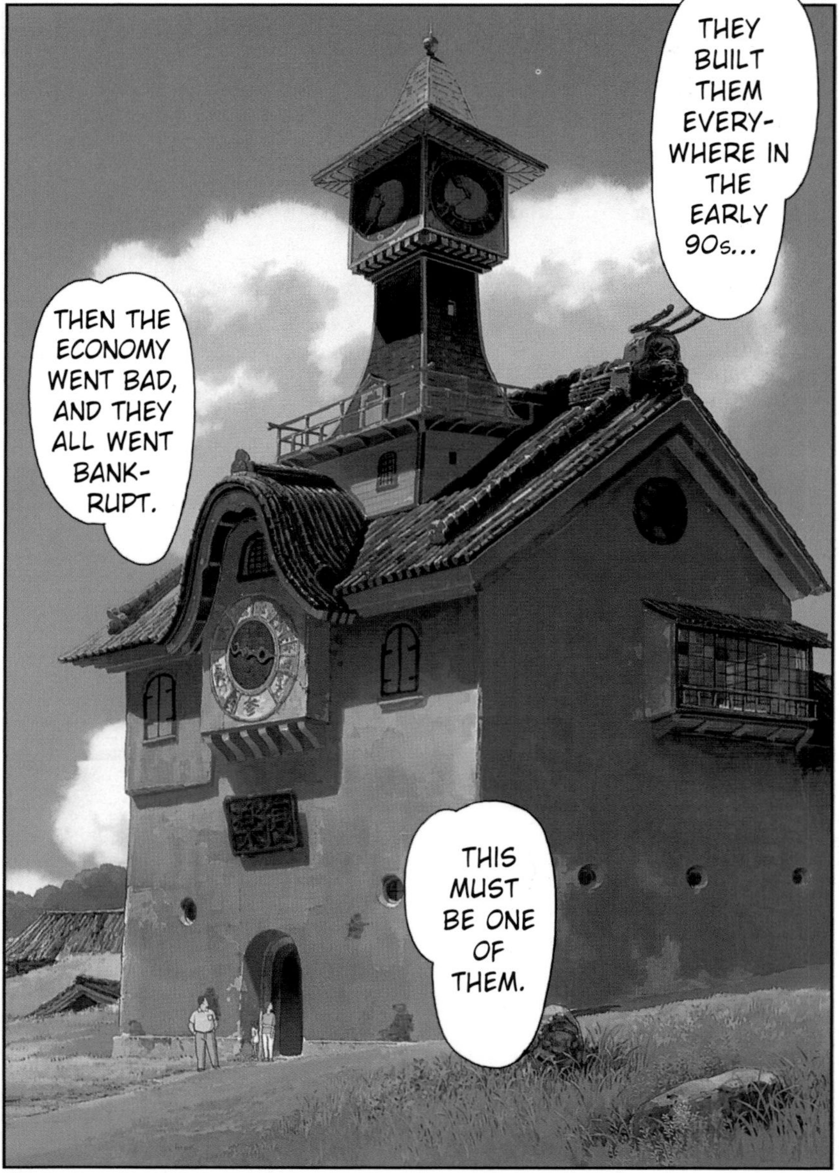
THEY BUILT THEM EVERY-WHERE IN THE EARLY 90s...
THEN THE ECONOMY WENT BAD, AND THEY ALL WENT BANK-RUPT.
THIS MUST BE ONE OF THEM.

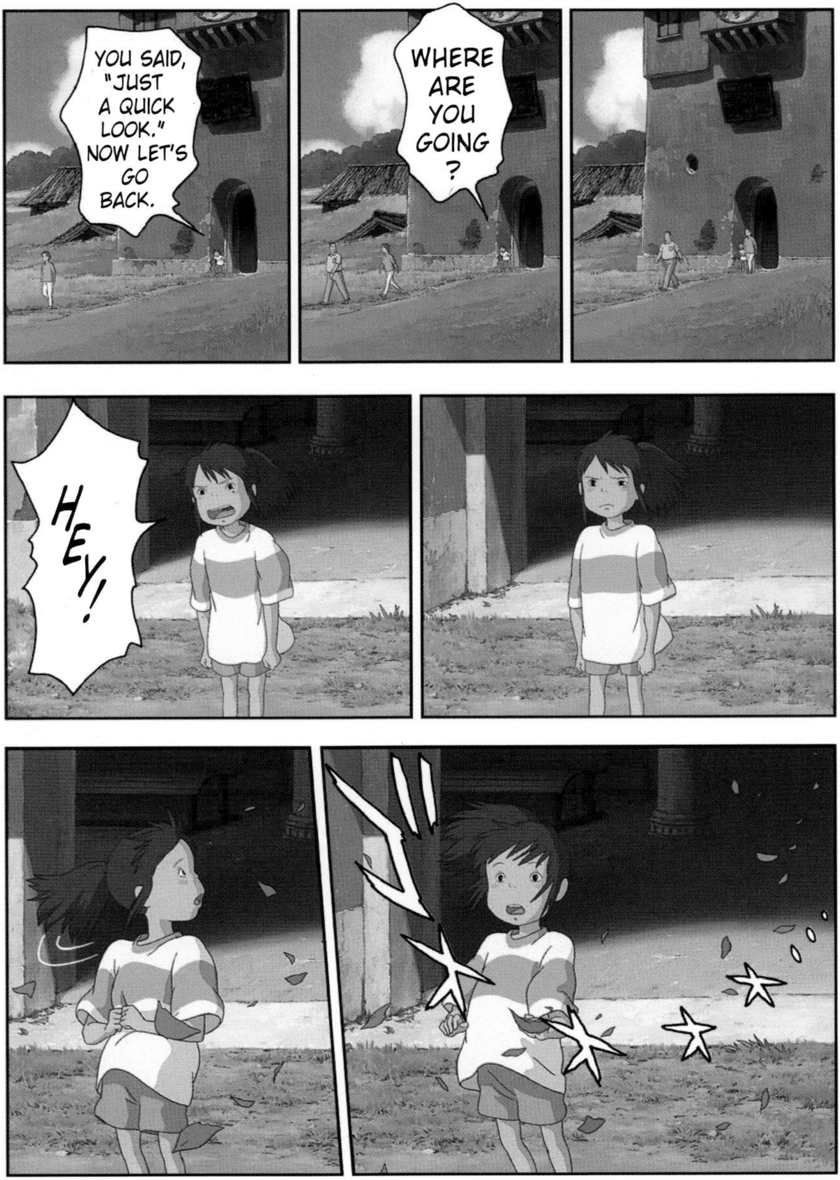
YOU SAID, "JUST A QUICK LOOK." NOW LET'S GO BACK.
WHERE ARE YOU GOING?
HEY!

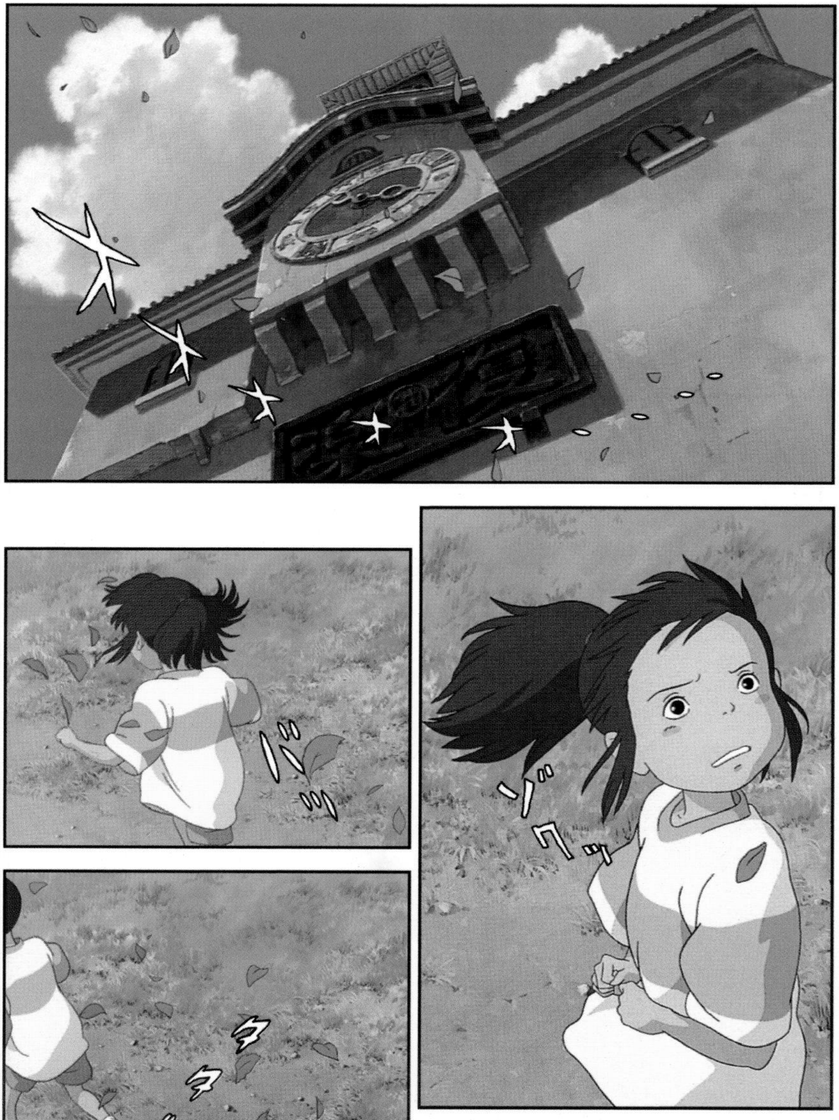
ゾクッ
バッ
タタッ

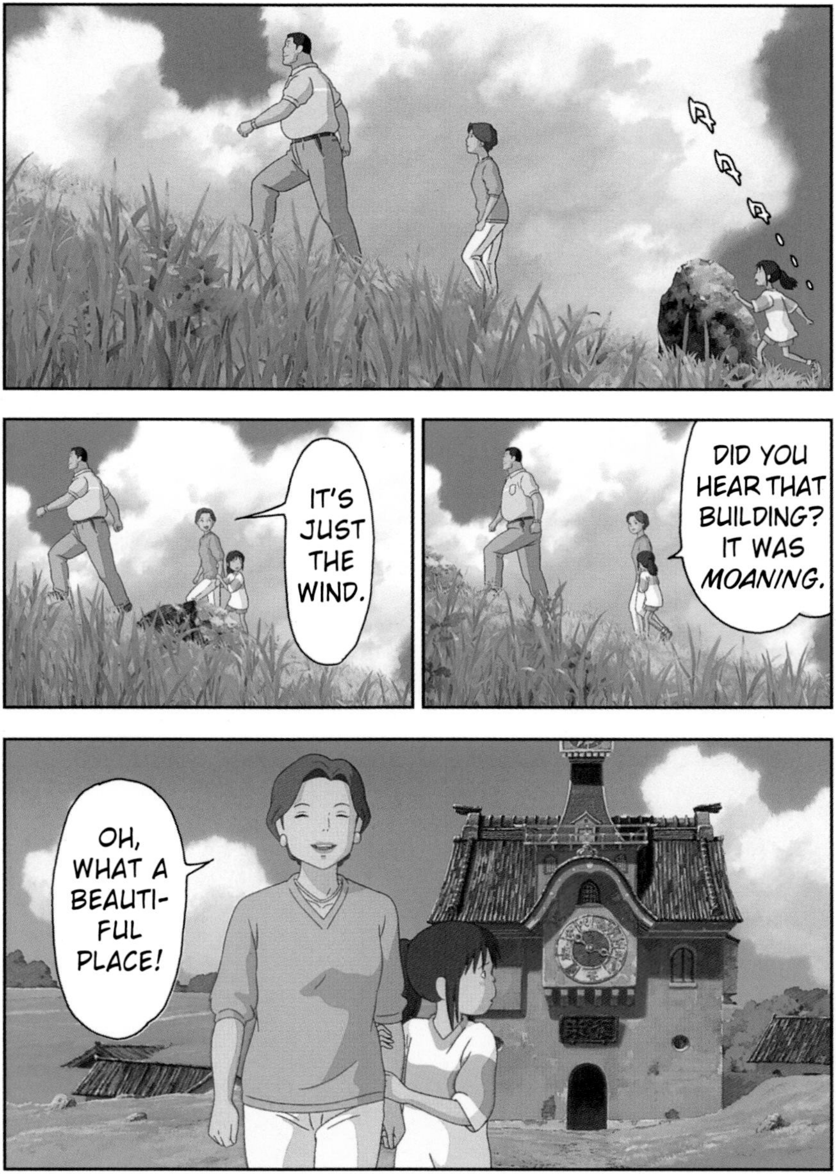
DID YOU HEAR THAT BUILDING? IT WAS *MOANING*.
IT'S JUST THE WIND.
OH, WHAT A BEAUTI-FUL PLACE!

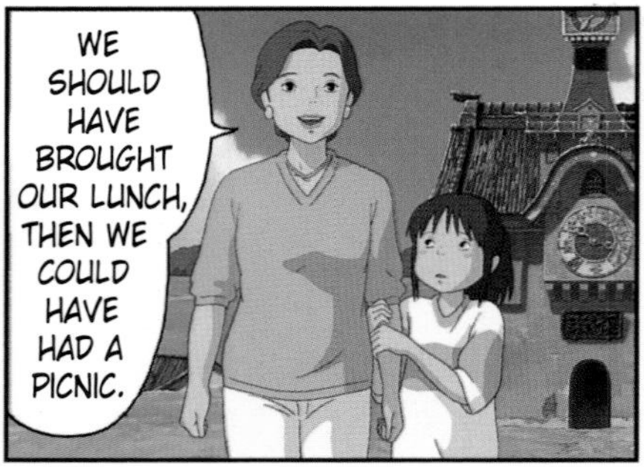
WE SHOULD HAVE BROUGHT OUR LUNCH, THEN WE COULD HAVE HAD A PICNIC.

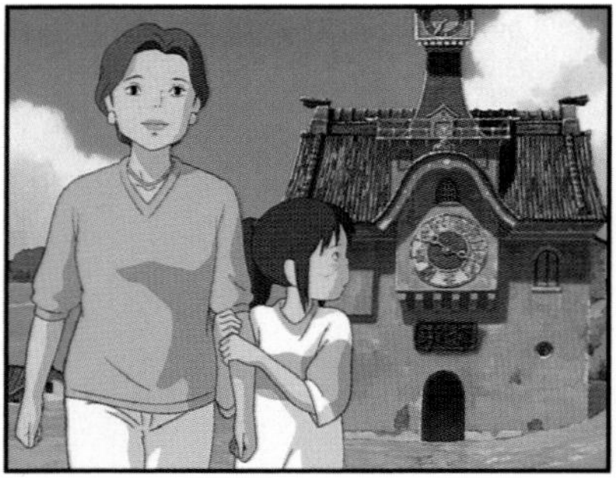

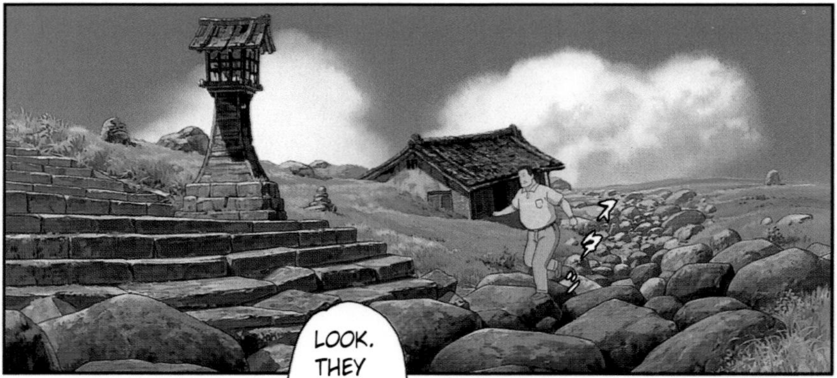

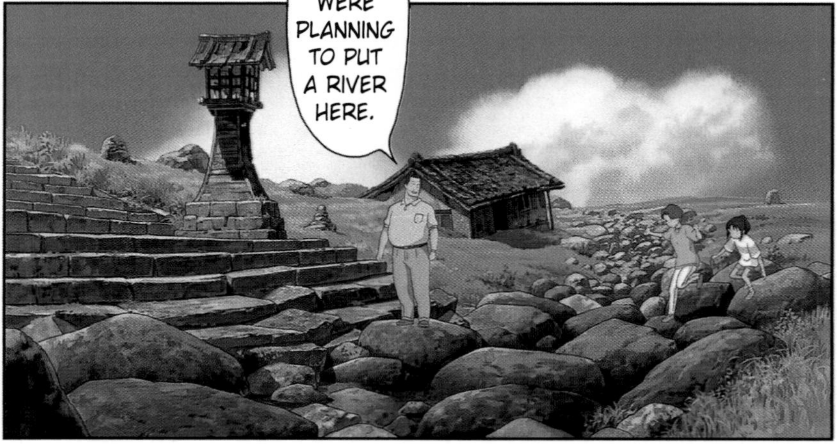
LOOK. THEY WERE PLANNING TO PUT A RIVER HERE.

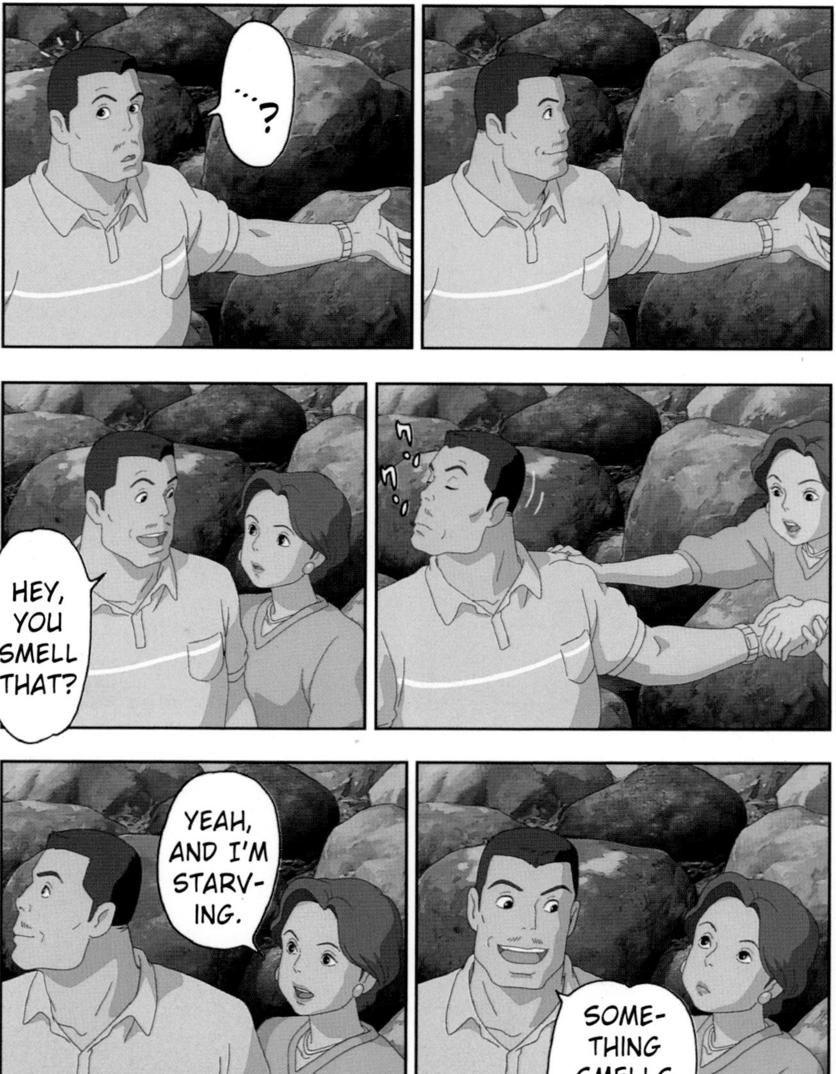
HEY, YOU SMELL THAT?
YEAH, AND I'M STARV-ING.
SOME-THING SMELLS DELI-CIOUS.

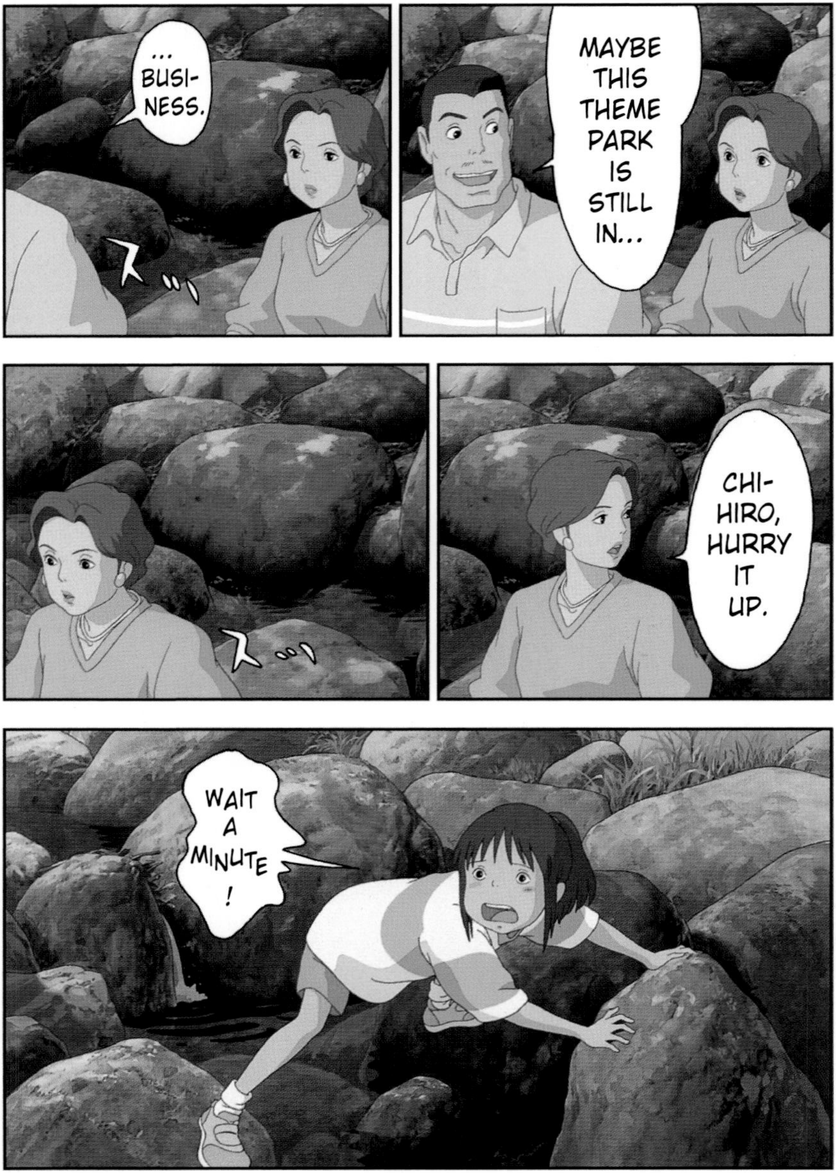
MAYBE THIS THEME PARK IS STILL IN...
... BUSI-NESS.
CHI-HIRO, HURRY IT UP.
WAIT A MINUTE!

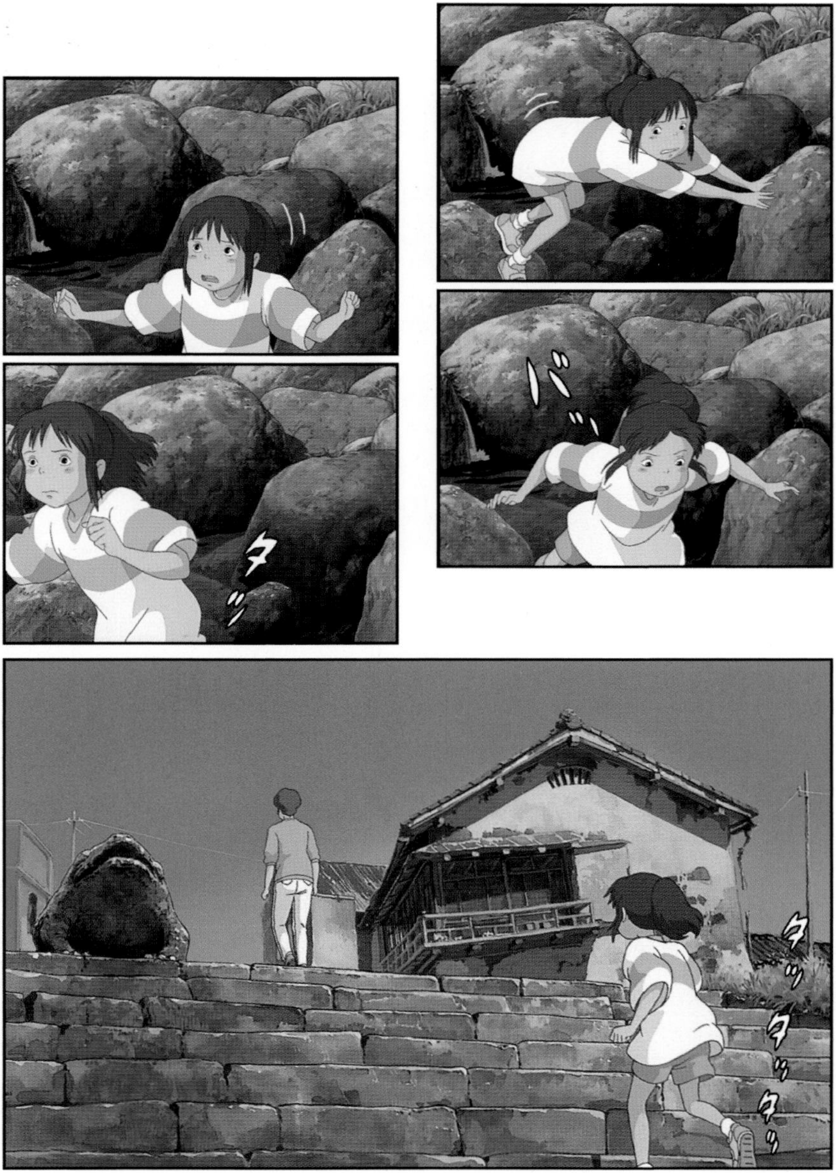
バッ
タッ
タッ
タッ
タッ

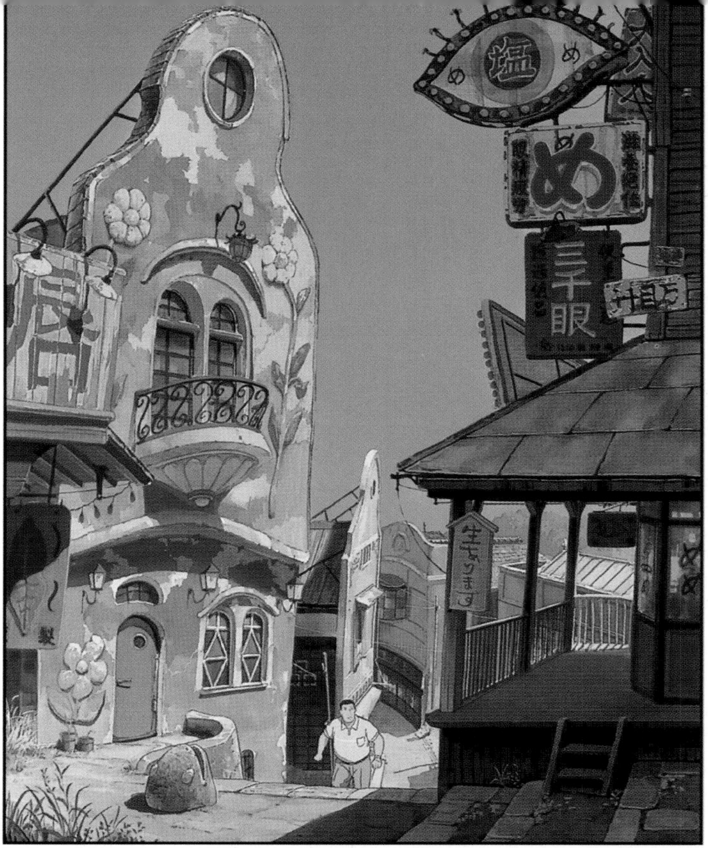
塩
め

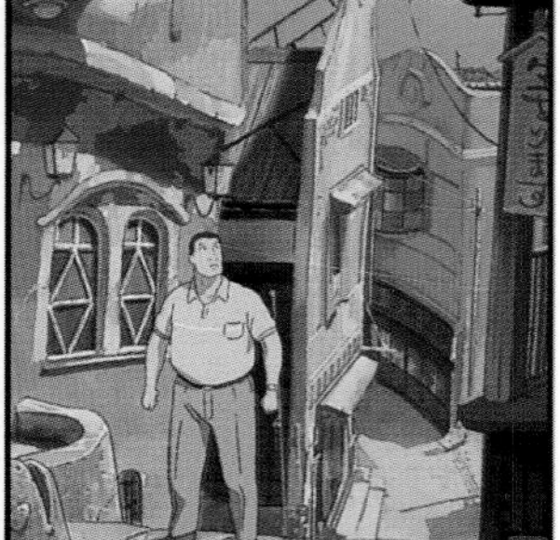

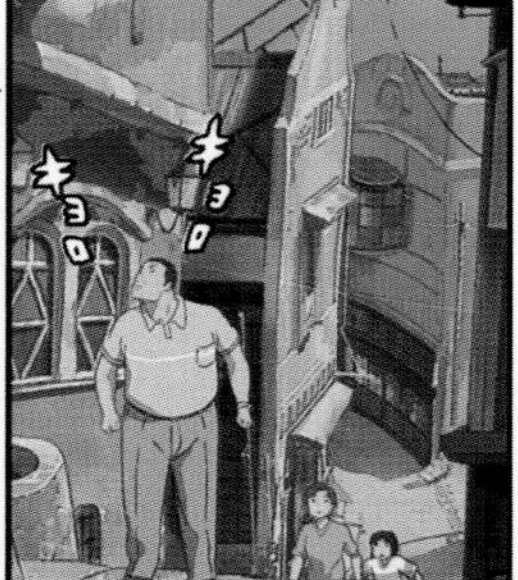
キョロ
キョロ

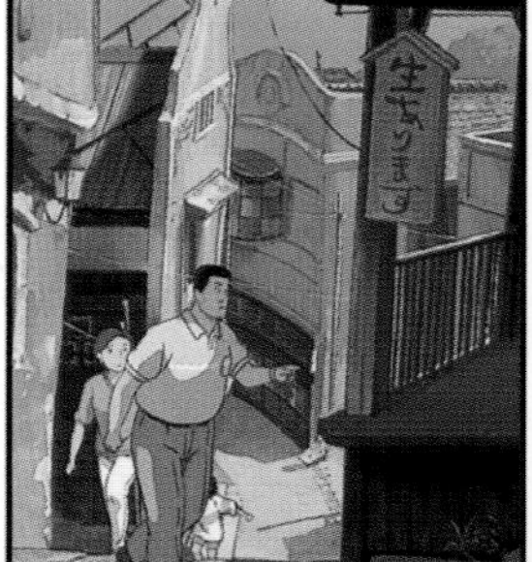

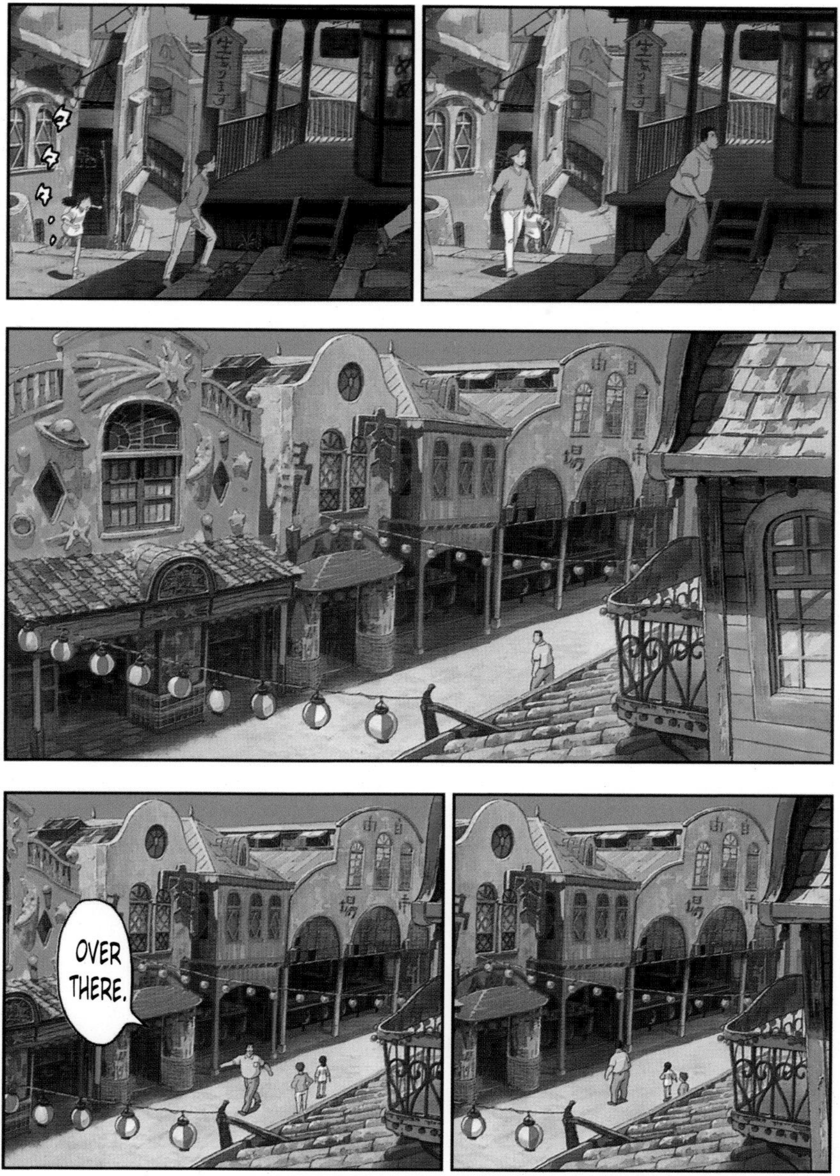
OVER THERE.

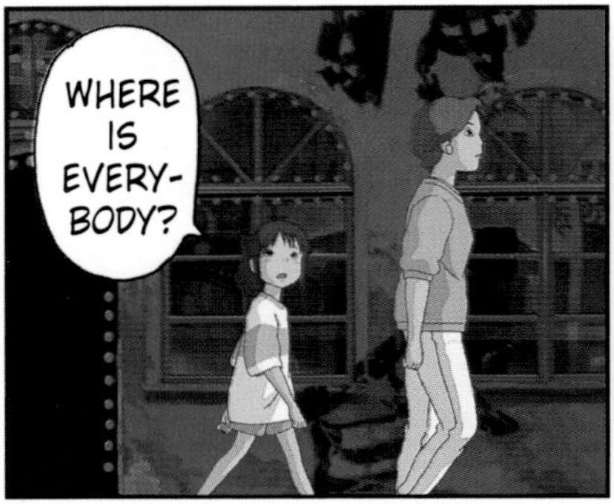
WHERE IS EVERY-BODY?

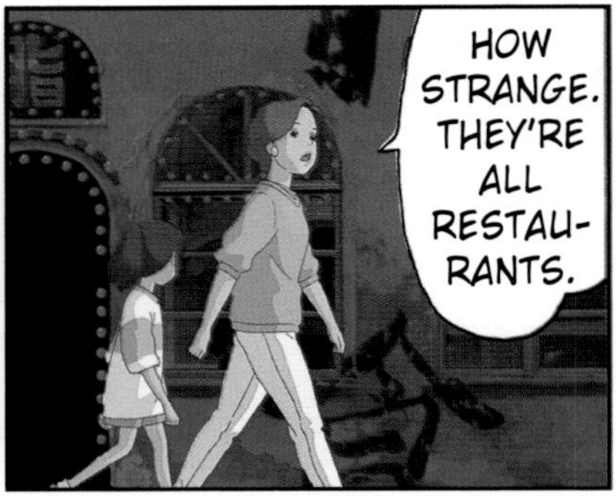
HOW STRANGE. THEY'RE ALL RESTAU-RANTS.

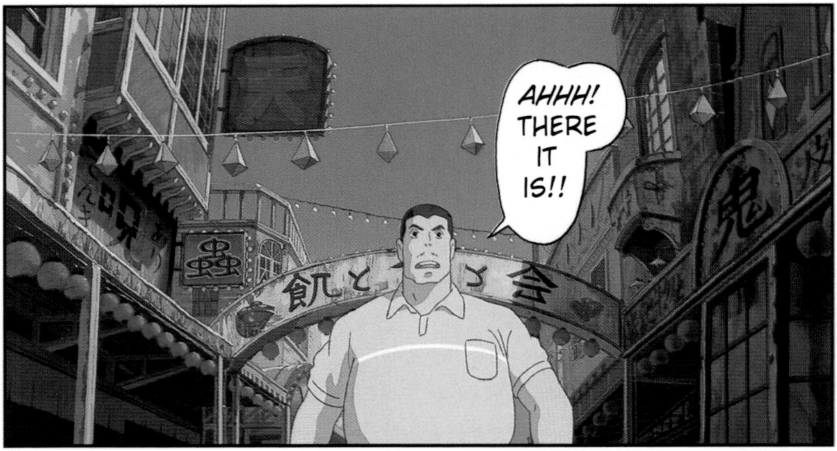
AHHH! THERE IT IS!!

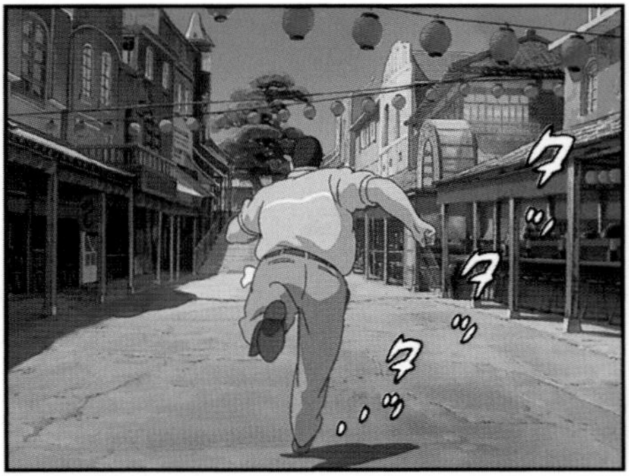
タッ
タッ
タッ

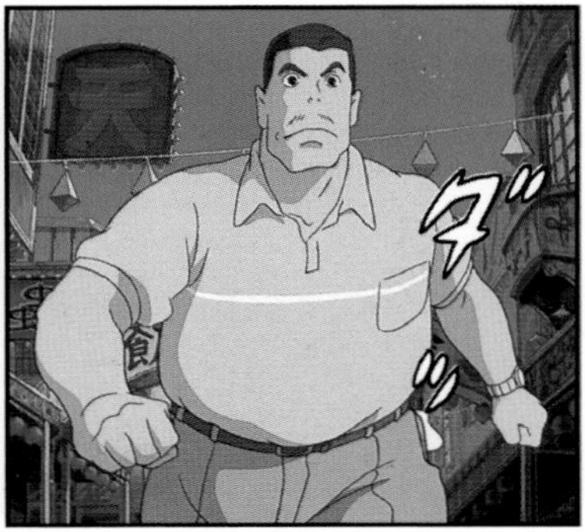
ダッ

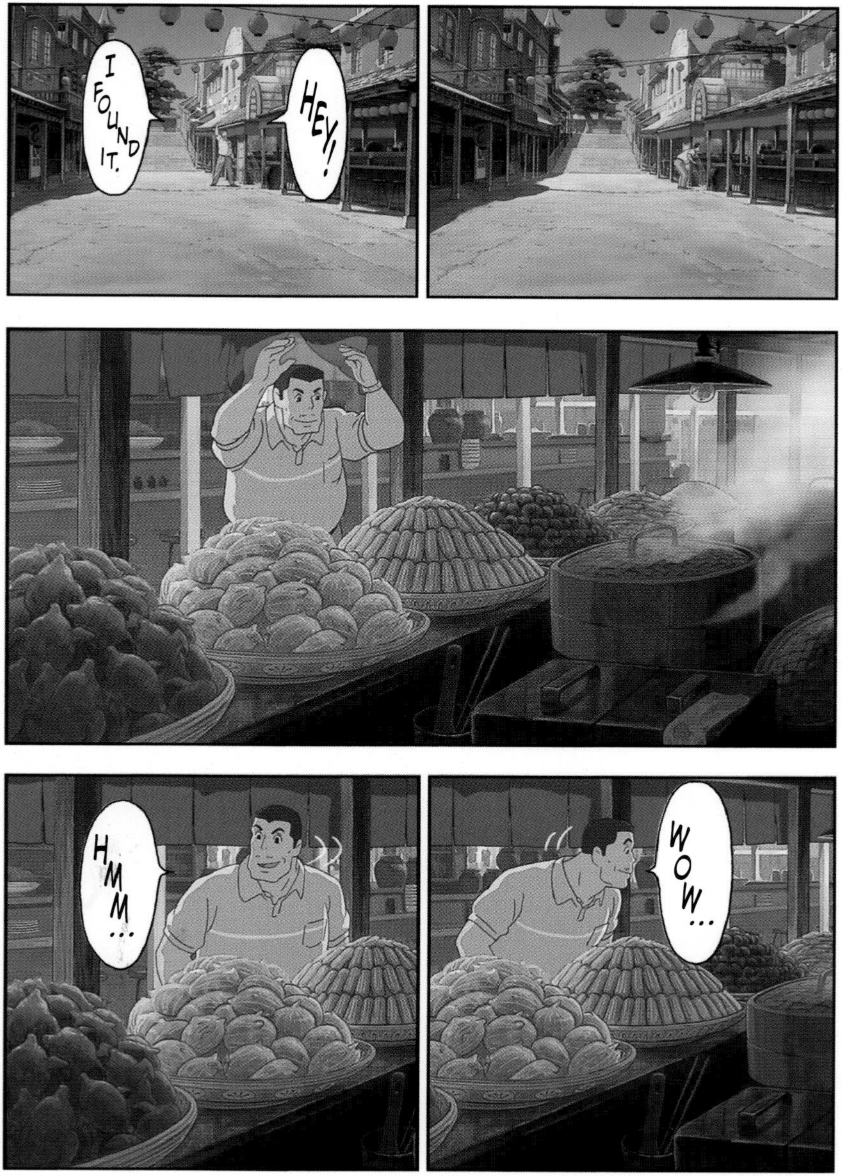
HEY!
I FOUND IT.
WOW...
HMM...

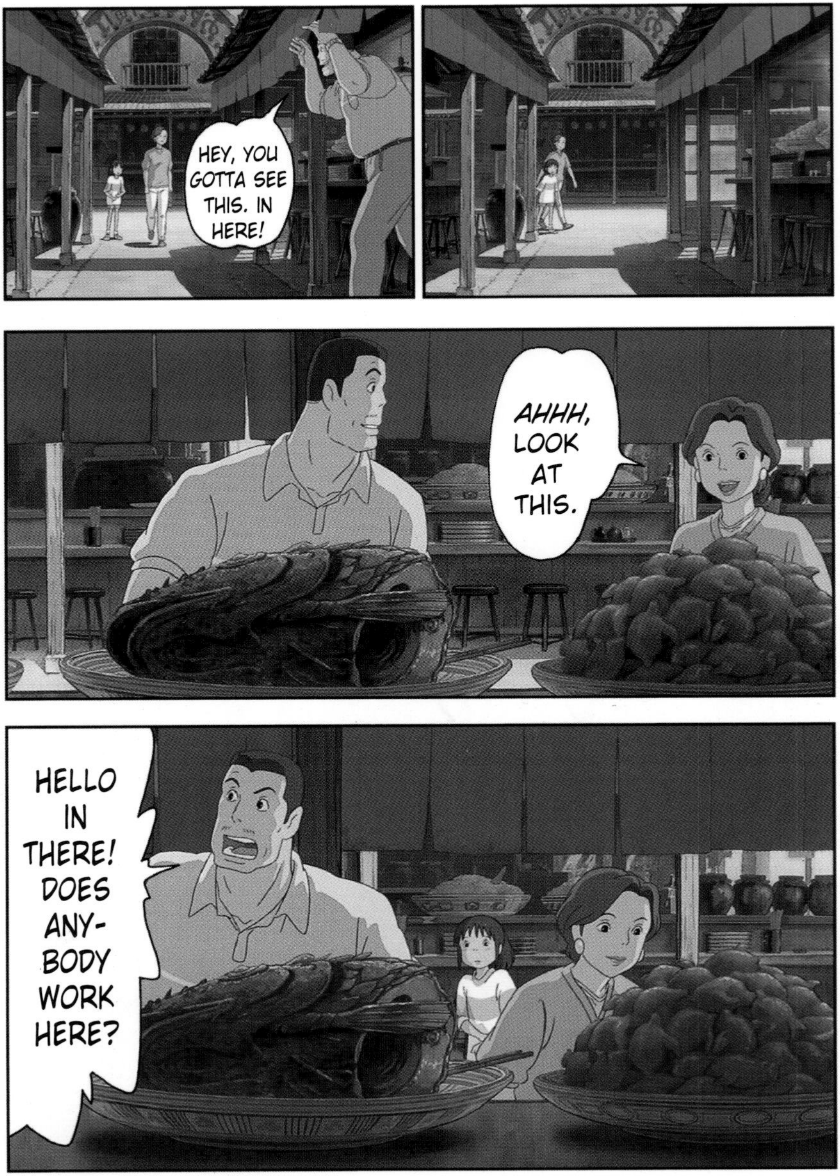
HEY, YOU GOTTA SEE THIS. IN HERE!
AHHH, LOOK AT THIS.
HELLO IN THERE! DOES ANY-BODY WORK HERE?

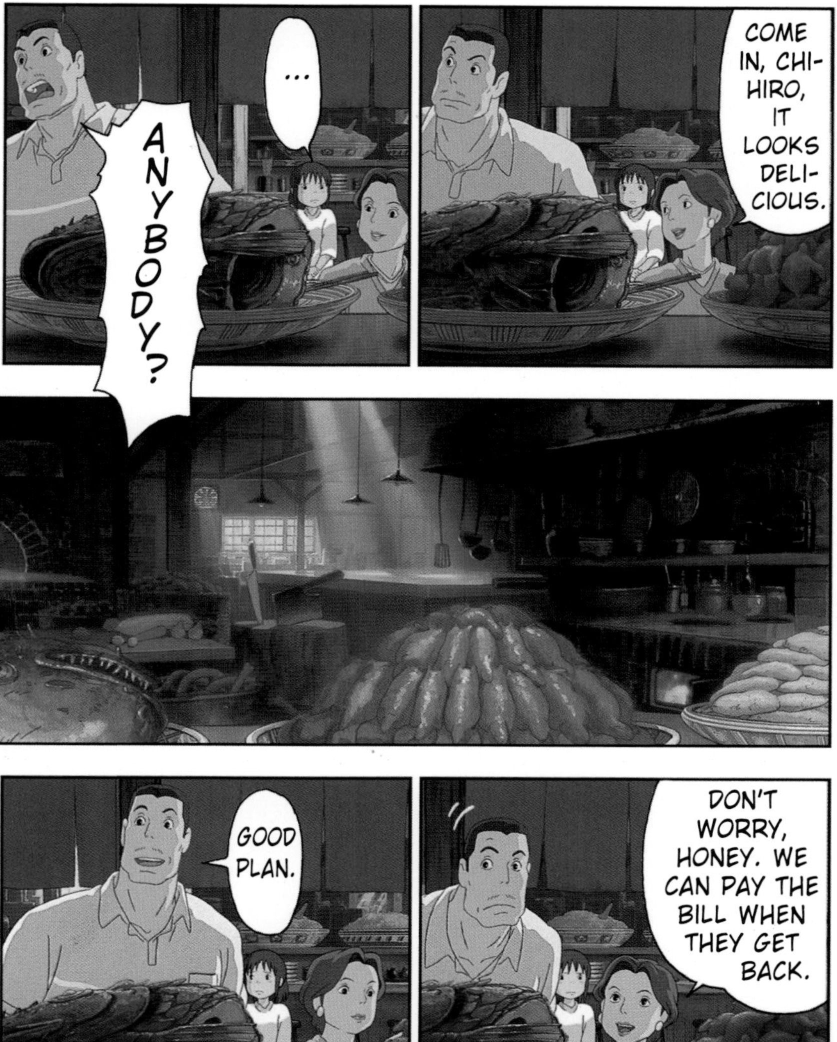
COME IN, CHIHIRO, IT LOOKS DELICIOUS.
ANYBODY?
...
DON'T WORRY, HONEY. WE CAN PAY THE BILL WHEN THEY GET BACK.
GOOD PLAN.

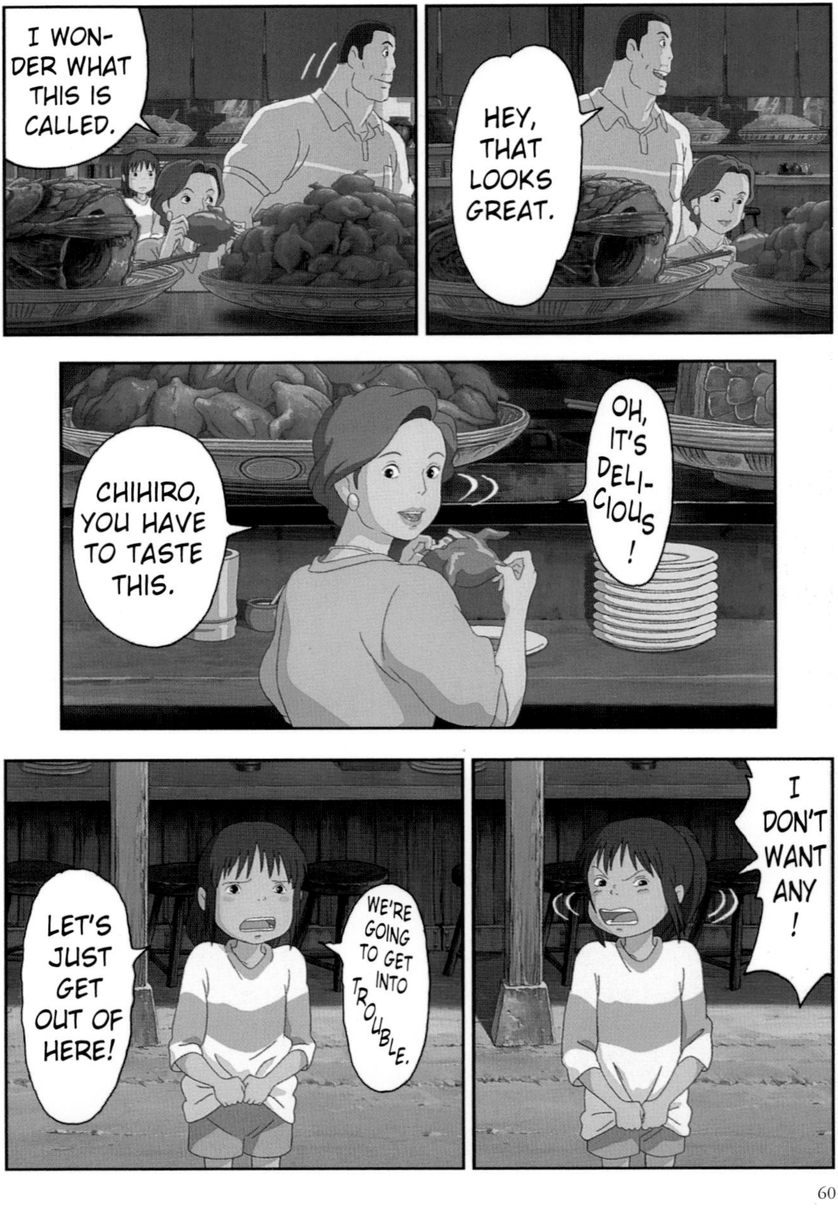
I WONDER WHAT THIS IS CALLED.
HEY, THAT LOOKS GREAT.
OH, IT'S DELICIOUS!
CHIHIRO, YOU HAVE TO TASTE THIS.
LET'S JUST GET OUT OF HERE!
WE'RE GOING TO GET INTO TROUBLE.
I DON'T WANT ANY!

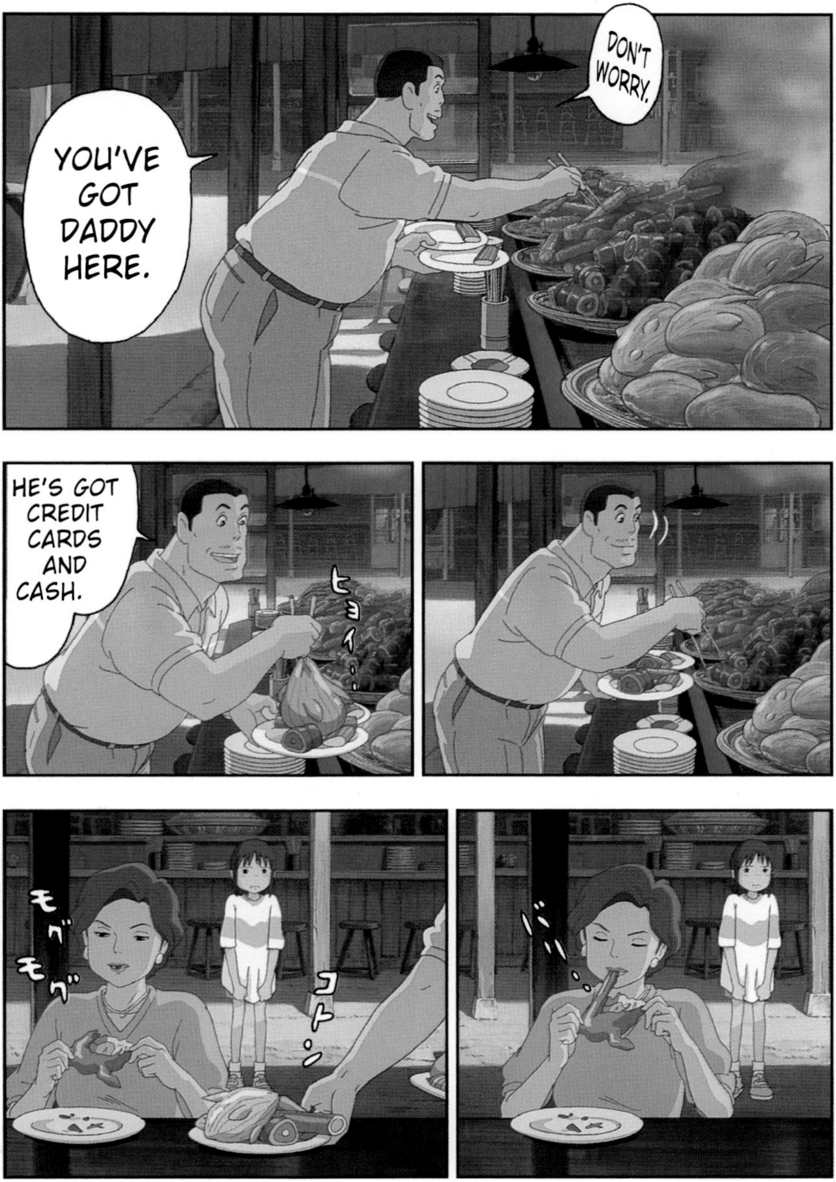

DON'T WORRY.
YOU'VE GOT DADDY HERE.
HE'S GOT CREDIT CARDS AND CASH.
ヒョイ・・
コト・・
モグ
モグ

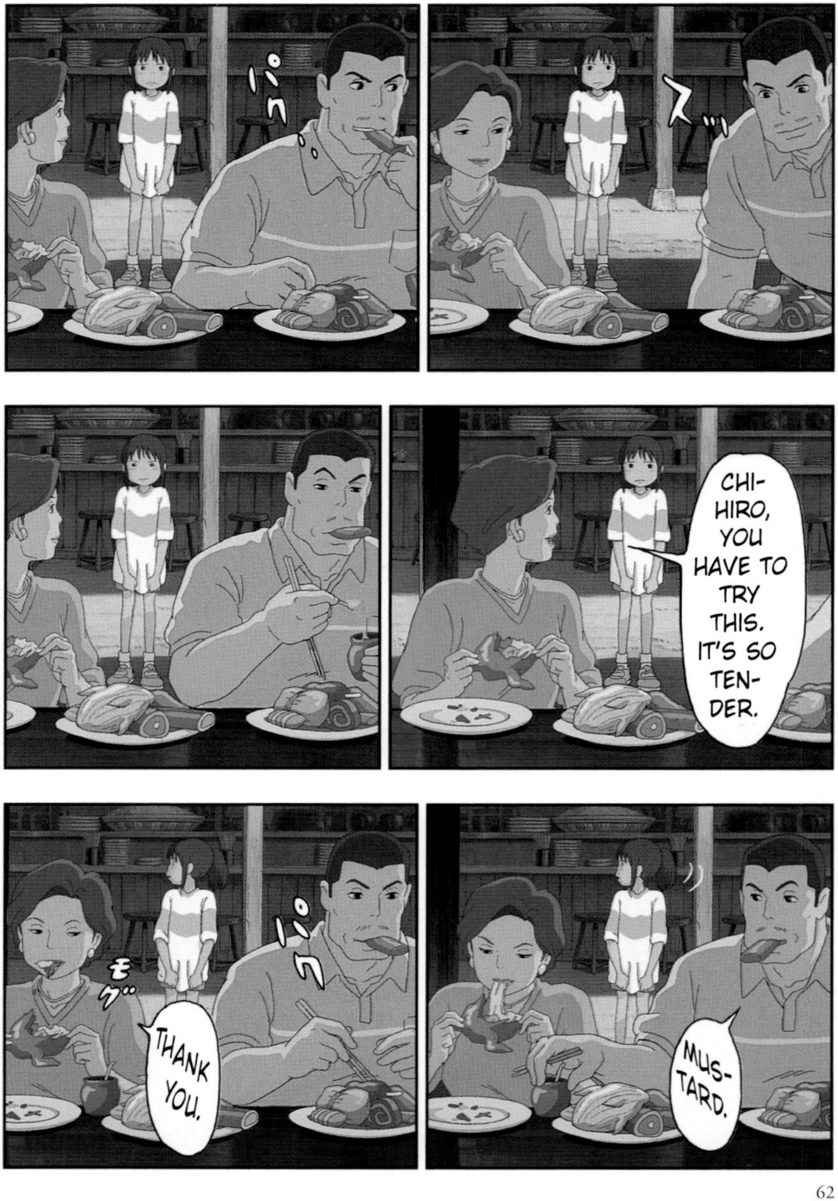
CHI-HIRO, YOU HAVE TO TRY THIS. IT'S SO TEN-DER.
MUS-TARD.
THANK YOU.

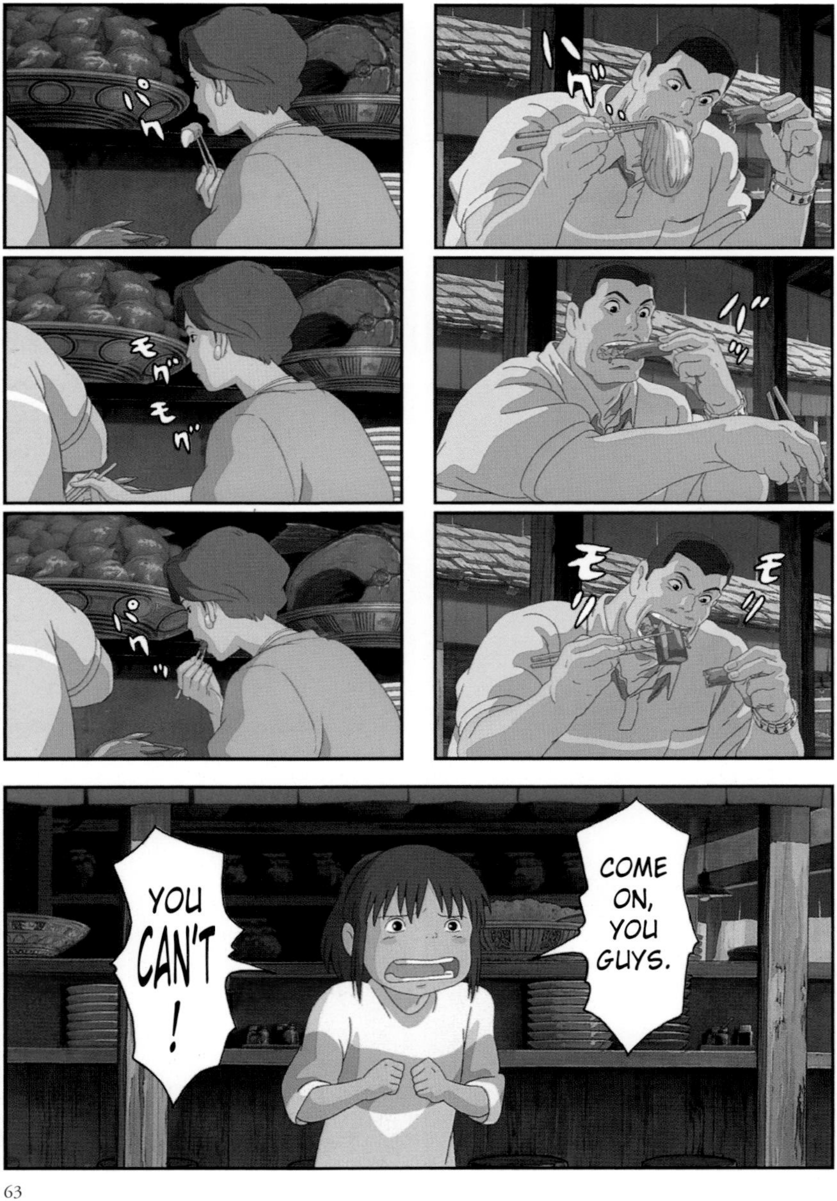
COME ON, YOU GUYS.
YOU CAN'T!

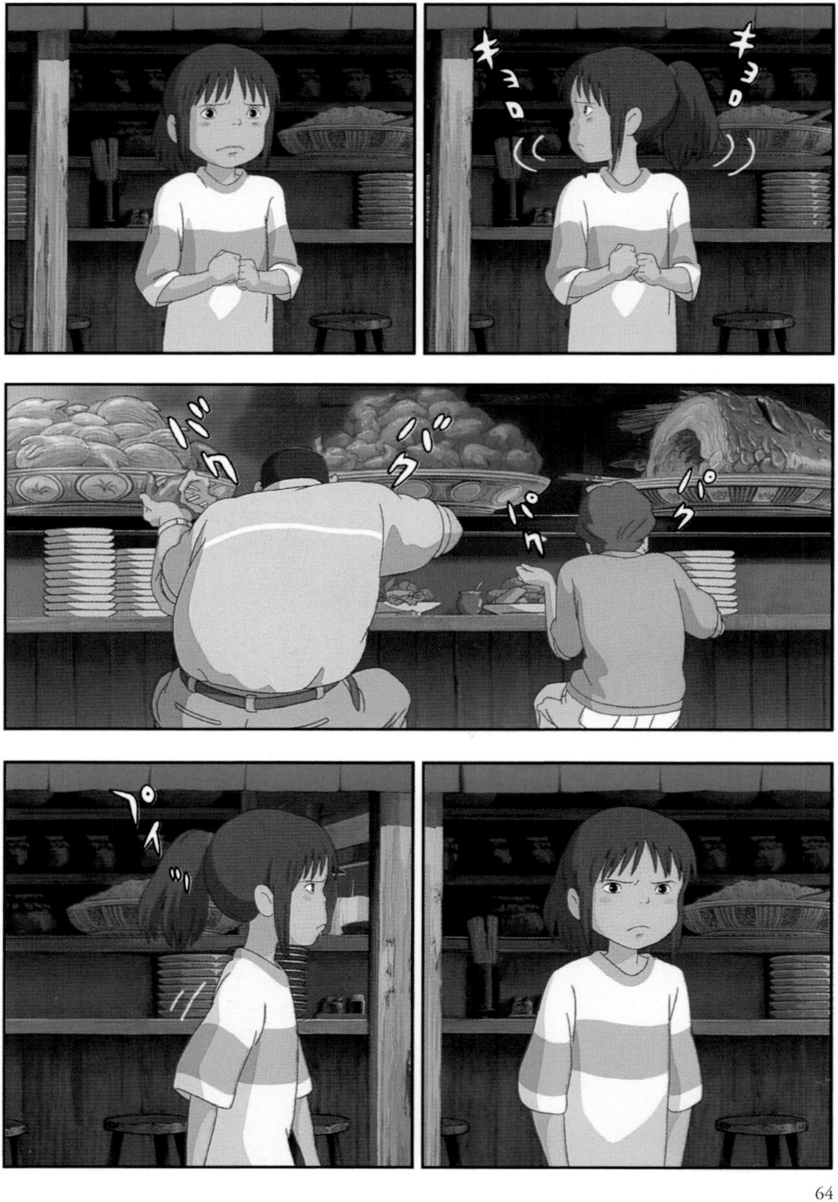
キョロ
キョロ
パク
パク
バク
バク
プイ

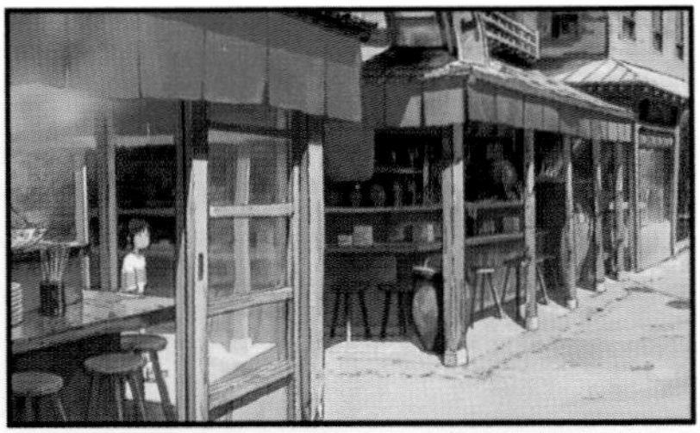
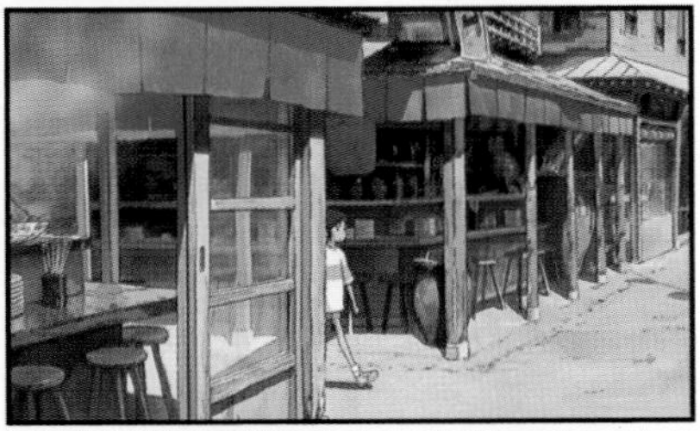
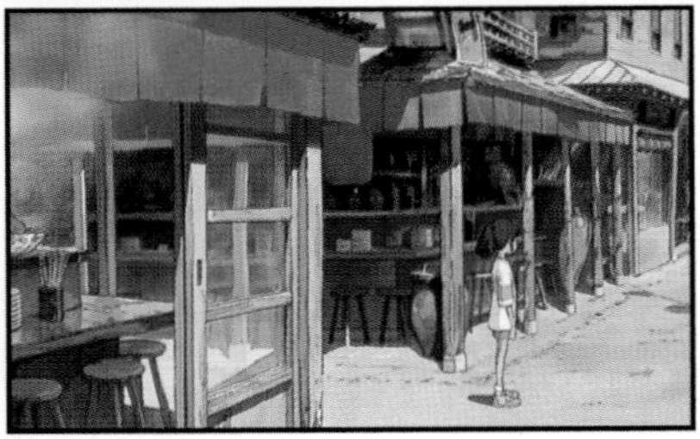
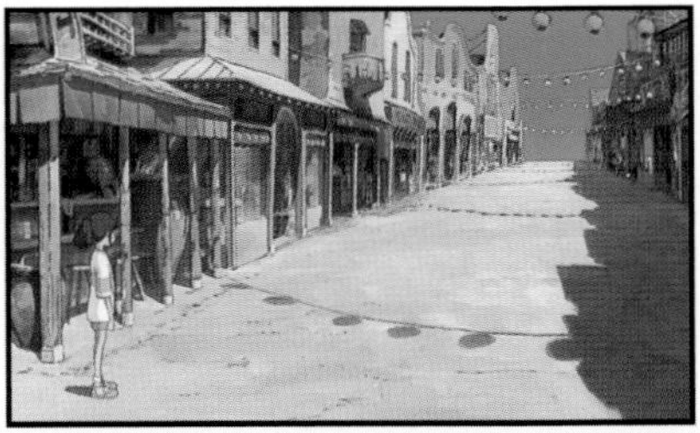
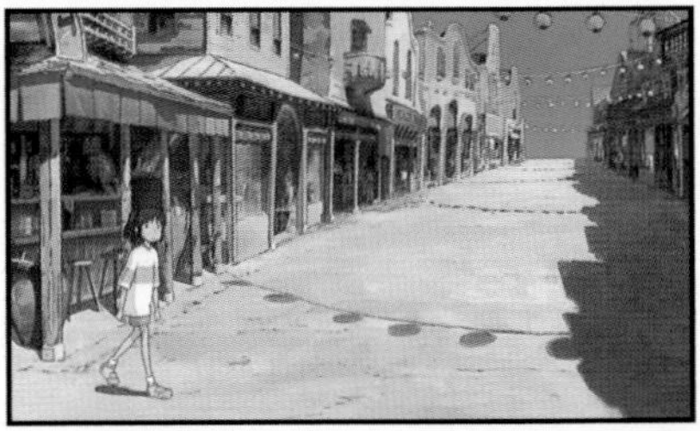
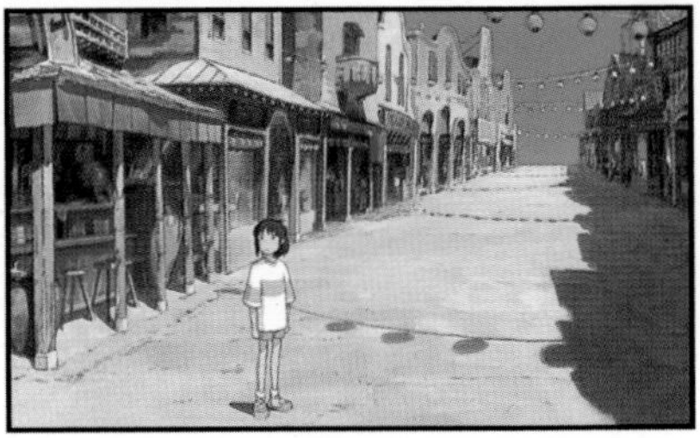
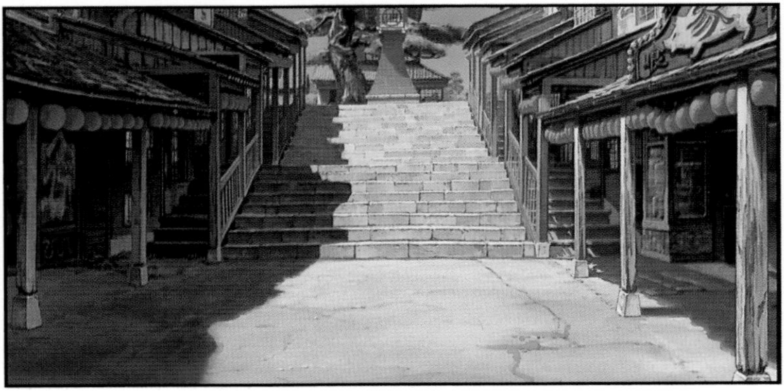

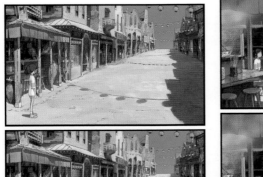

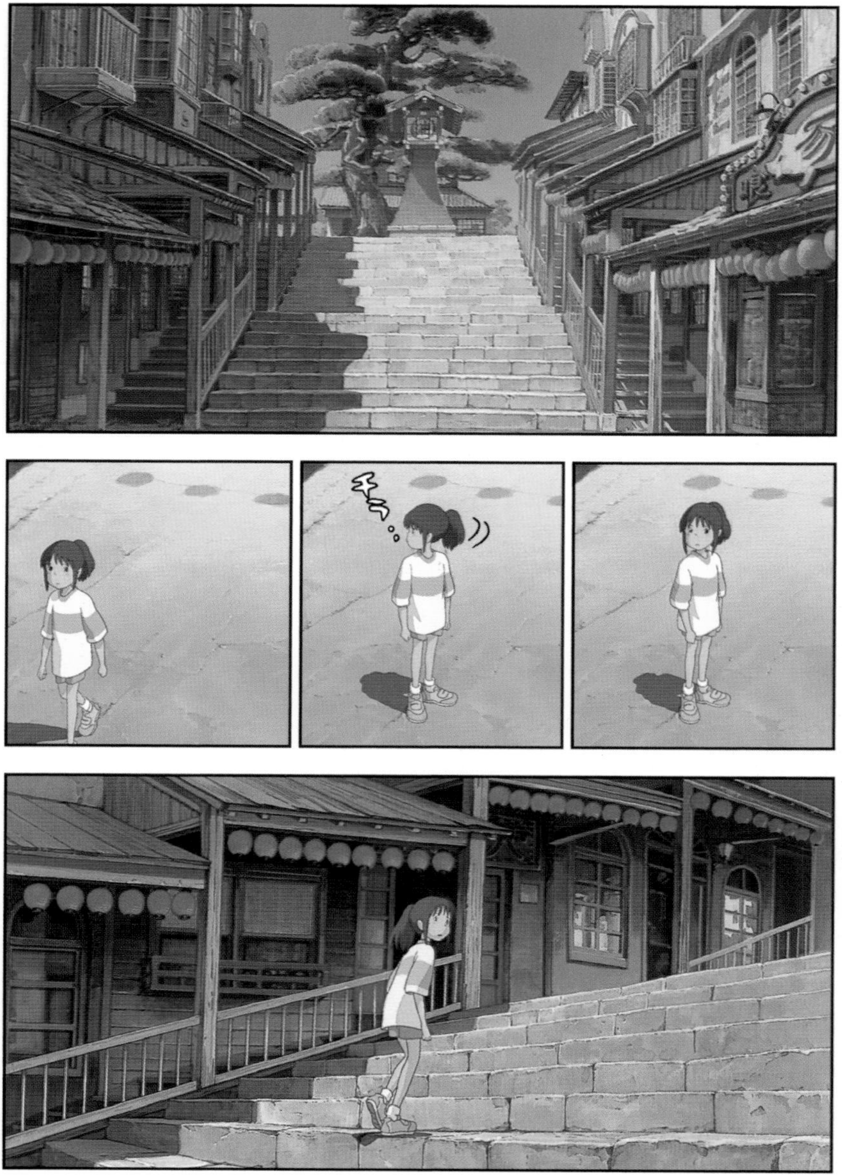
チラ

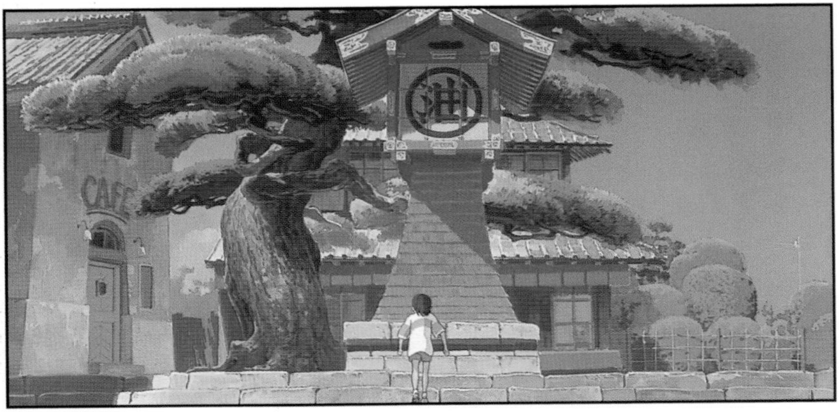
油
CAFE
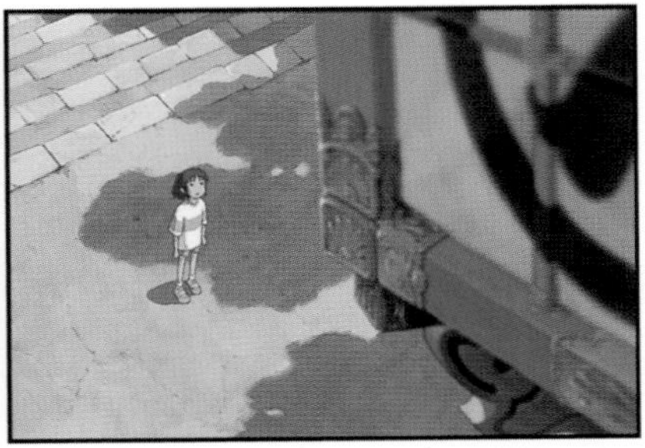
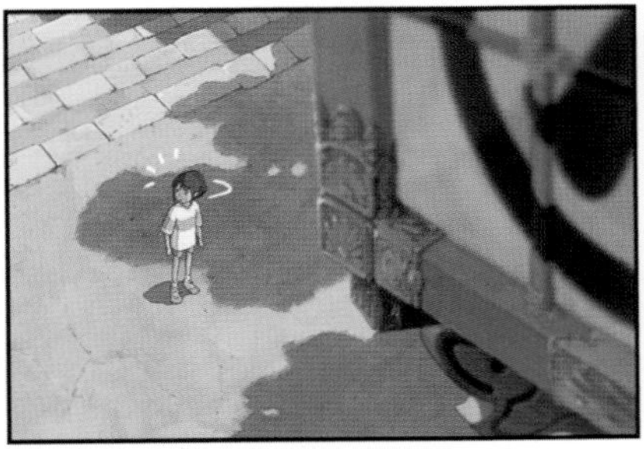
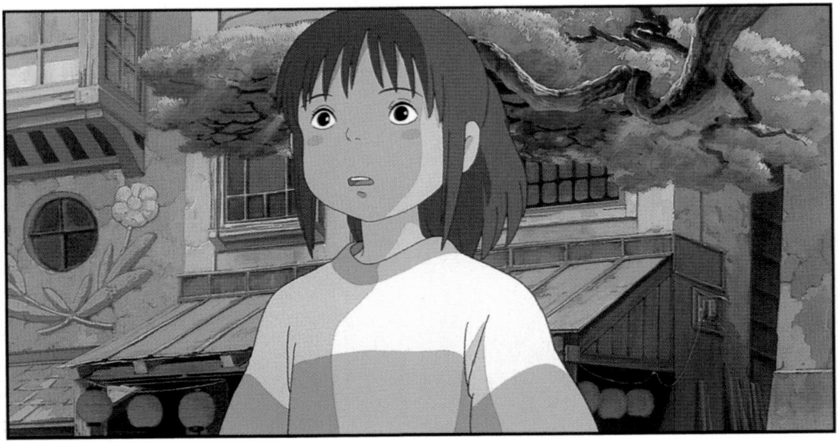

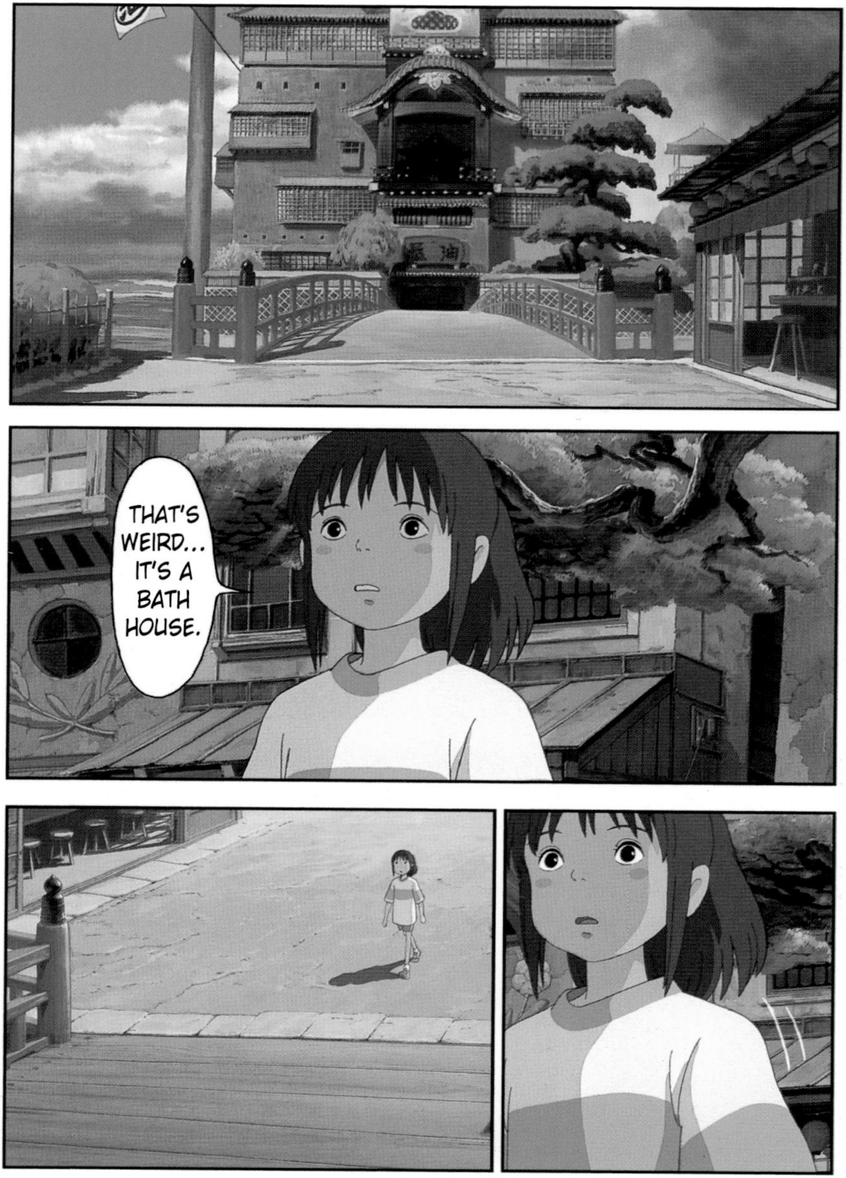
THAT'S WEIRD... IT'S A BATH HOUSE.

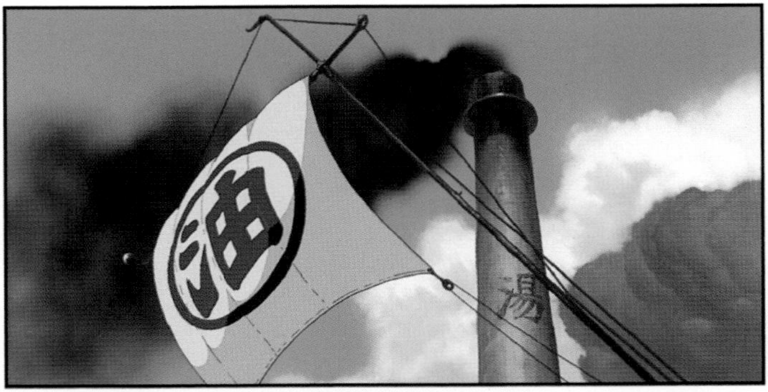
油
湯

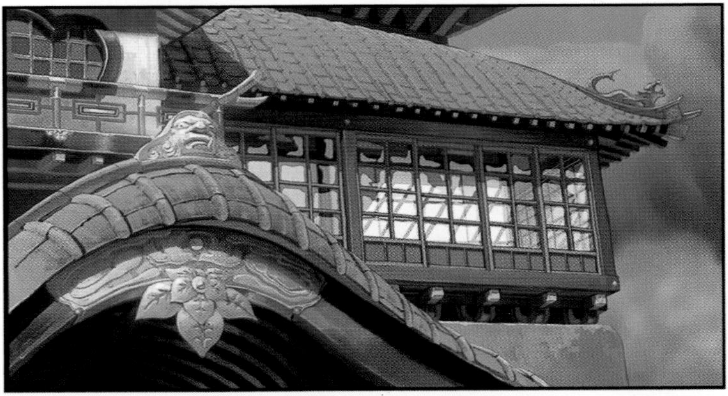

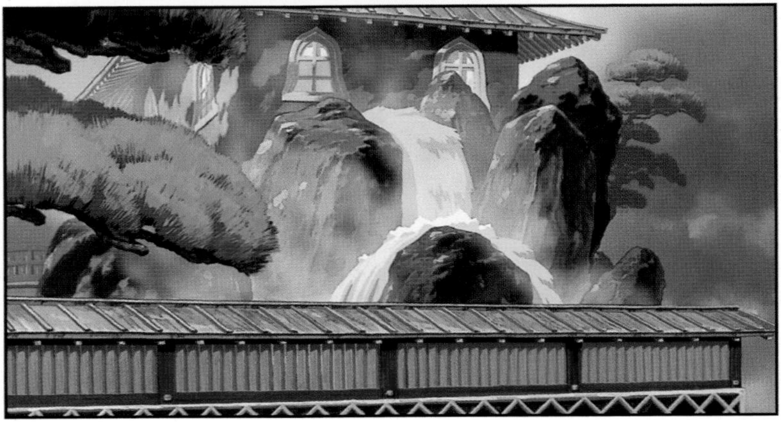

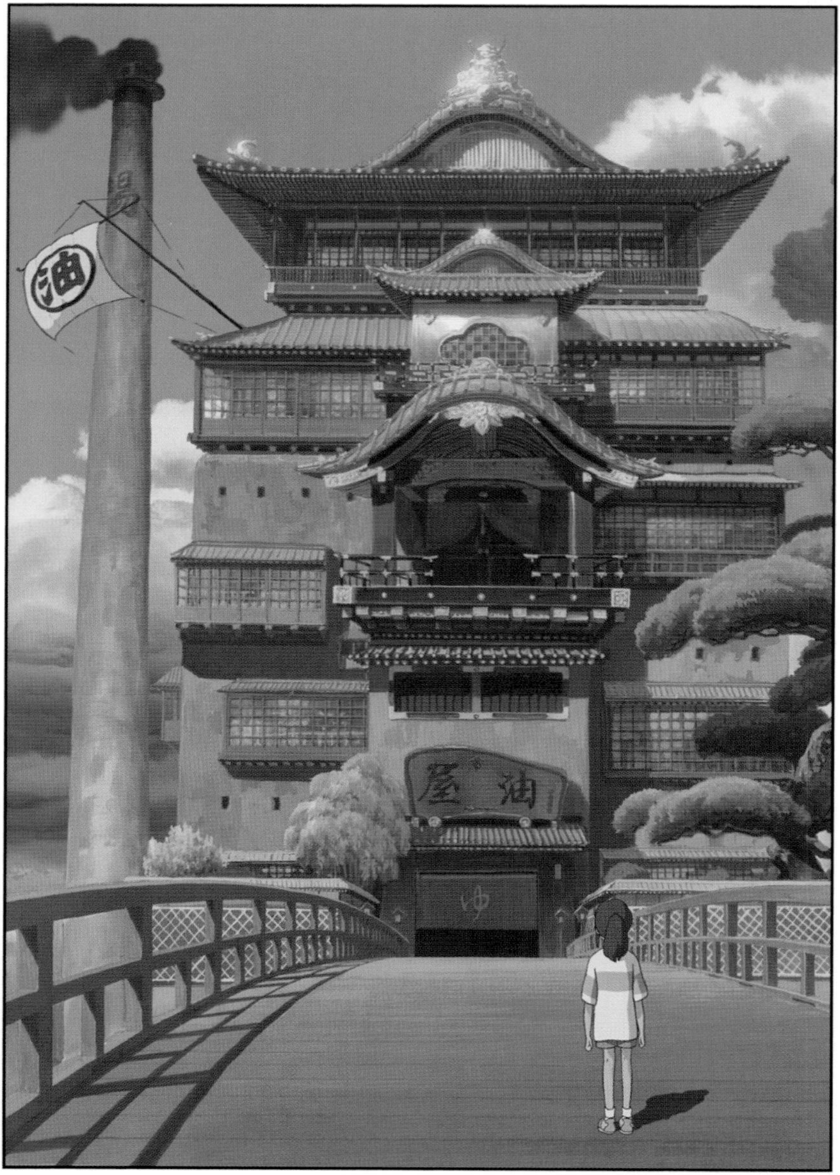
油
油屋
ゆ

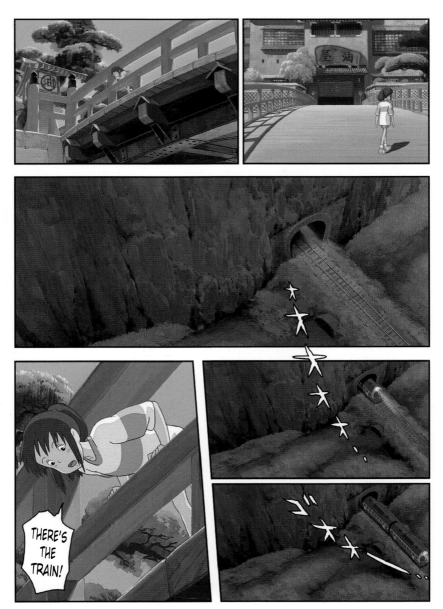

THERE'S THE TRAIN!

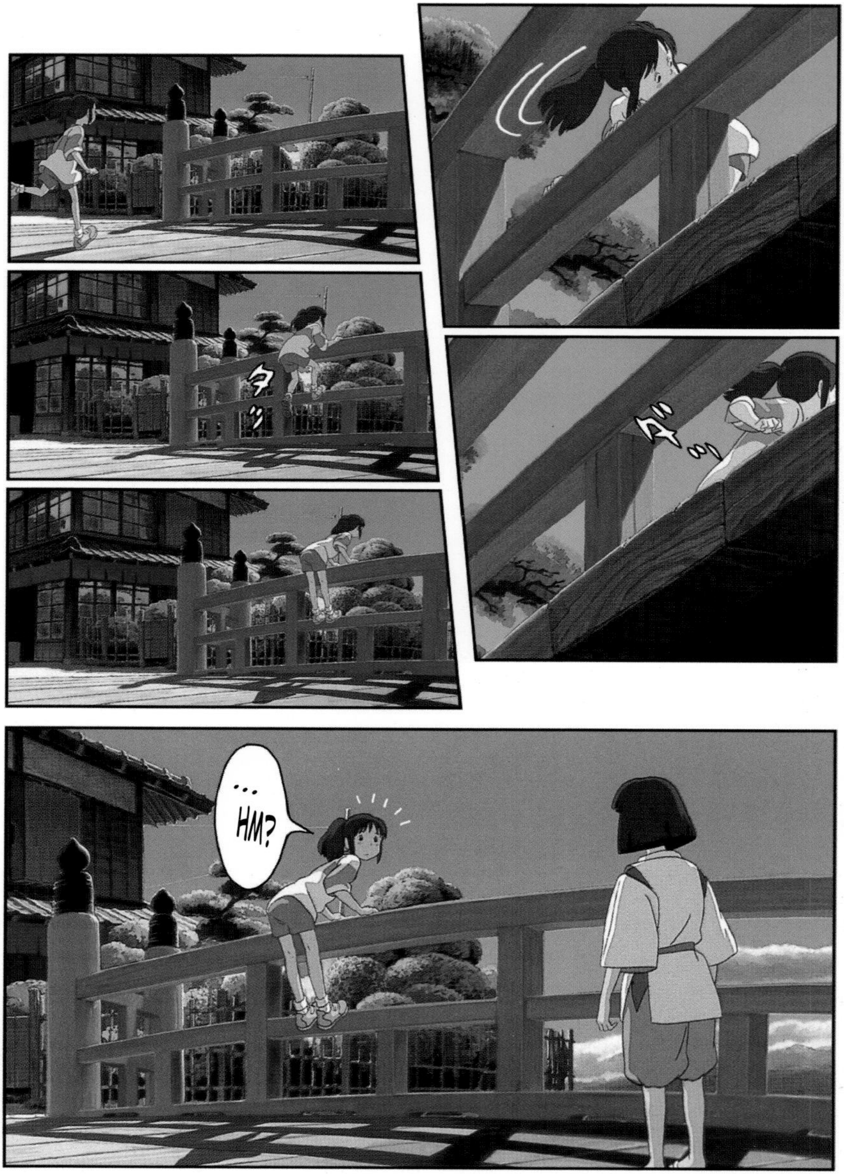
... HM?

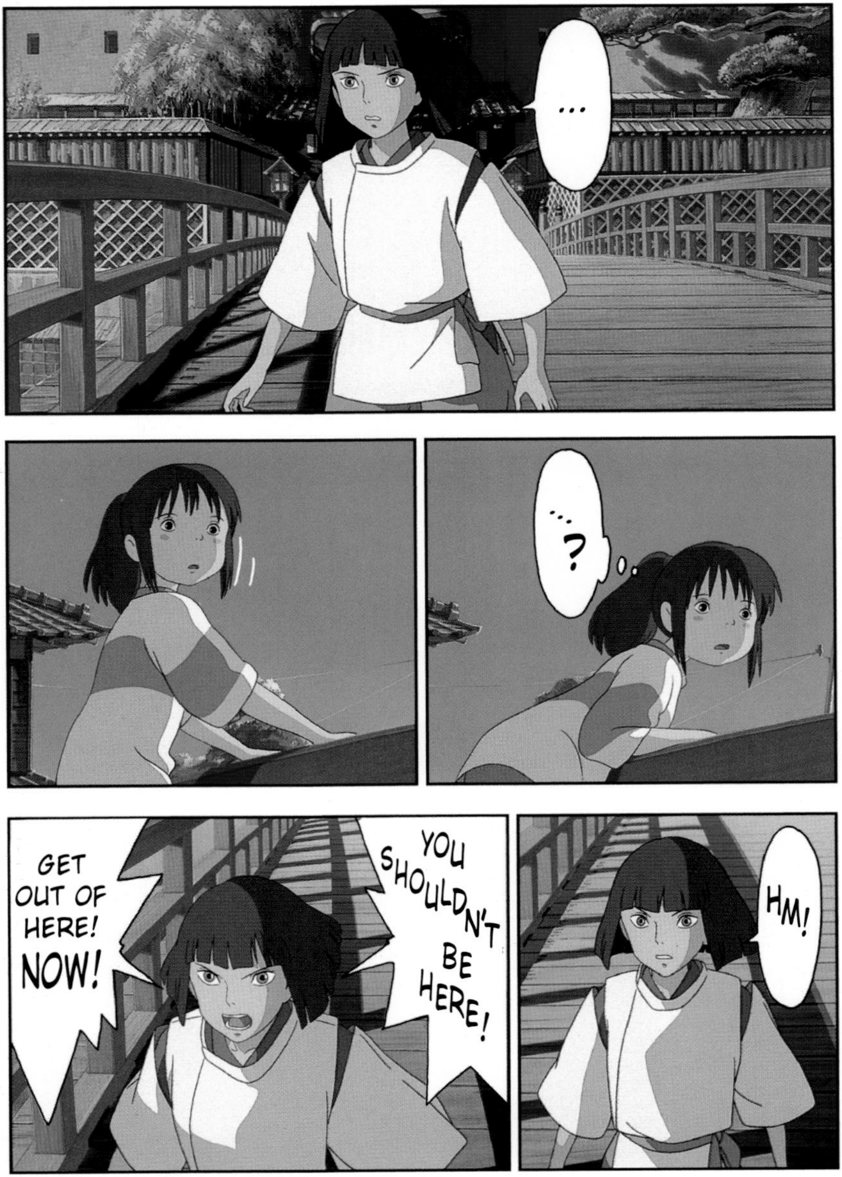
...
...?
HM!
YOU SHOULDN'T BE HERE!
GET OUT OF HERE! NOW!

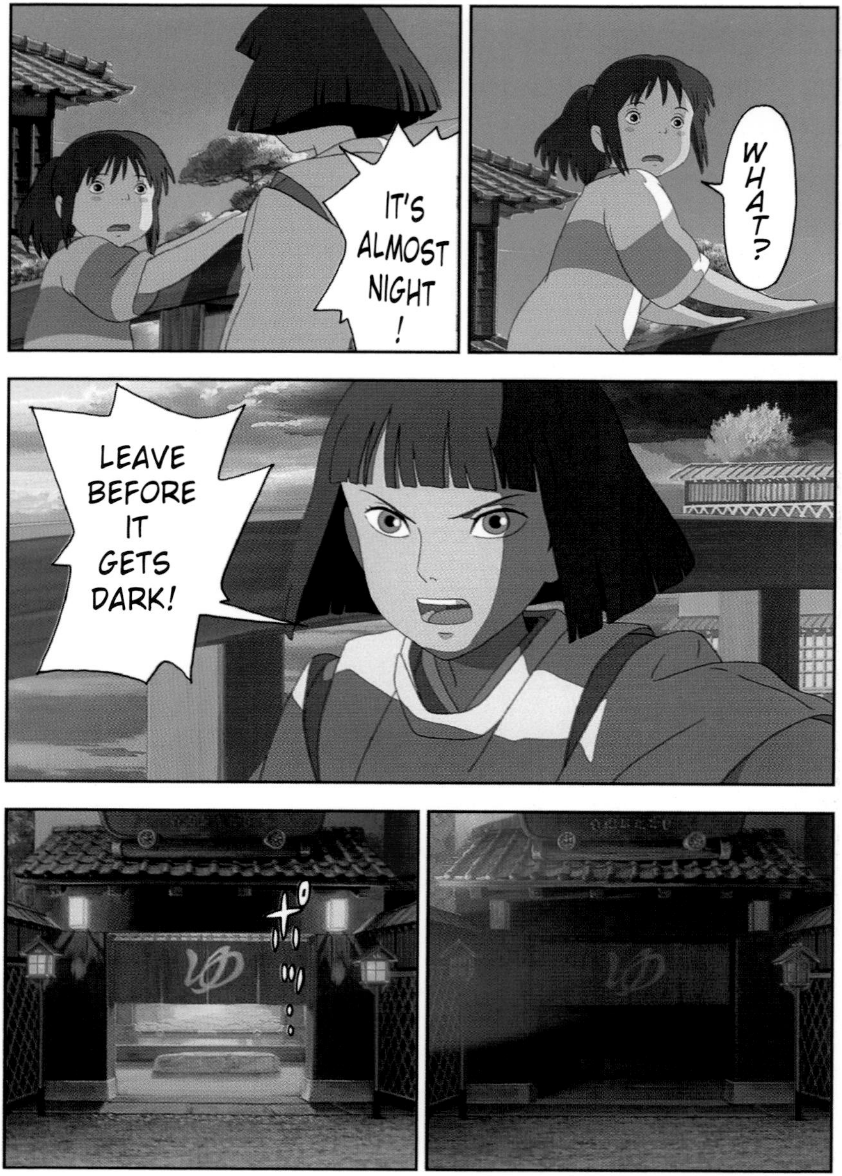
IT'S ALMOST NIGHT!
WHAT?
LEAVE BEFORE IT GETS DARK!

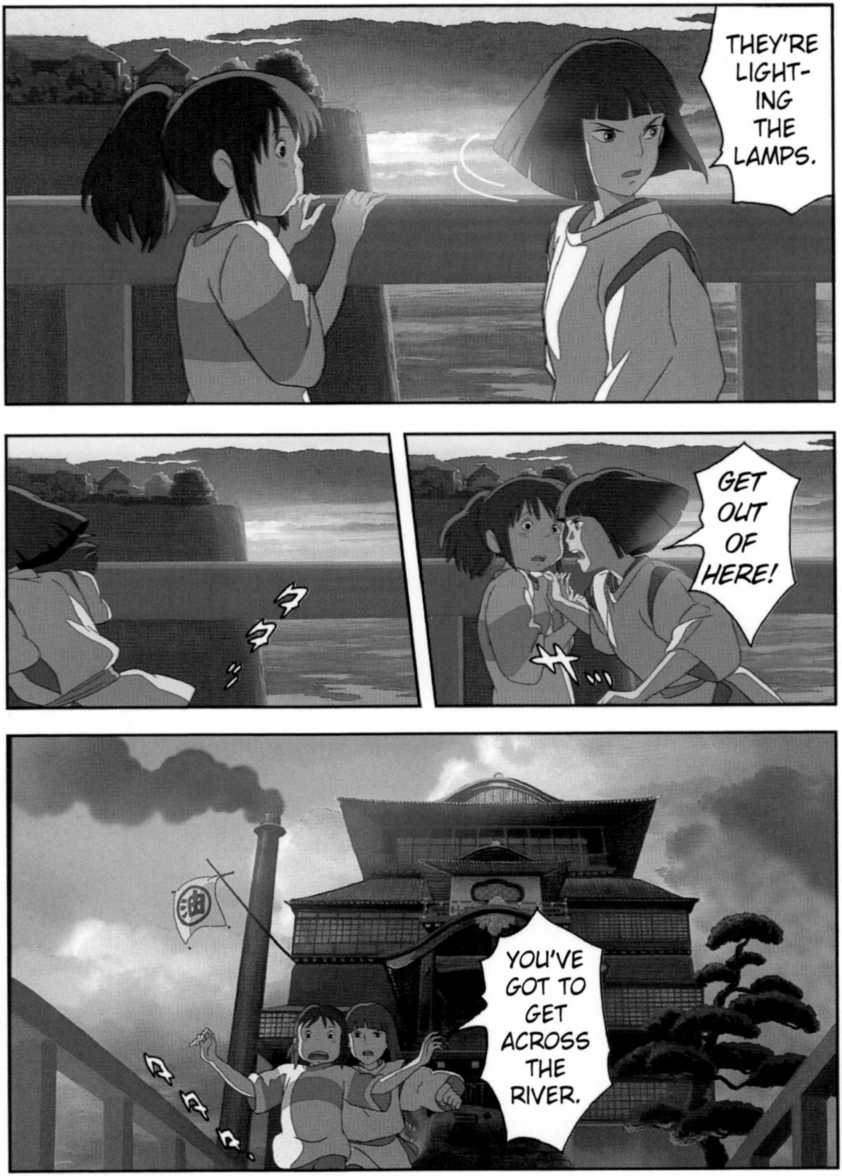
THEY'RE LIGHT-ING THE LAMPS.
GET OUT OF HERE!
YOU'VE GOT TO GET ACROSS THE RIVER.

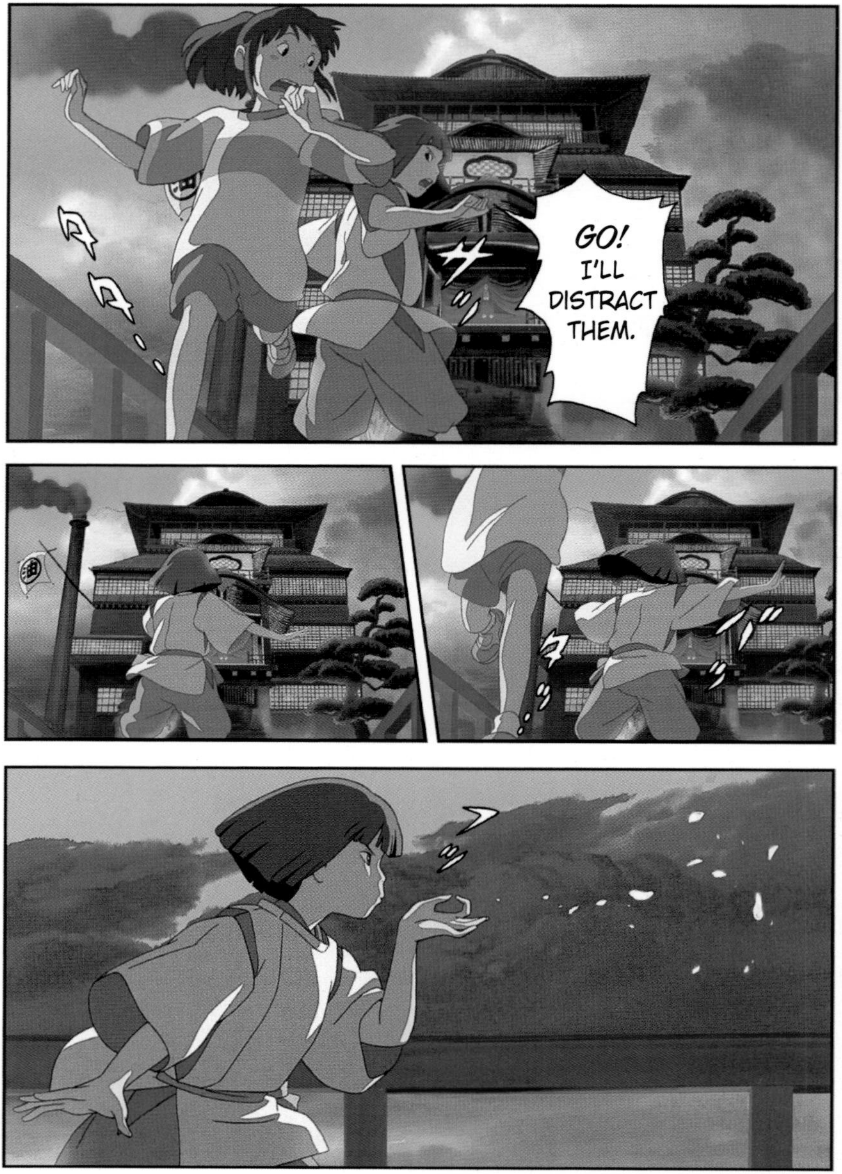
GO! I'LL DISTRACT THEM.

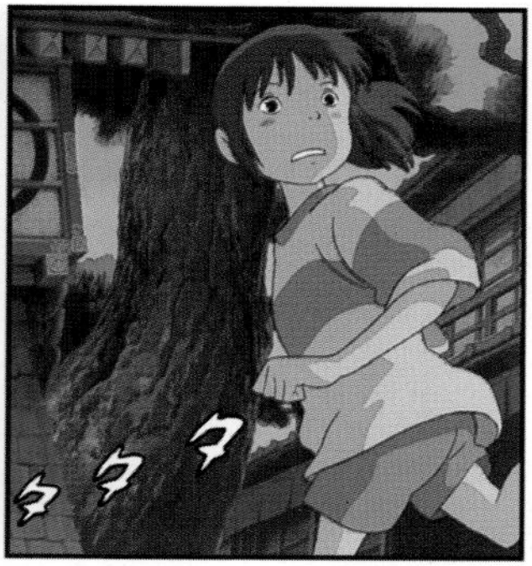
タタタタ
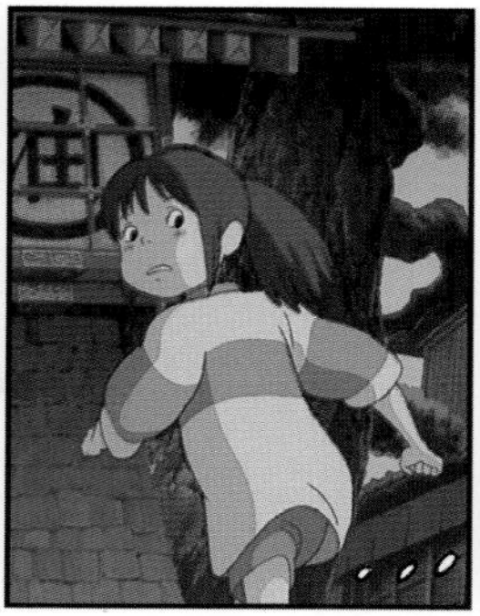
・・・
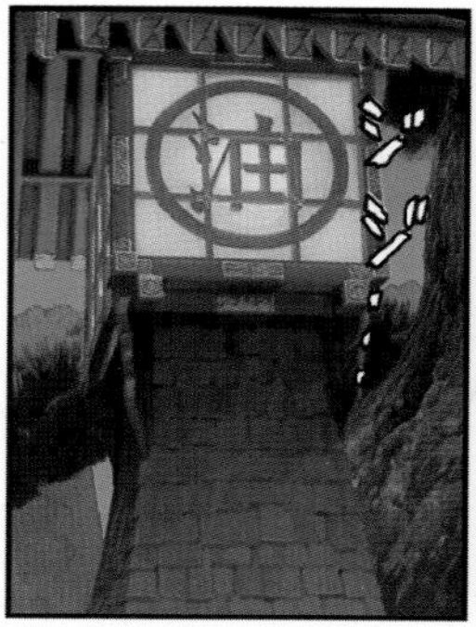
ジジ…
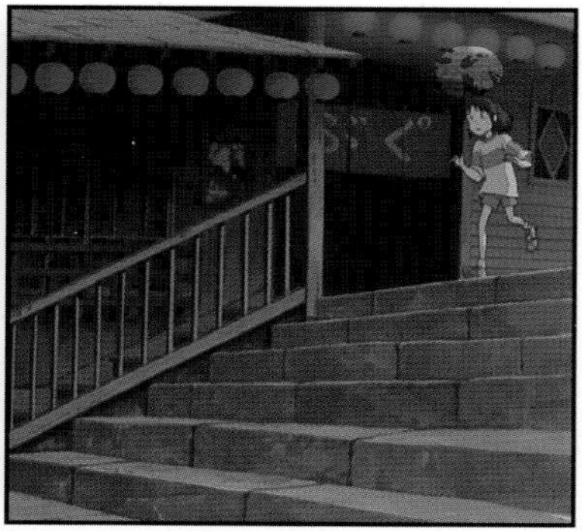
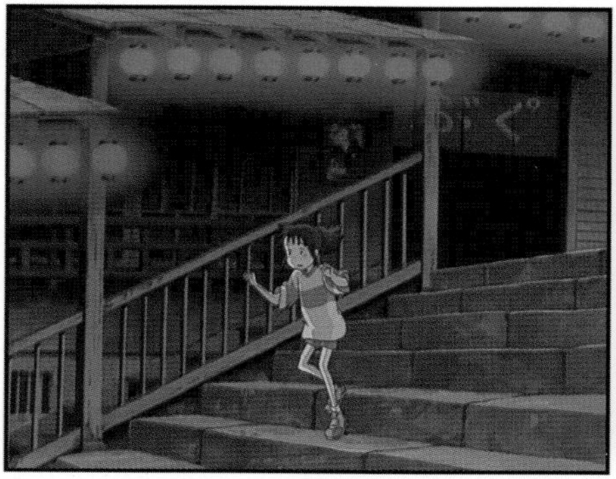
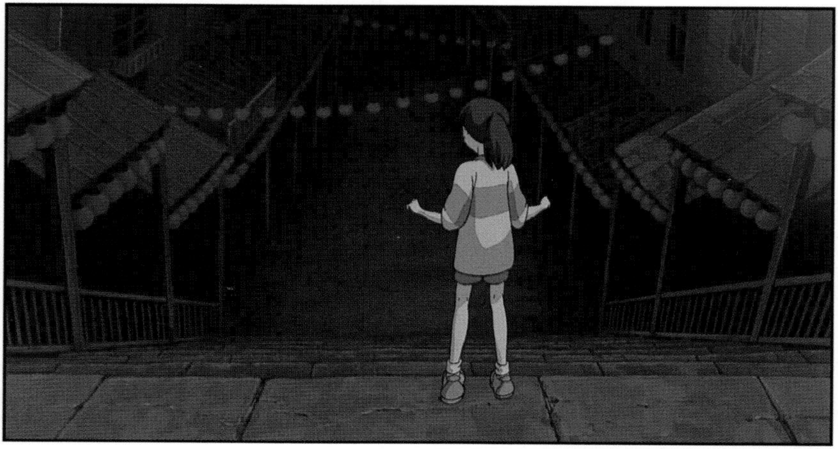

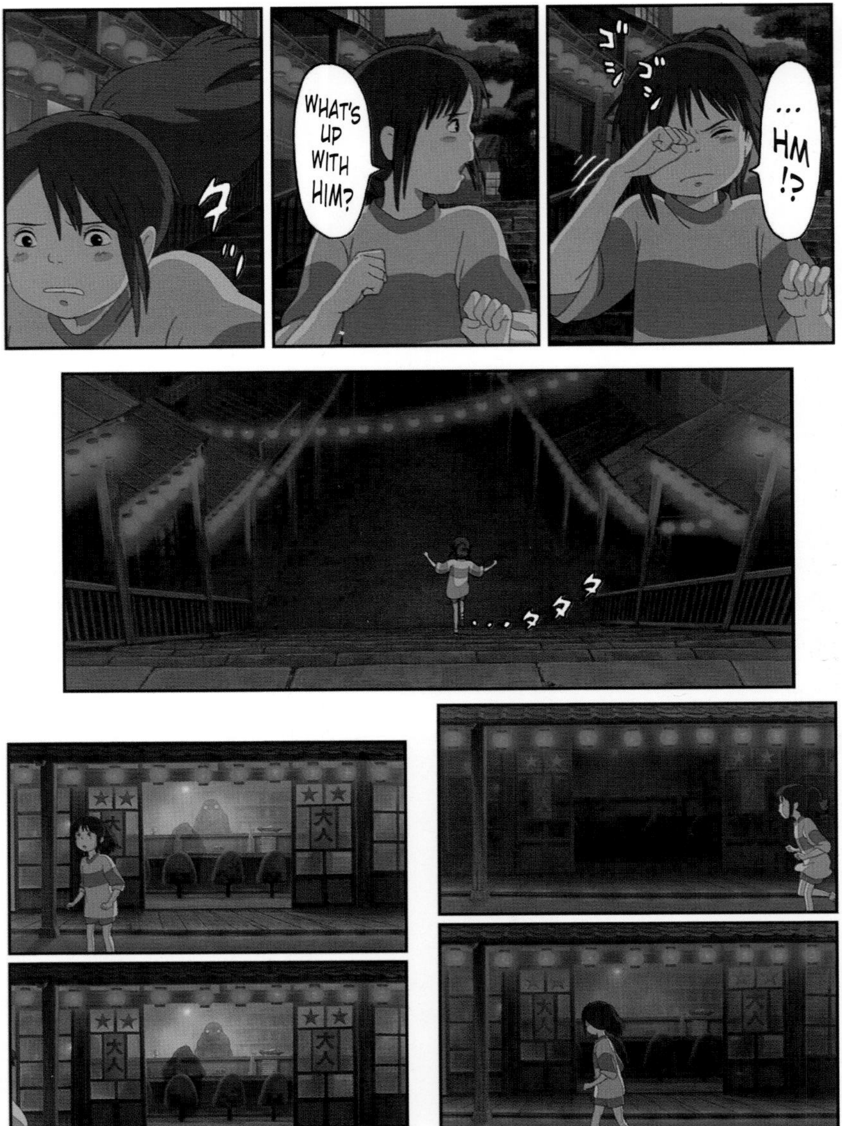
WHAT'S UP WITH HIM?
... HM !?

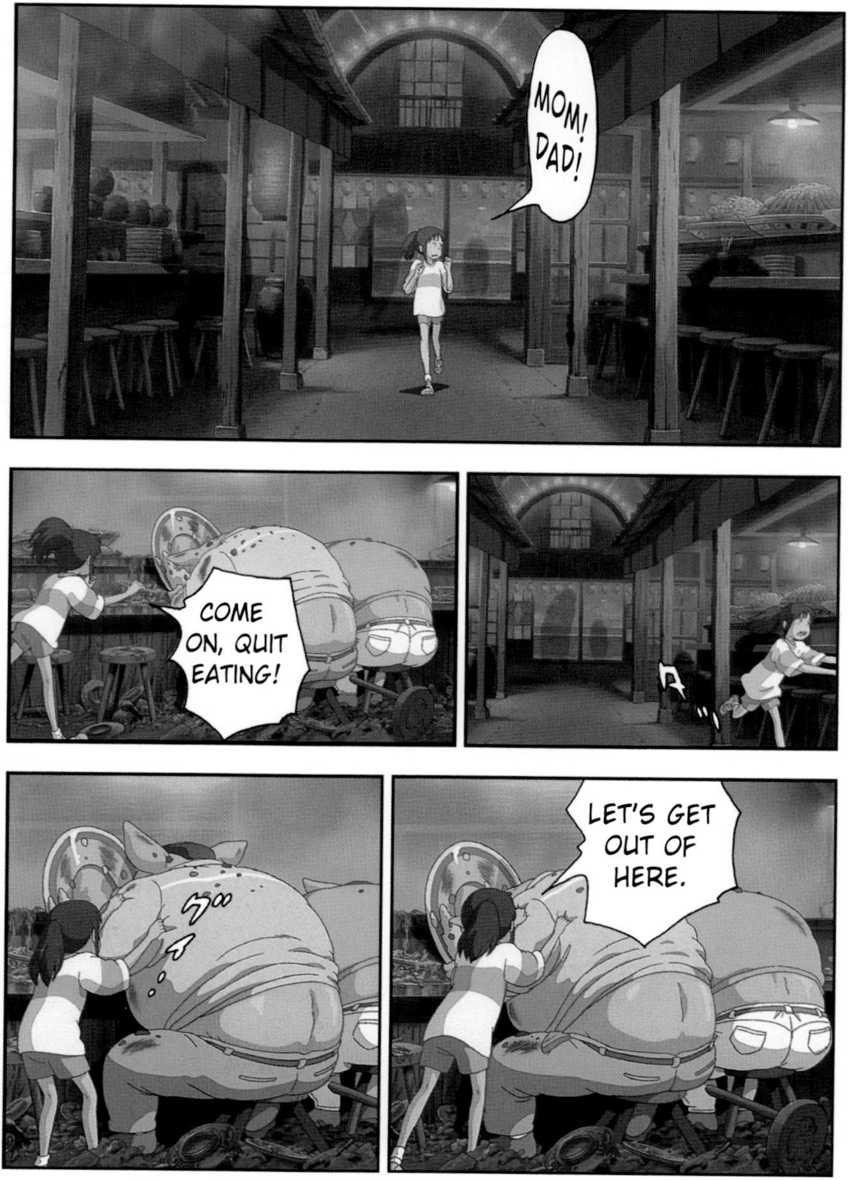
MOM! DAD!
COME ON, QUIT EATING!
LET'S GET OUT OF HERE.

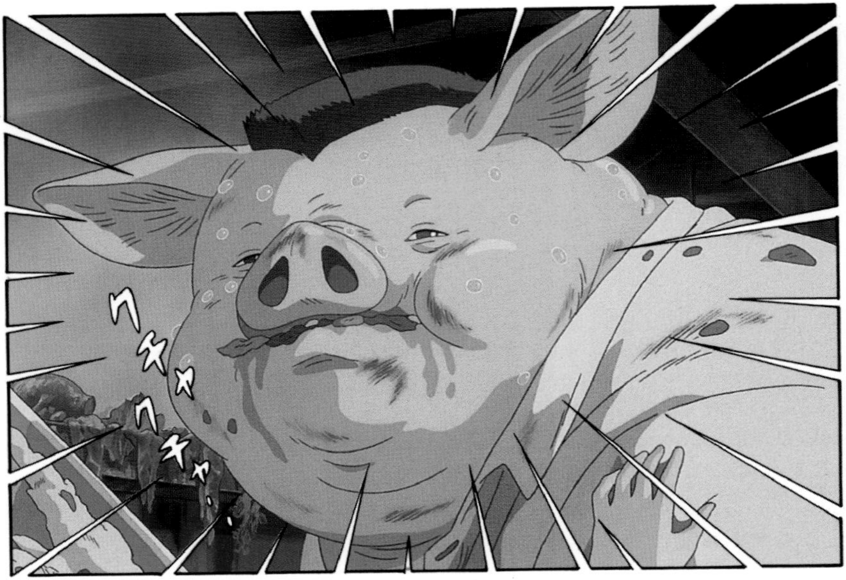

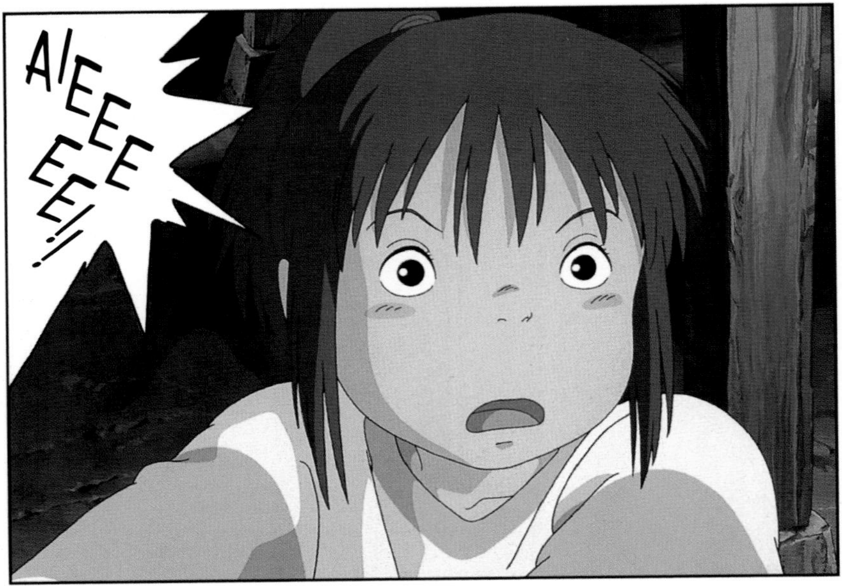
AIEEEEEE!!

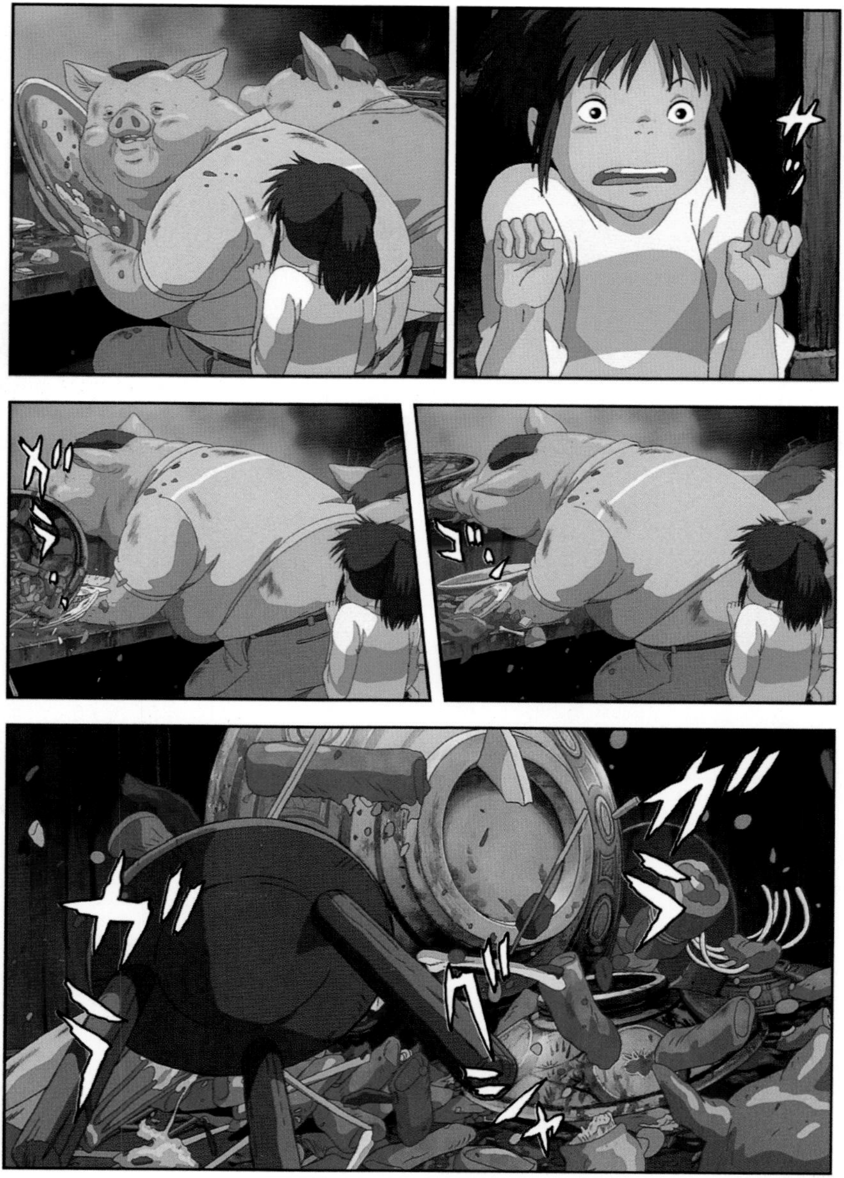
サッ
ゴッ
ガシャ

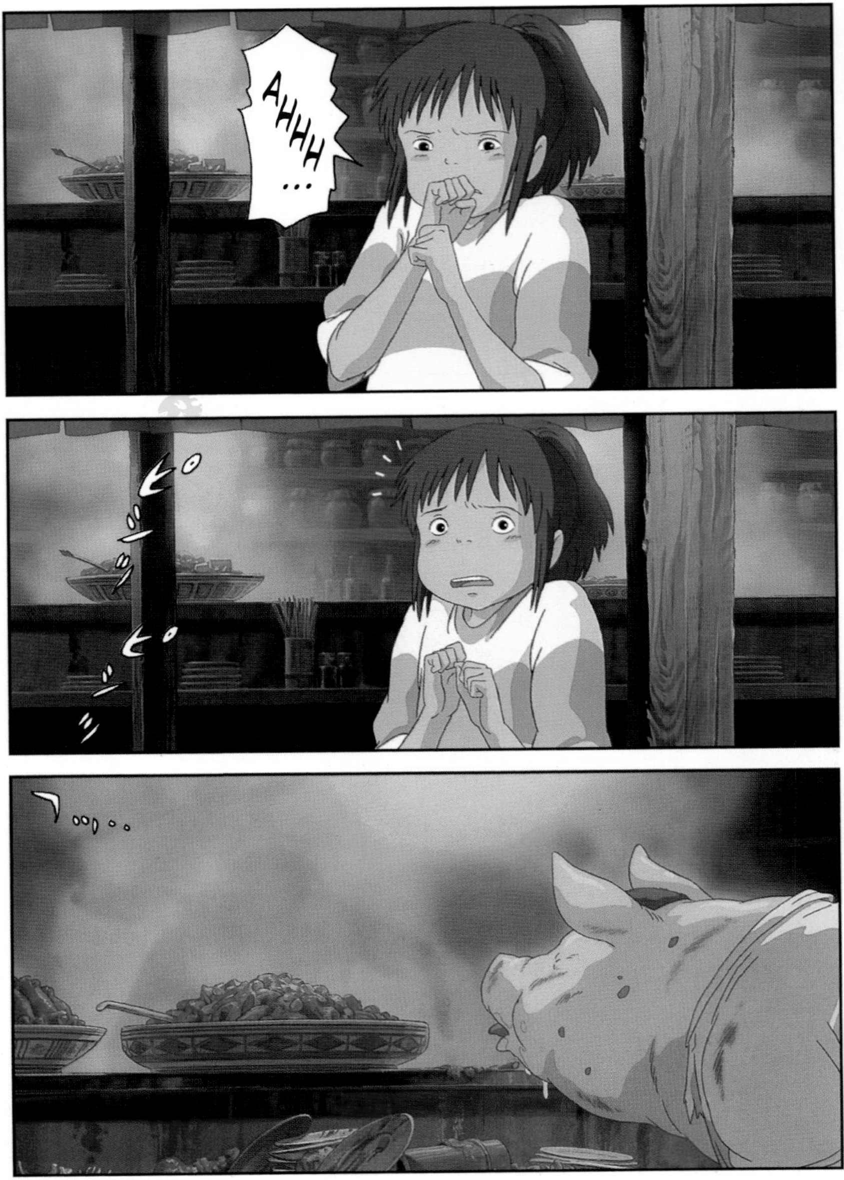
AHHH ...

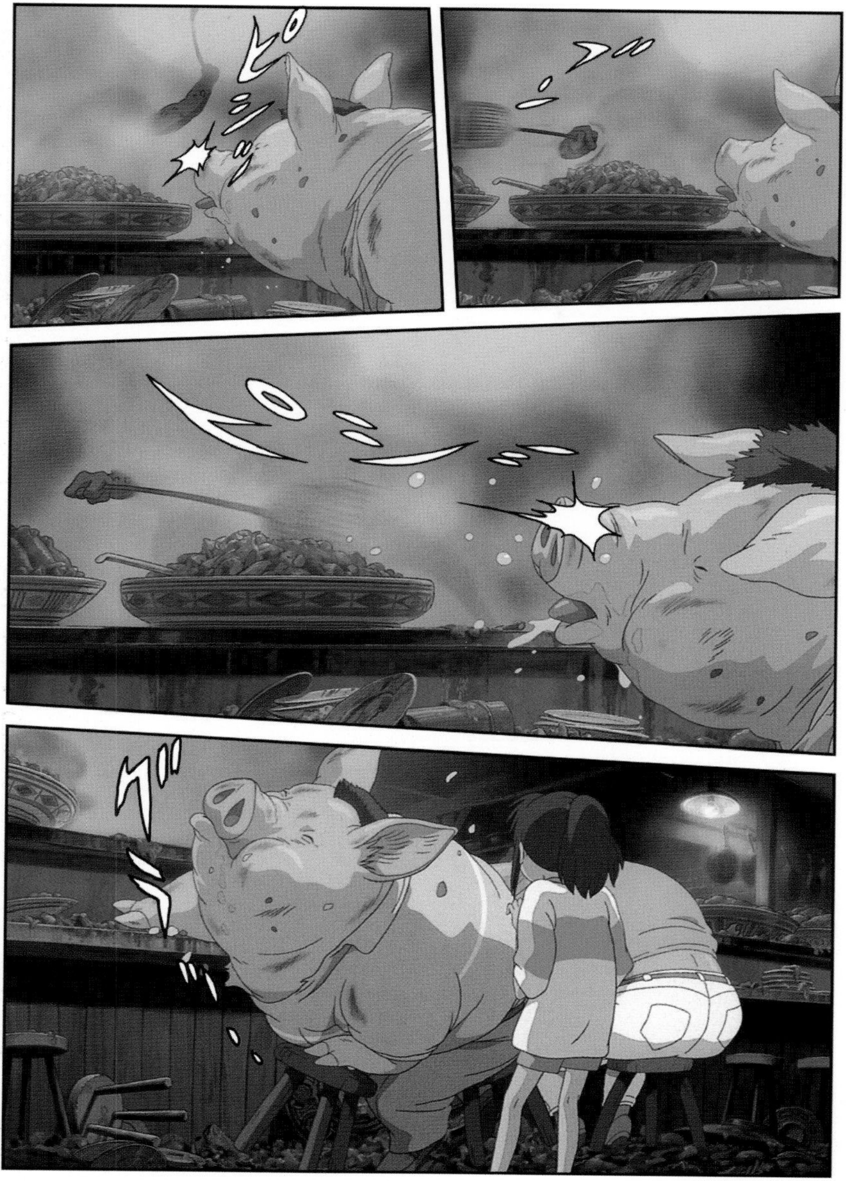
ピシッ
パシーッ

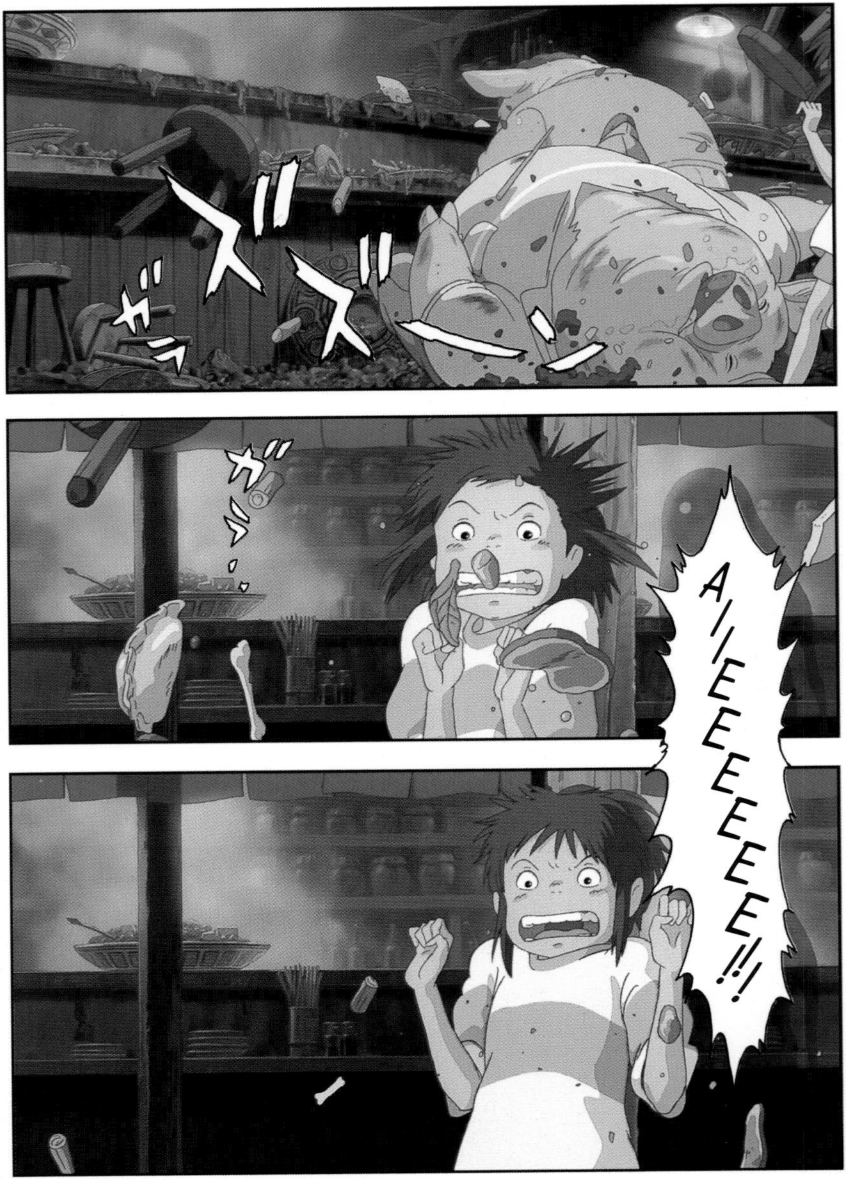
AIIEEEEEE!!!

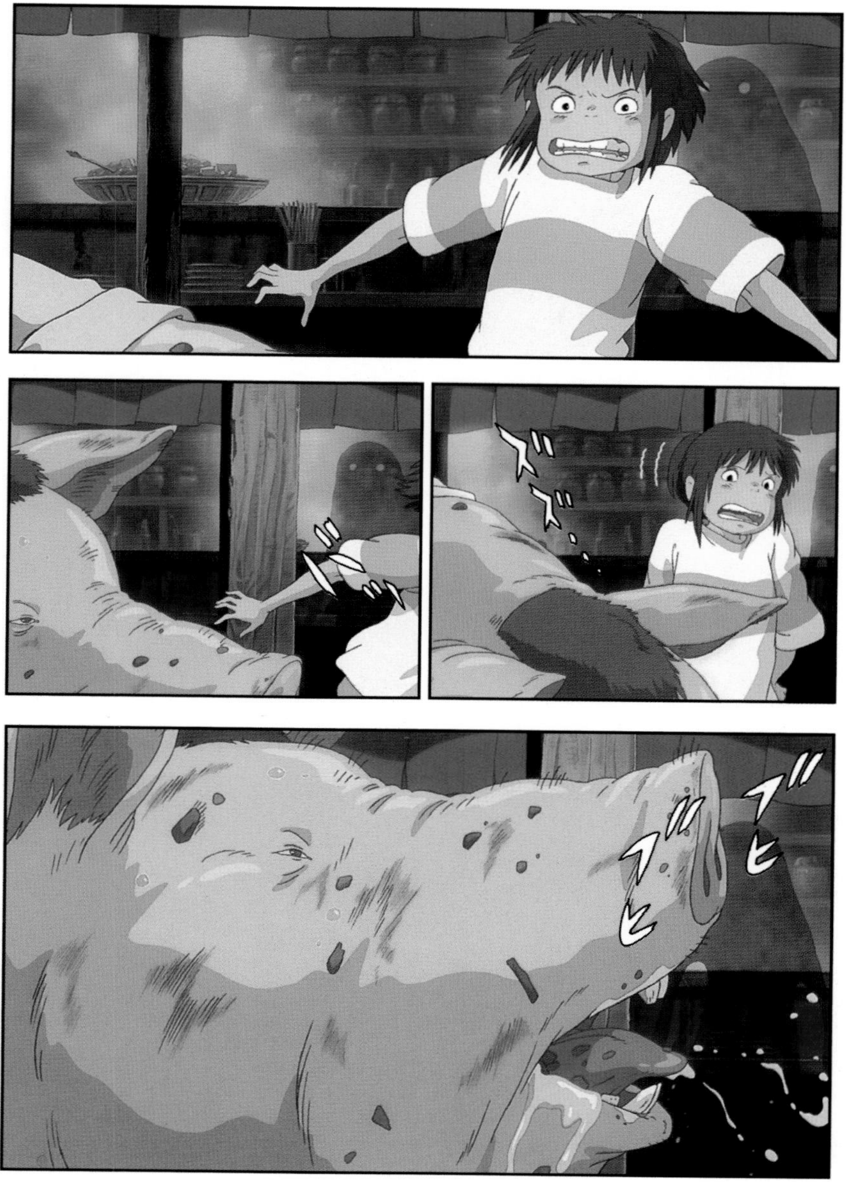
ズズ…
ブヒ
ブヒ

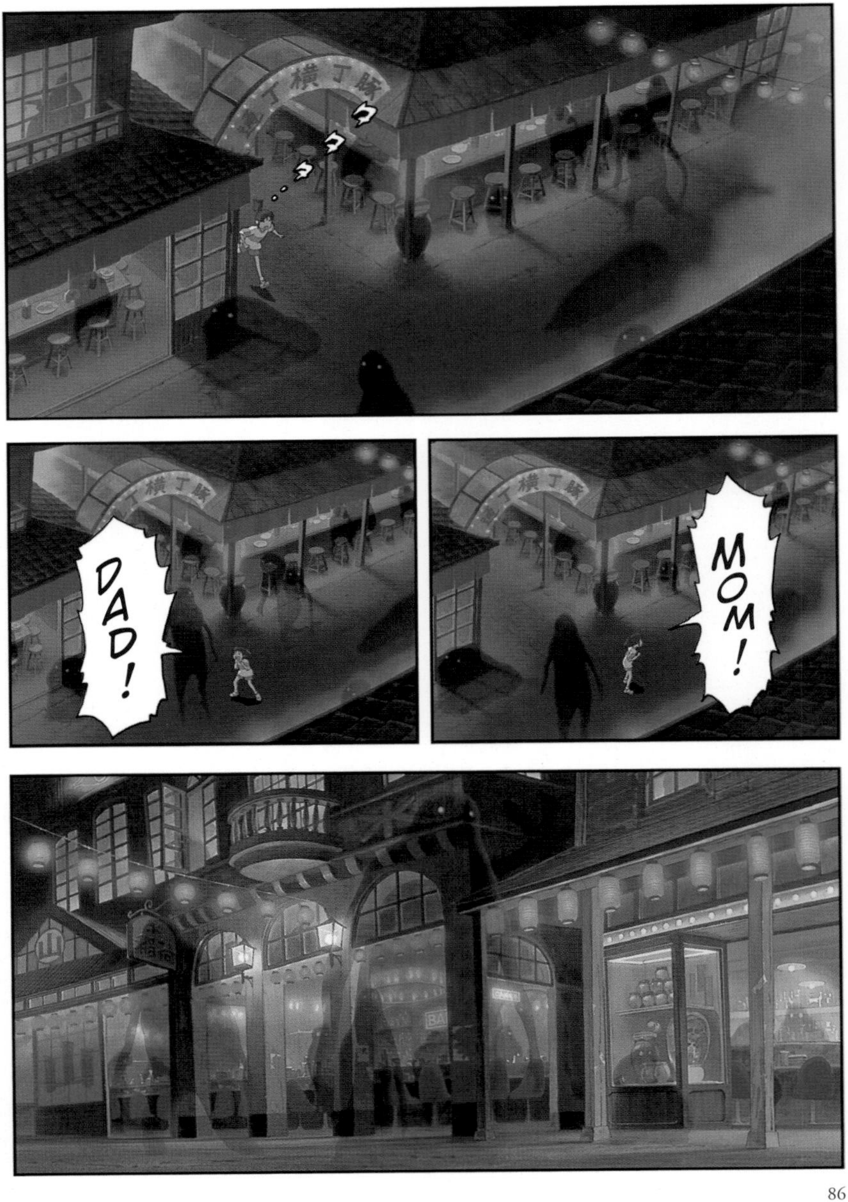
MOM!
DAD!

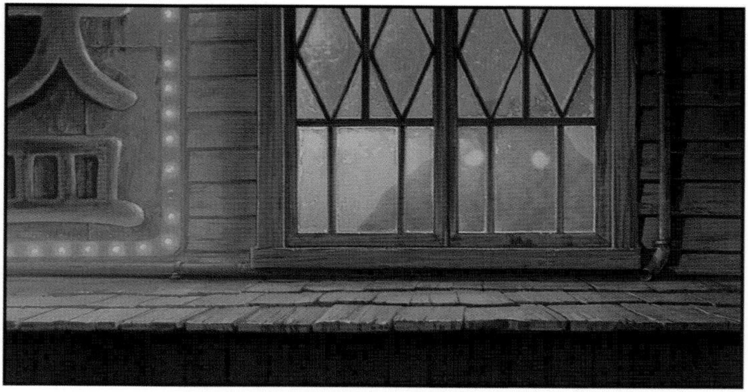

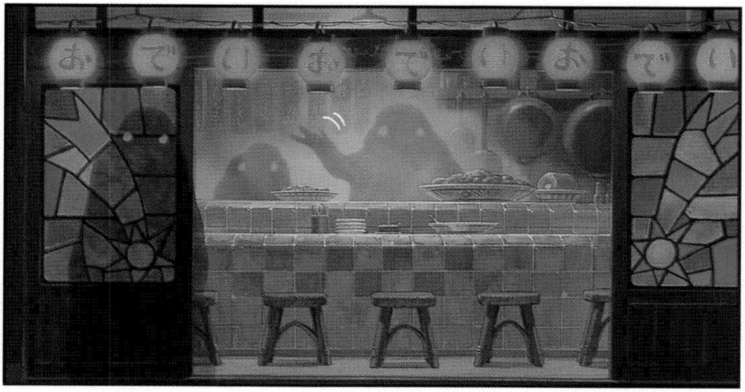

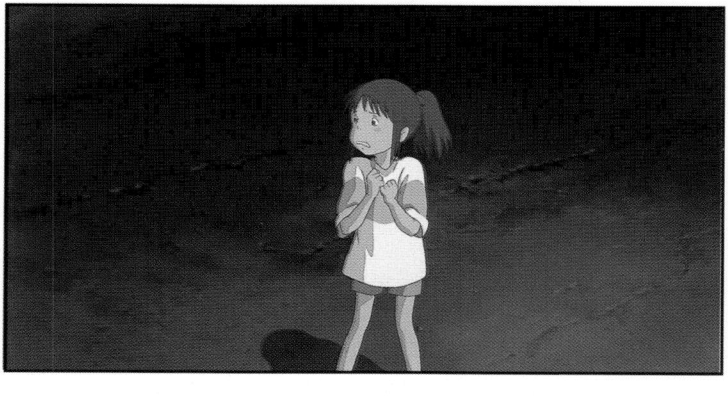

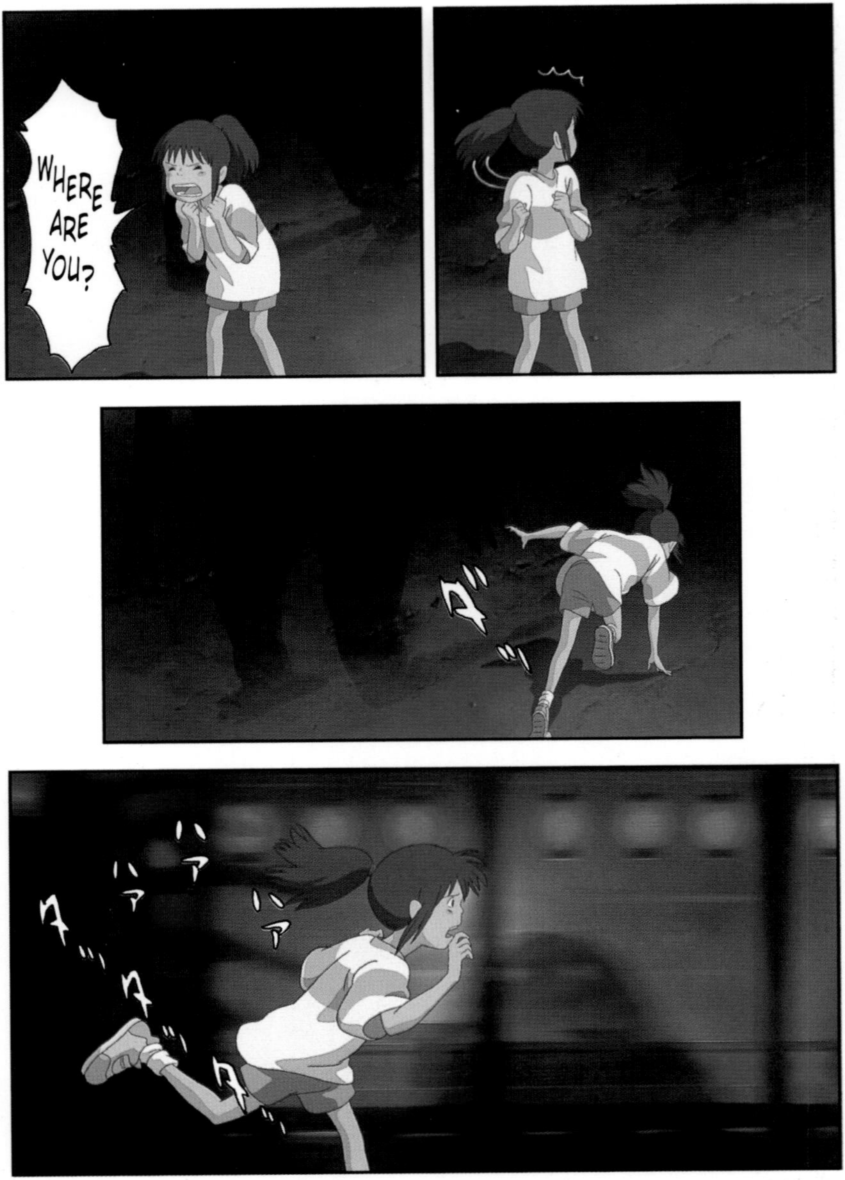
WHERE ARE YOU?
ダッ
ハァ ハァ
タッ タッ タッ

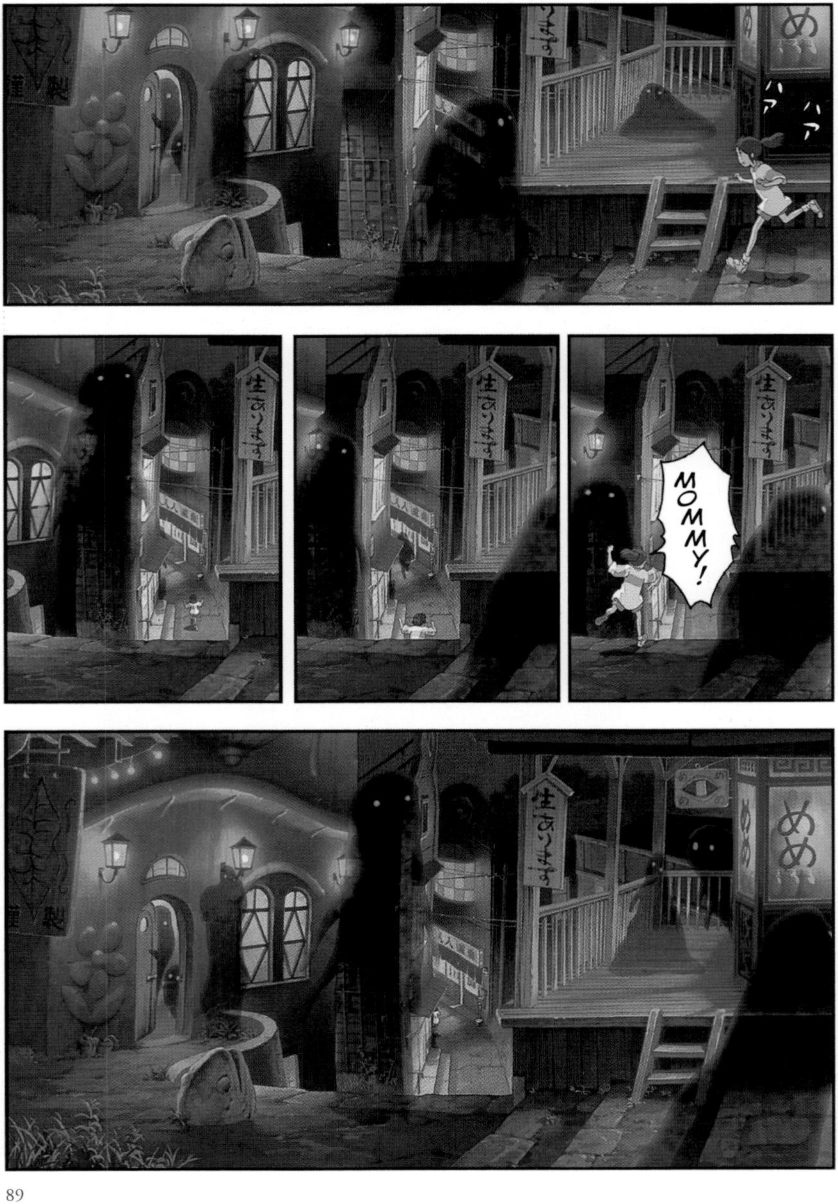
ハア ハア
MOMMY!

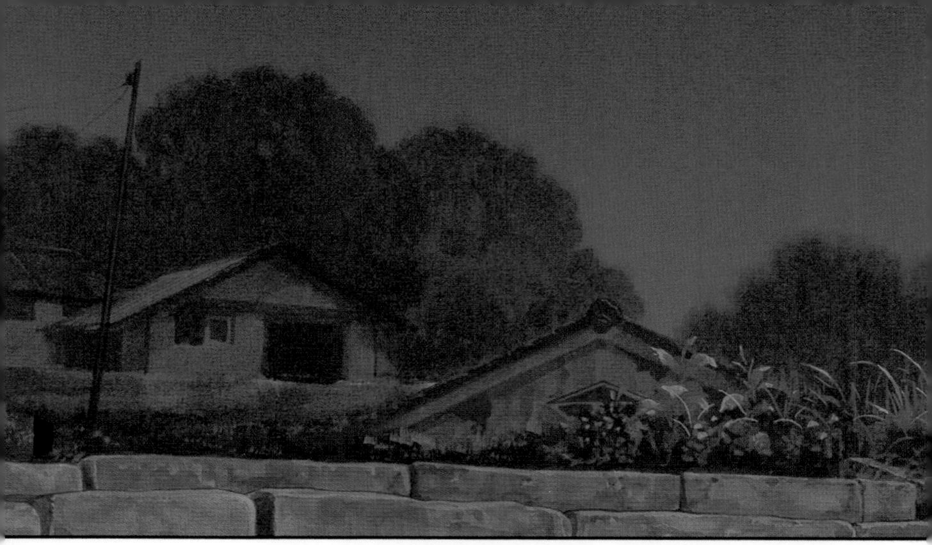

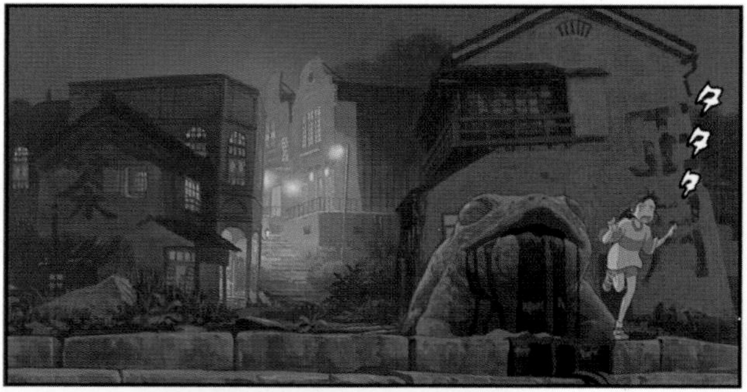

タタタ

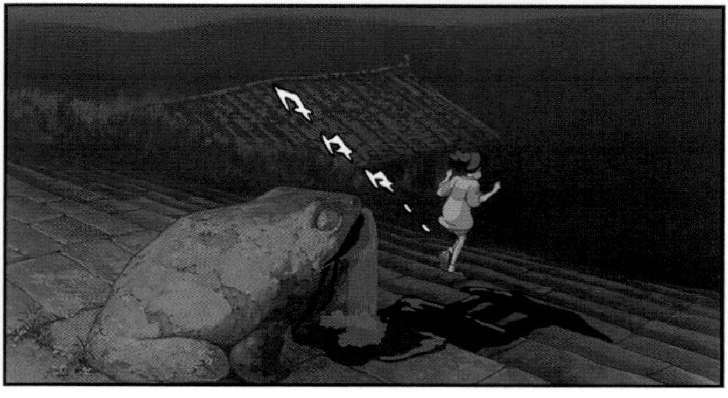

タタタ‥

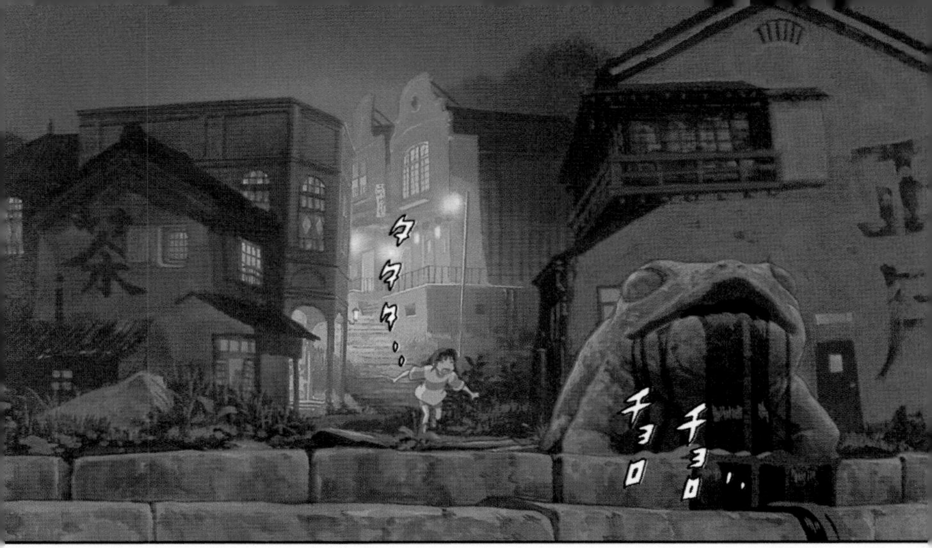
チョロ
チョロ
タタタ…

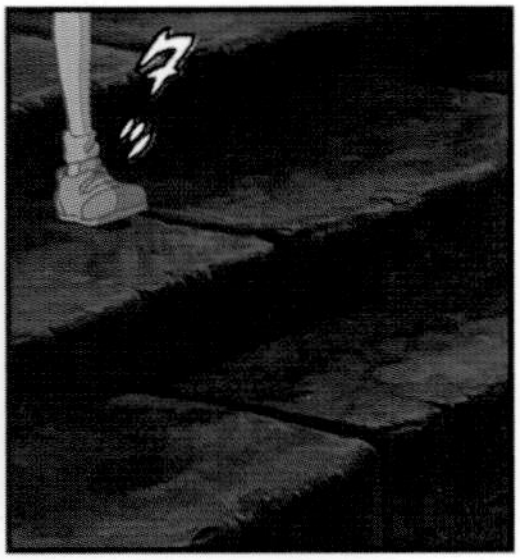
タッ

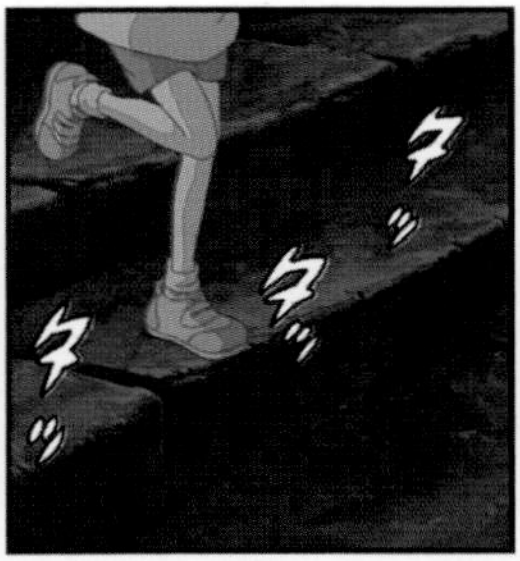
タッ
タッ
タッ

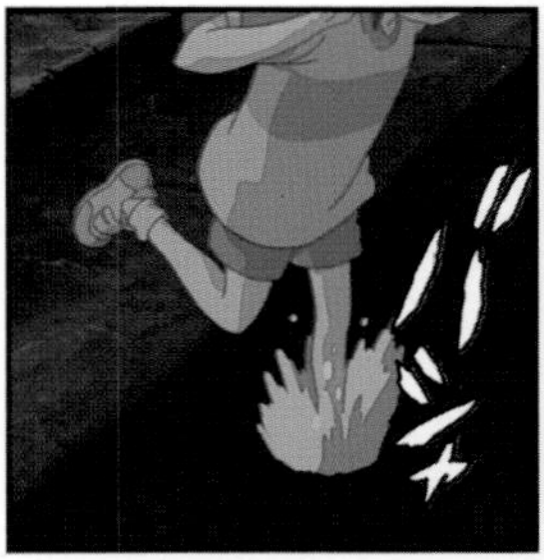
バシャ

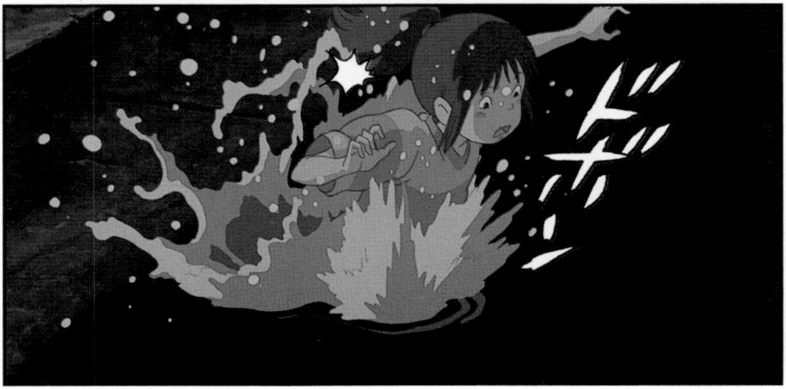
ドボーン

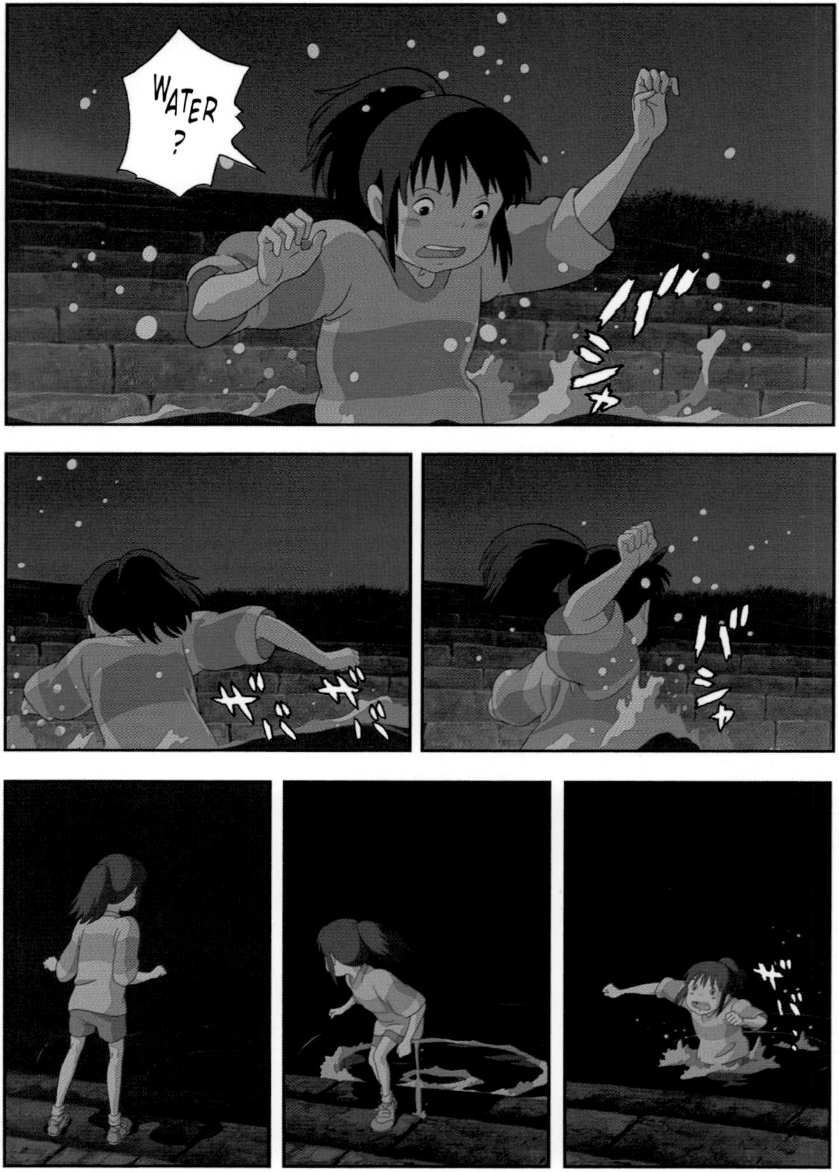
WATER ?
バシャ
バシャ
ザバ ザバ
ザバ

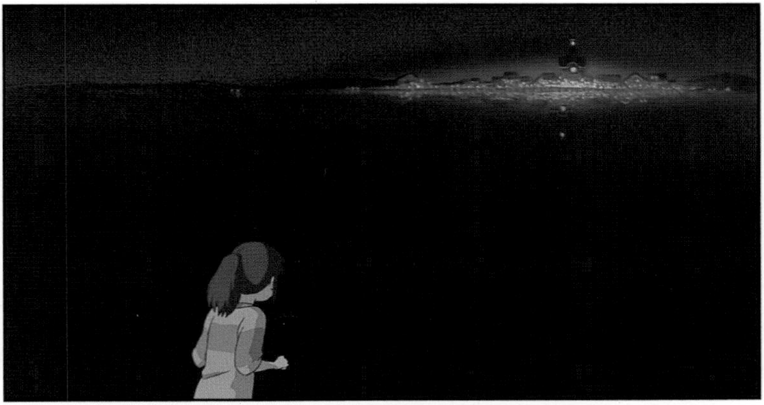

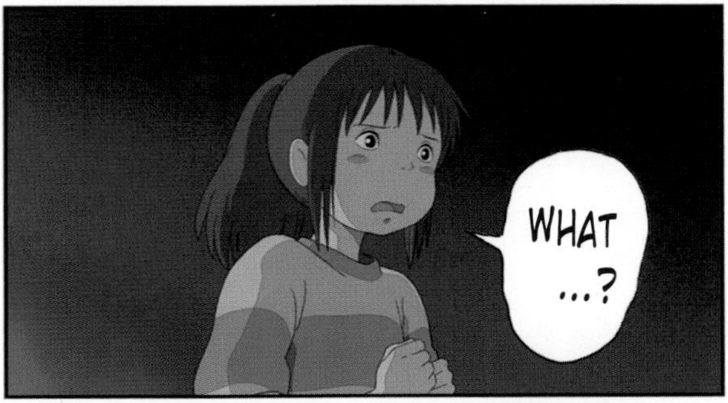
WHAT ...?

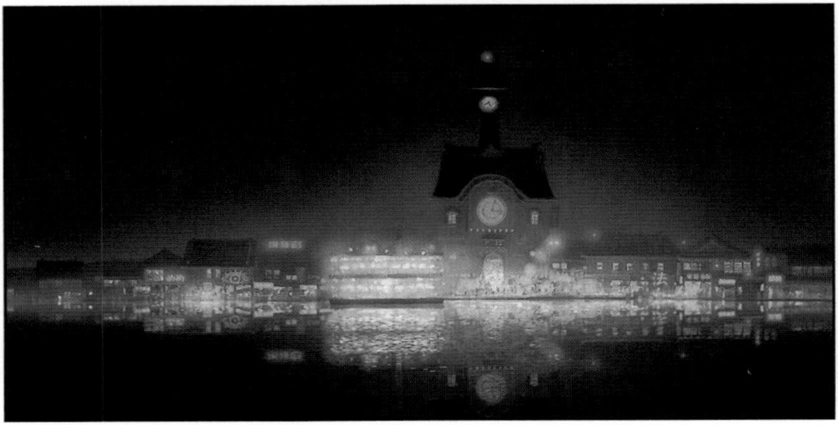

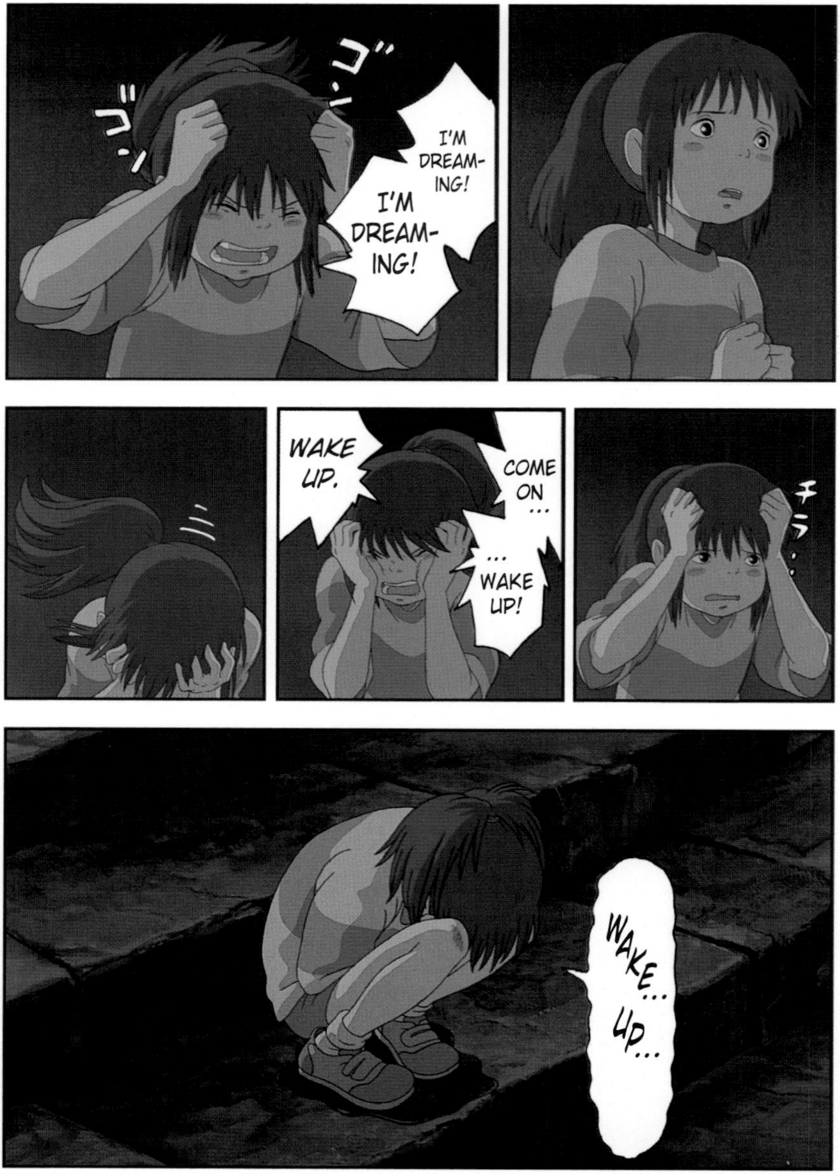
I'M DREAMING!
I'M DREAMING!
COME ON...
WAKE UP.
...WAKE UP!
WAKE... UP...

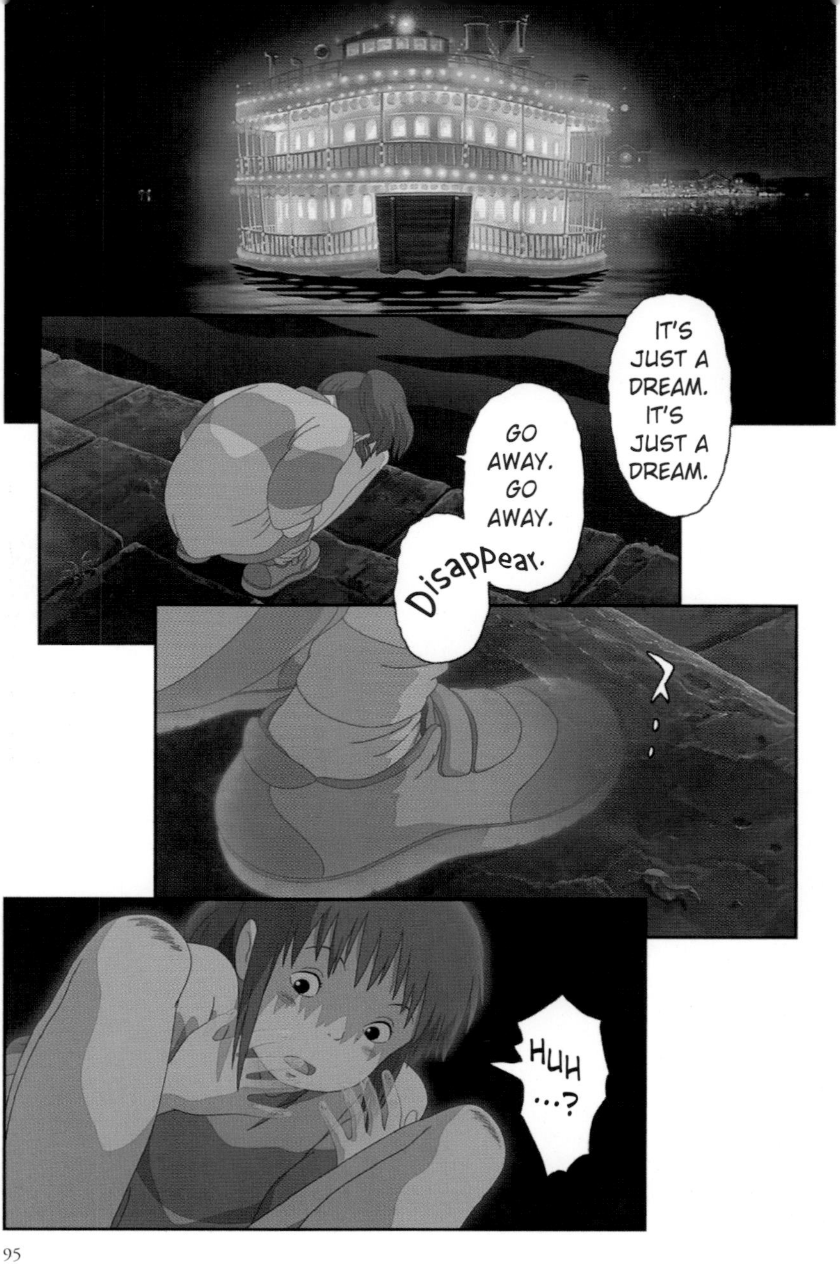
IT'S JUST A DREAM. IT'S JUST A DREAM.
GO AWAY. GO AWAY.
Disappear.
Huh ...?

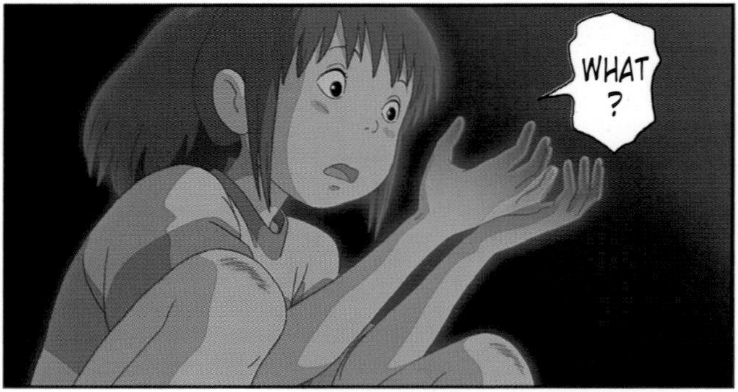
WHAT?
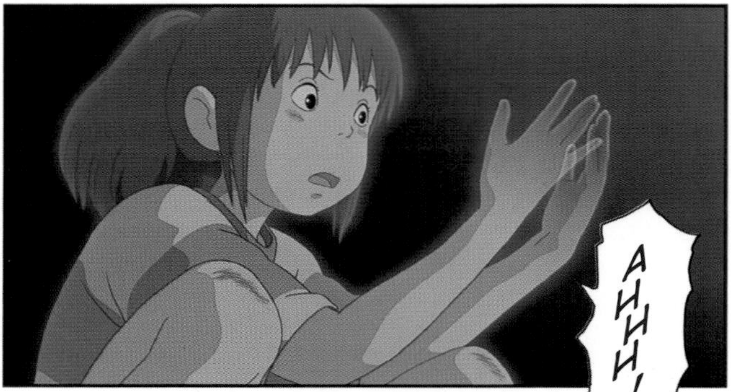
AHHH!
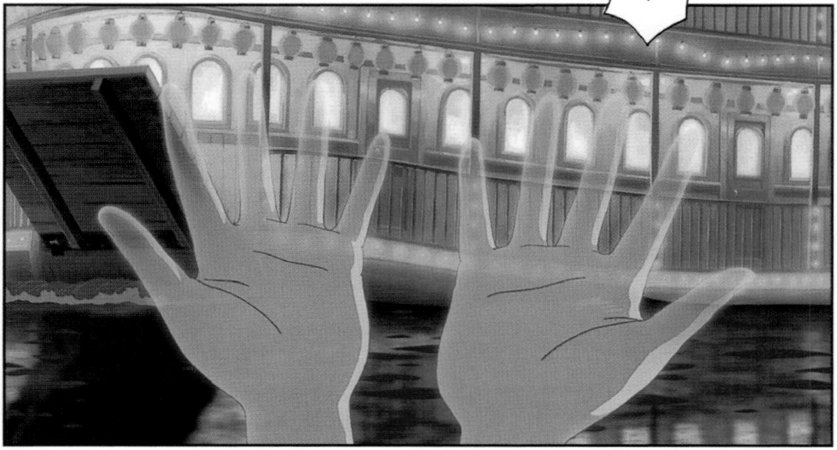

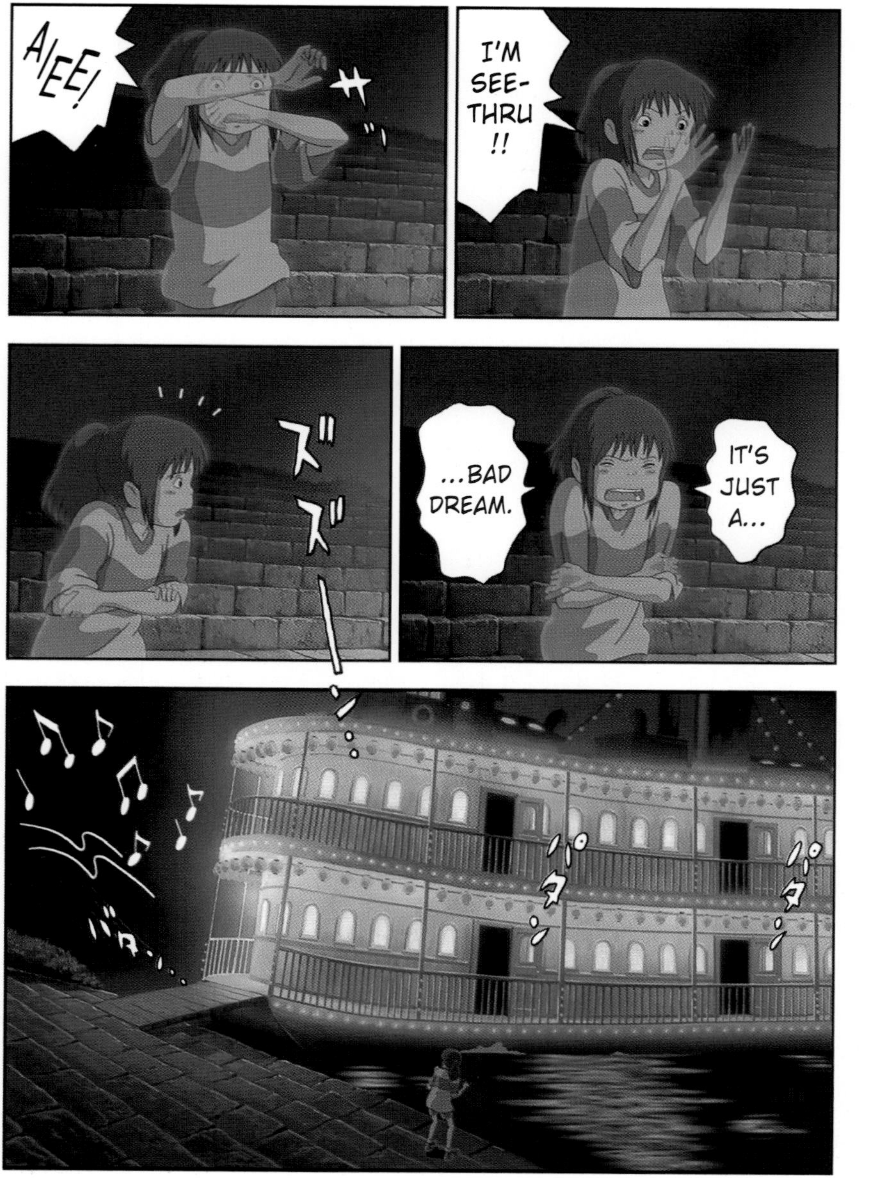
I'M SEE-THRU !!
AIEE!
IT'S JUST A...
...BAD DREAM.

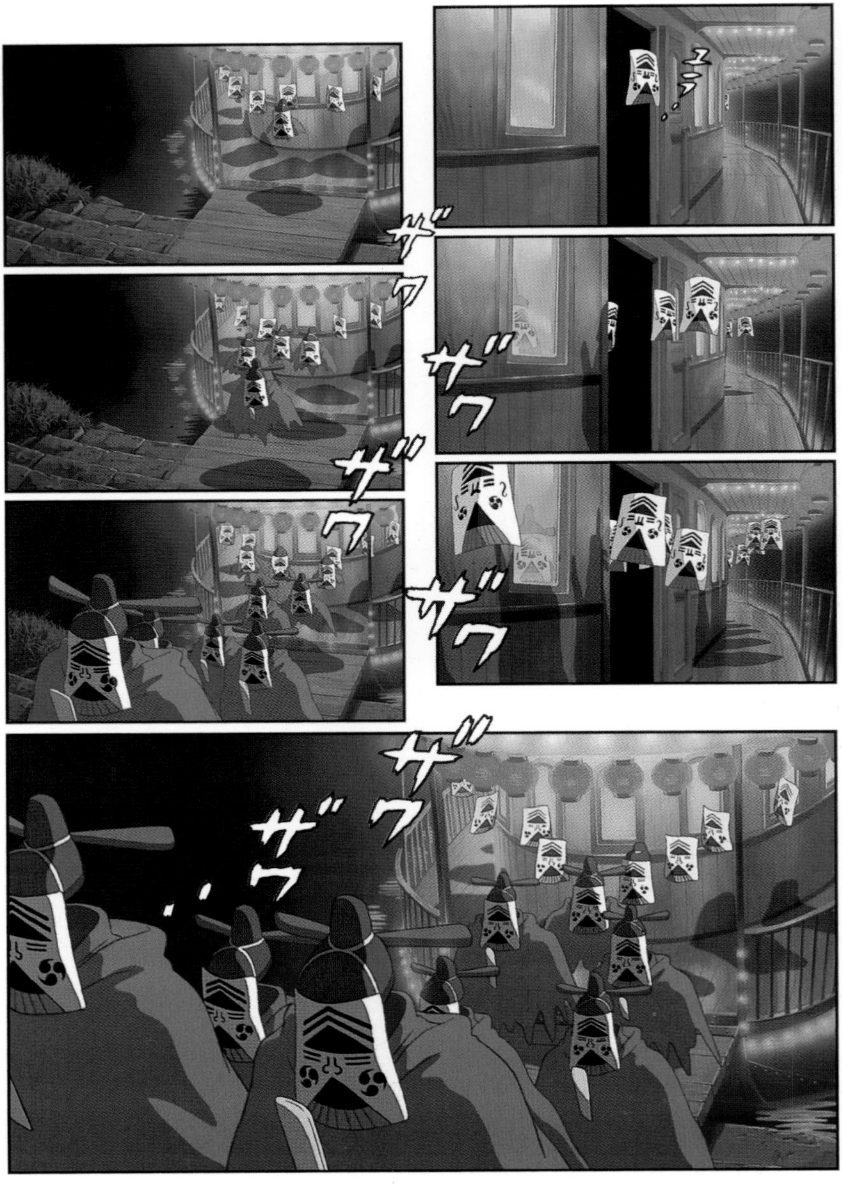
ザワ
ザワ
ザワ
ザワ
ザワ
ザワ..

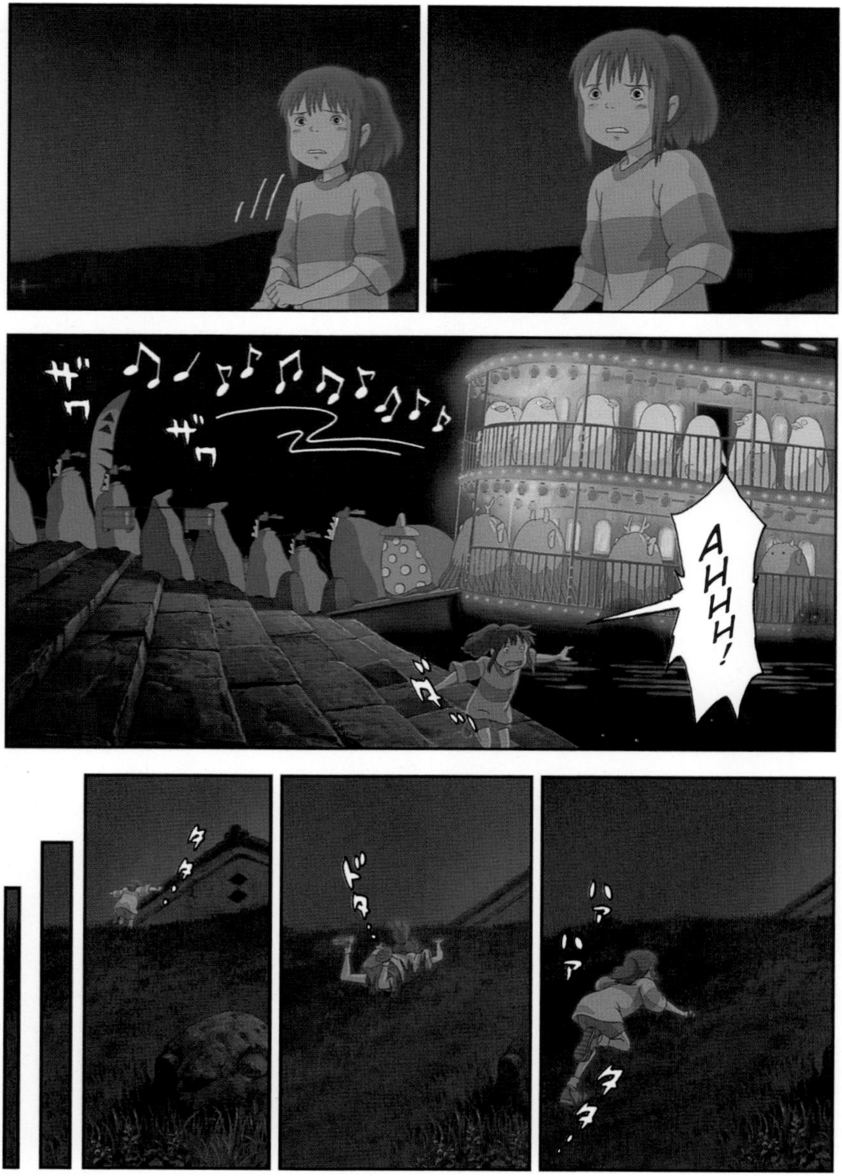
AHHHH!
ザワ
ザワ
ハァ
ハァ
タタ…
ドタ…
タタ…

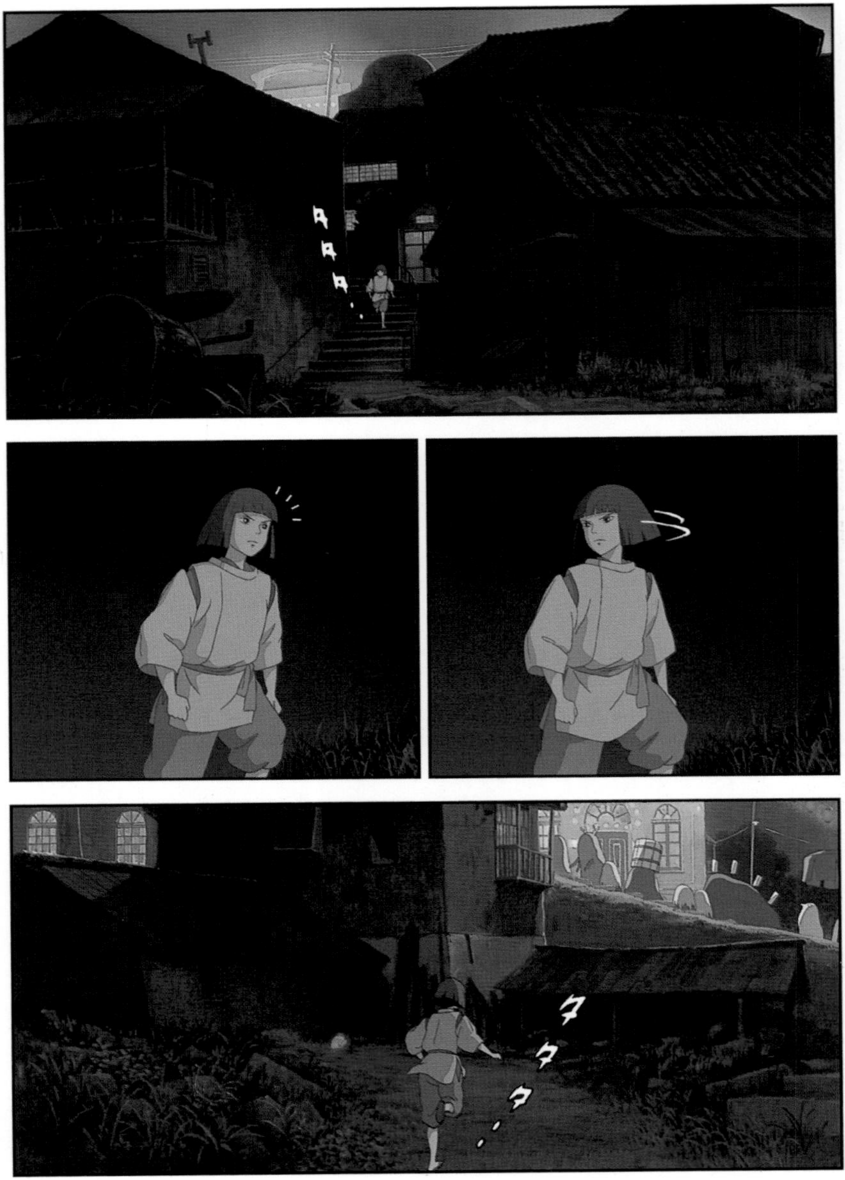
タタタ‥

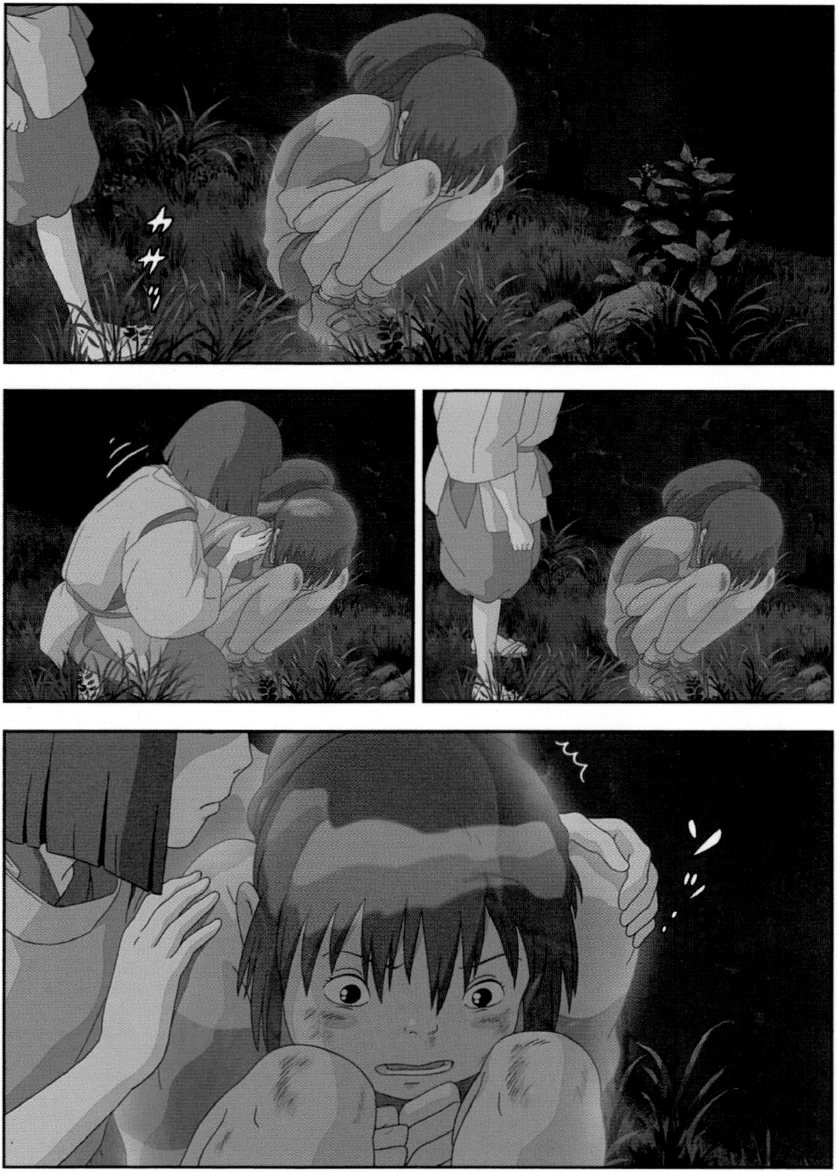
カサッ
ソッ

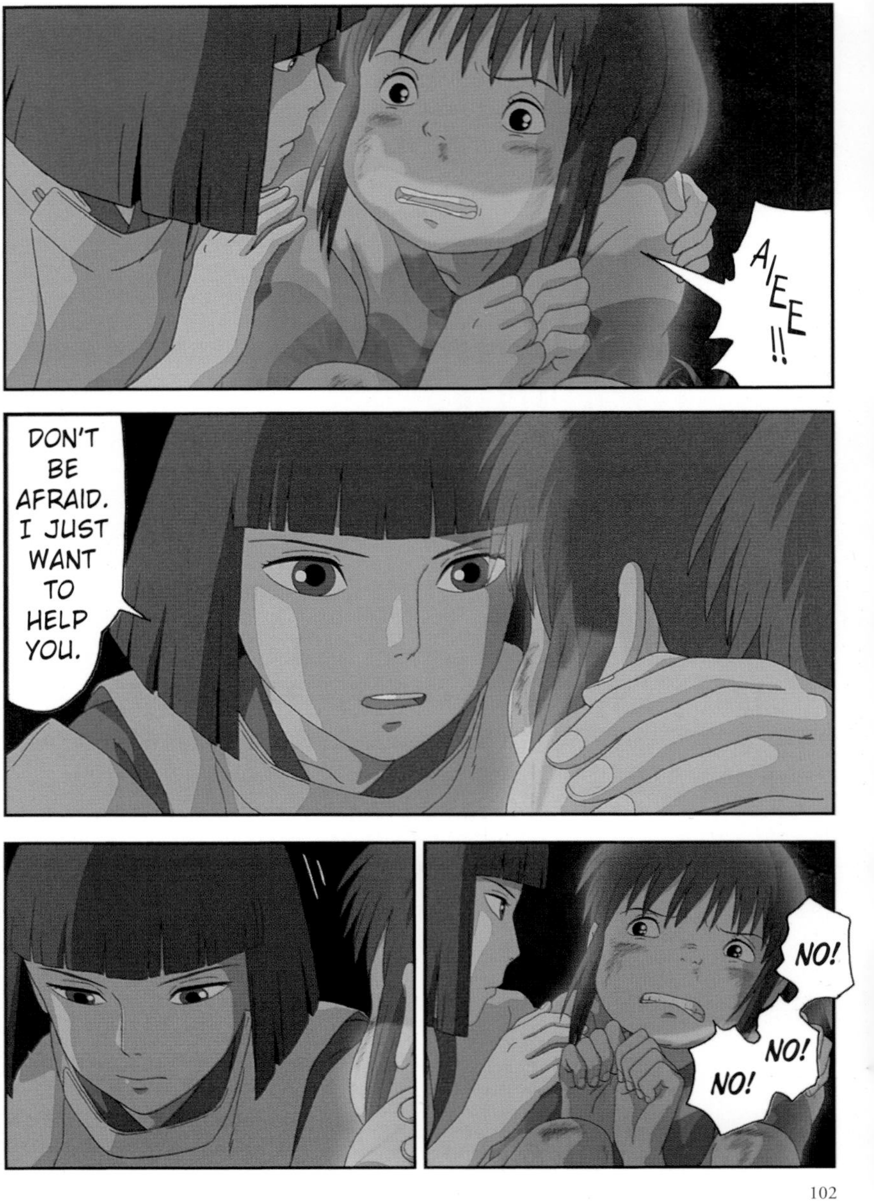
AIEE!!
DON'T BE AFRAID. I JUST WANT TO HELP YOU.
NO!
NO!
NO!

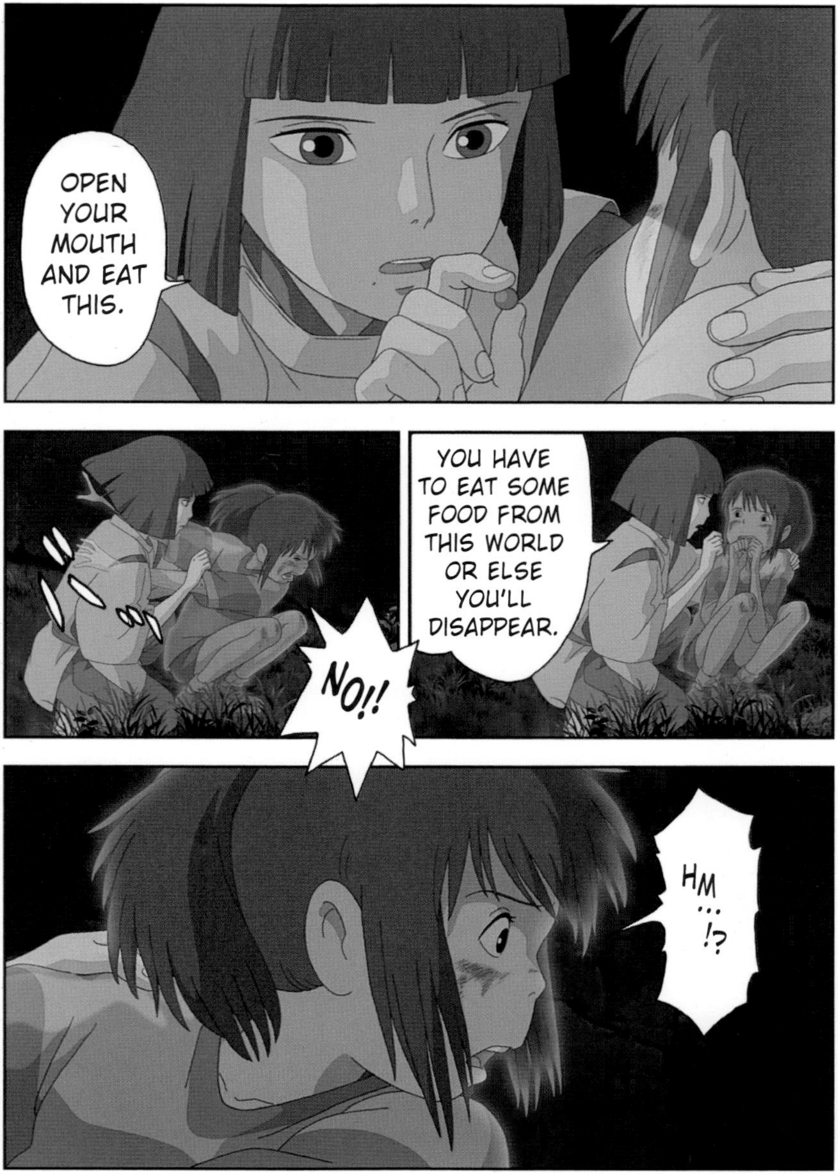

OPEN YOUR MOUTH AND EAT THIS.
YOU HAVE TO EAT SOME FOOD FROM THIS WORLD OR ELSE YOU'LL DISAPPEAR.
NO!!
HM...!?

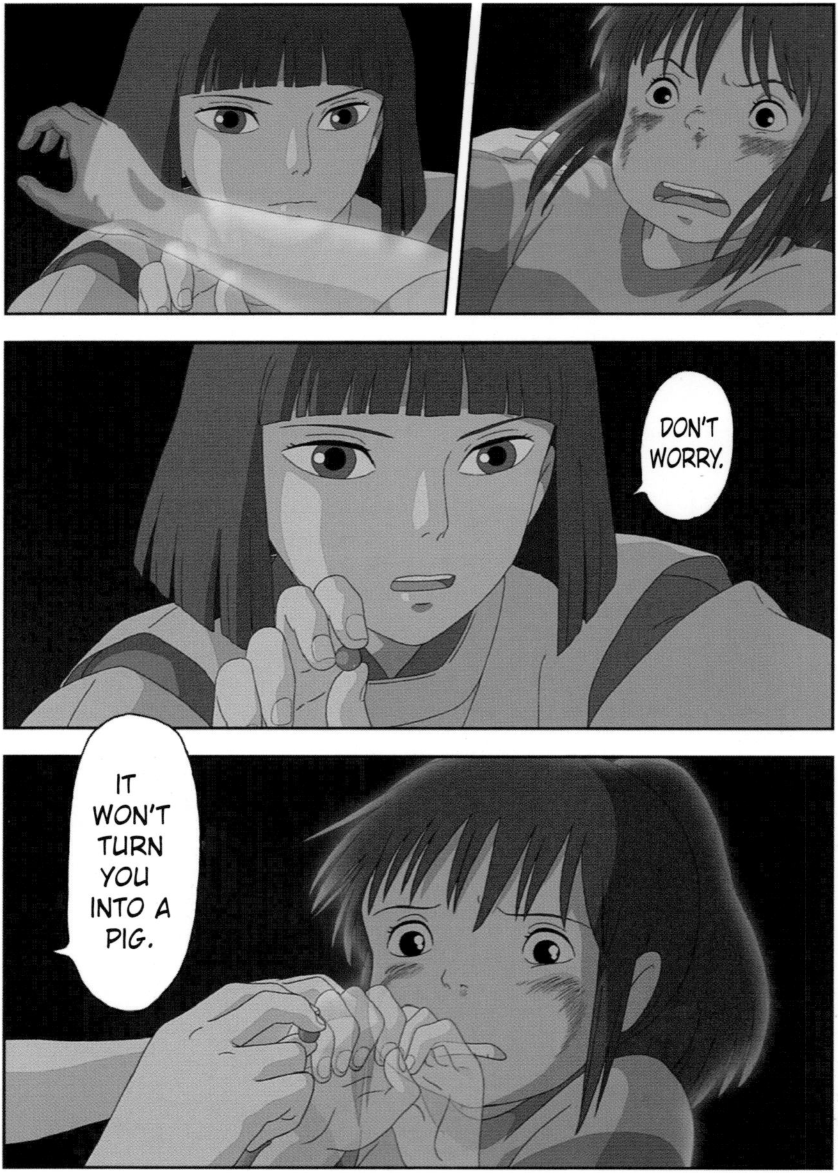
DON'T WORRY.
IT WON'T TURN YOU INTO A PIG.

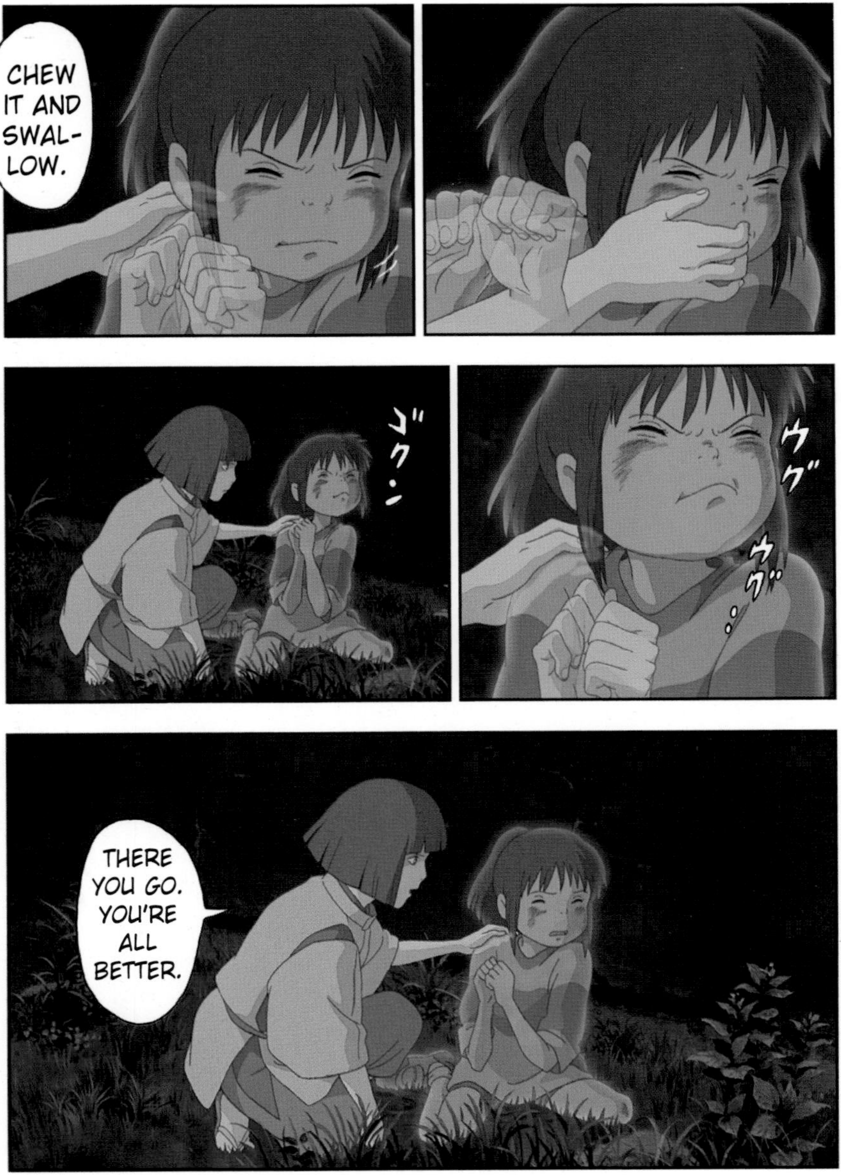
CHEW IT AND SWAL-LOW.
ウグ
ウグ…
ゴクン
THERE YOU GO. YOU'RE ALL BETTER.

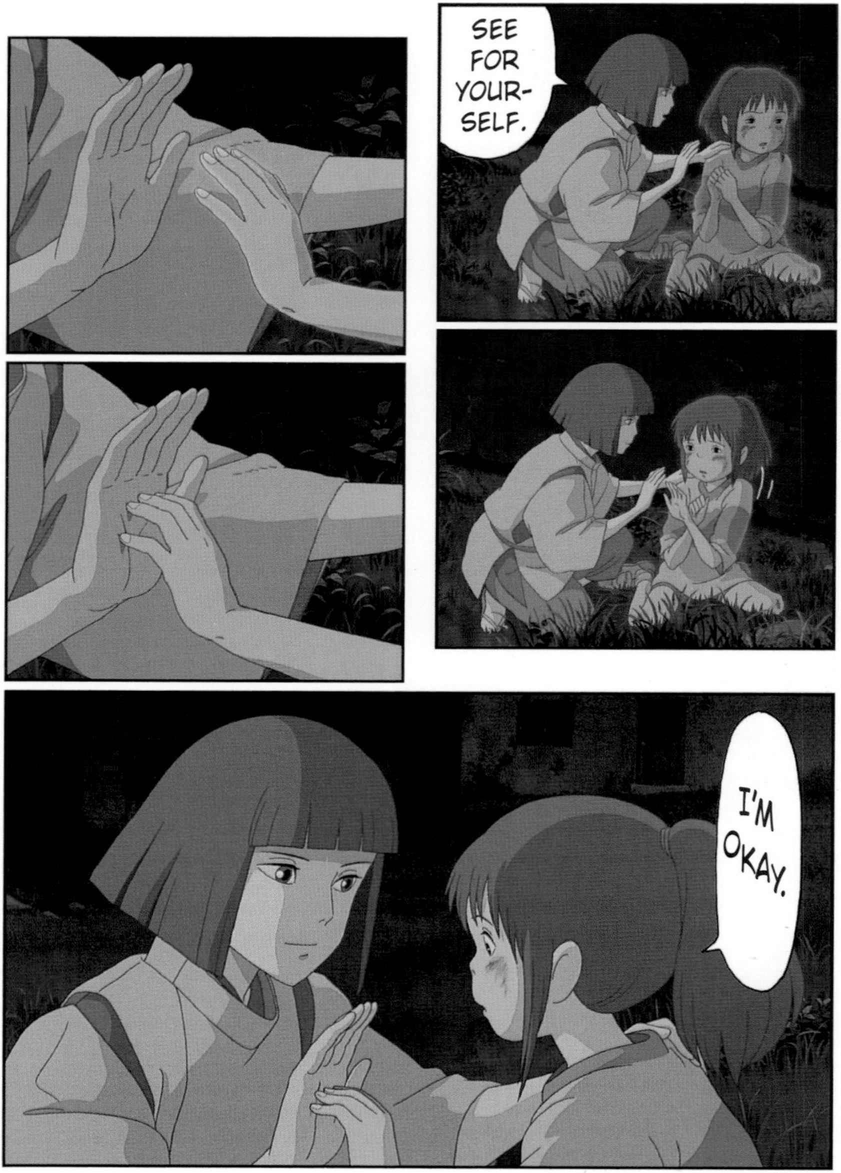
SEE FOR YOUR-SELF.
I'M OKAY.

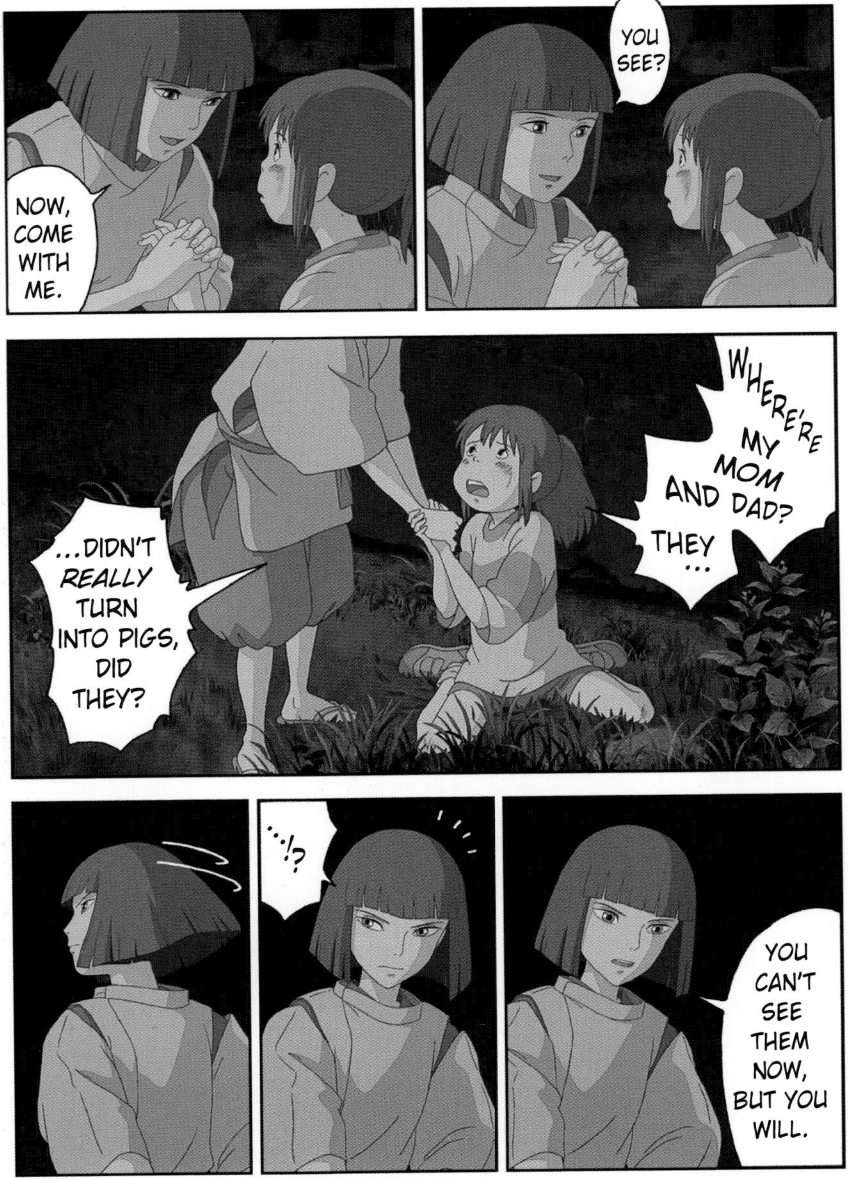
NOW, COME WITH ME.
YOU SEE?
WHERE'RE MY MOM AND DAD? THEY...
...DIDN'T REALLY TURN INTO PIGS, DID THEY?
...!?
YOU CAN'T SEE THEM NOW, BUT YOU WILL.

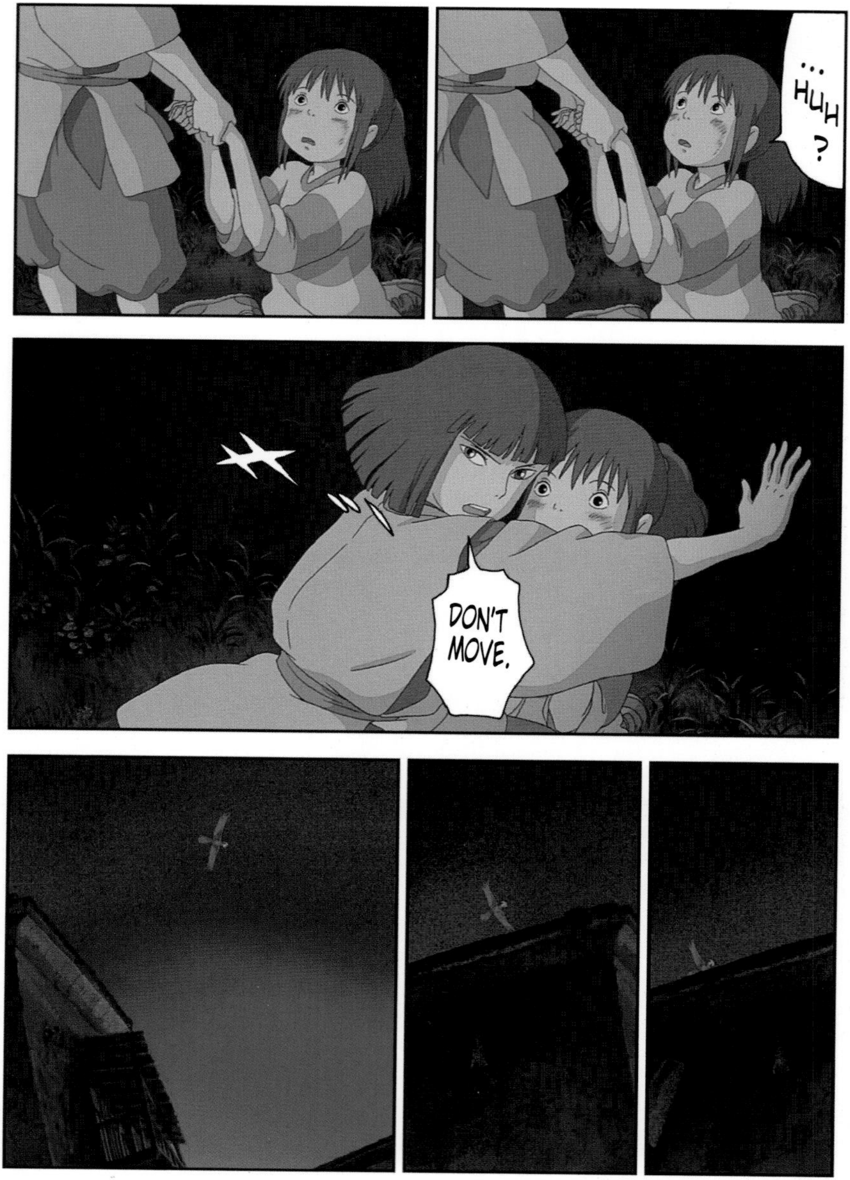
...HUH?
DON'T MOVE.

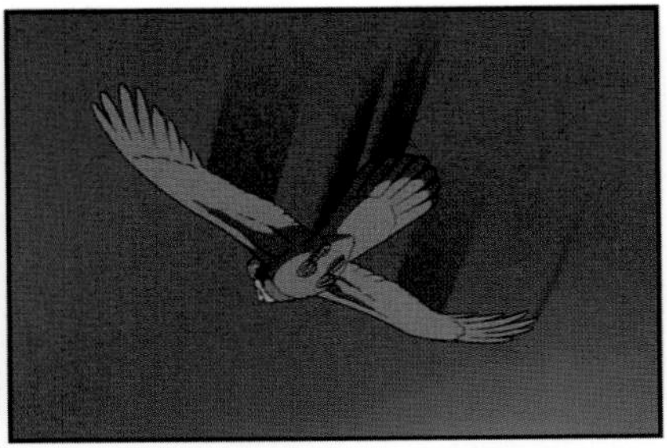
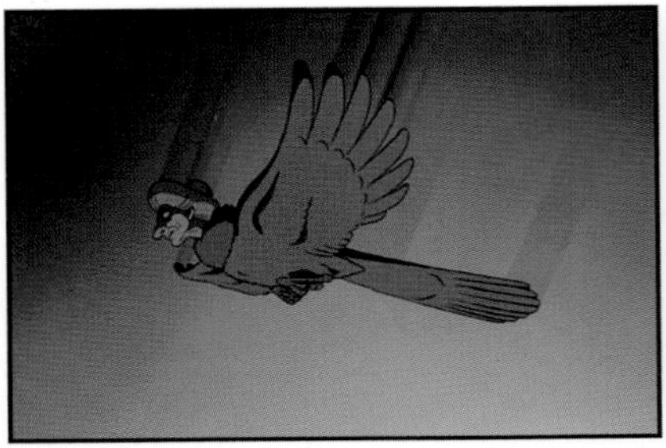
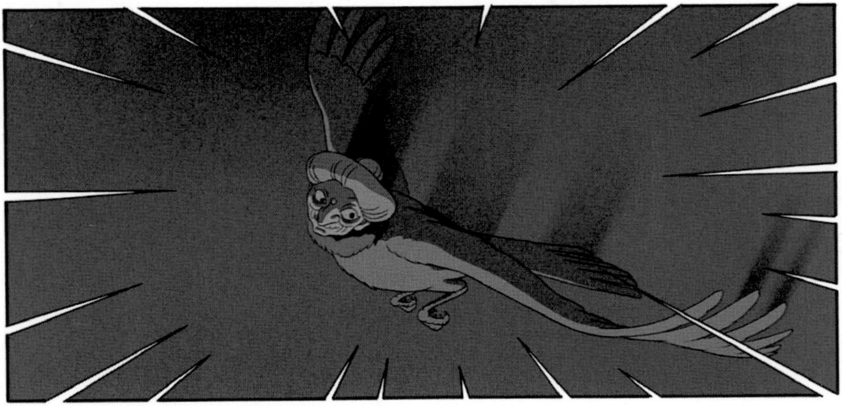
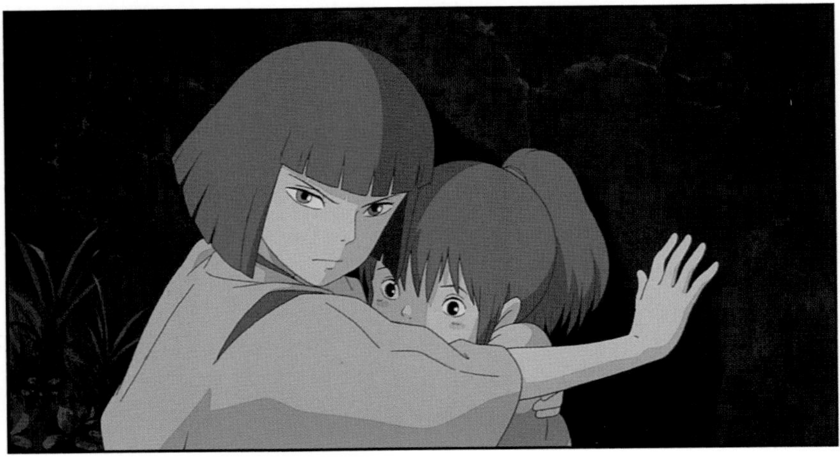

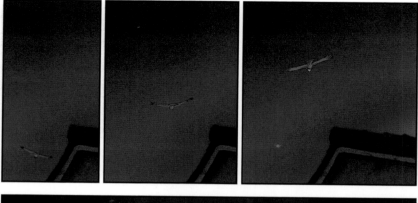

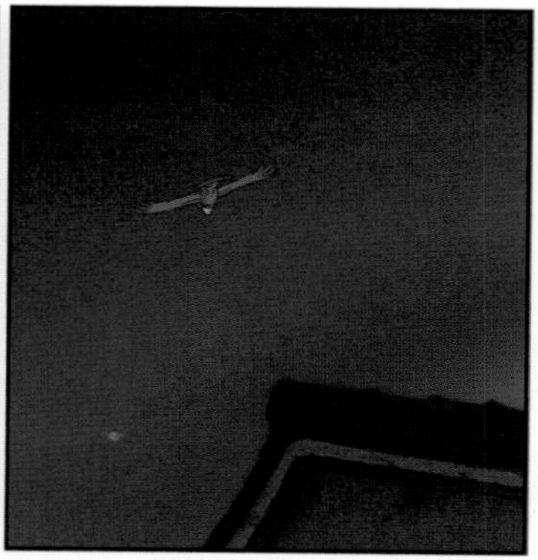
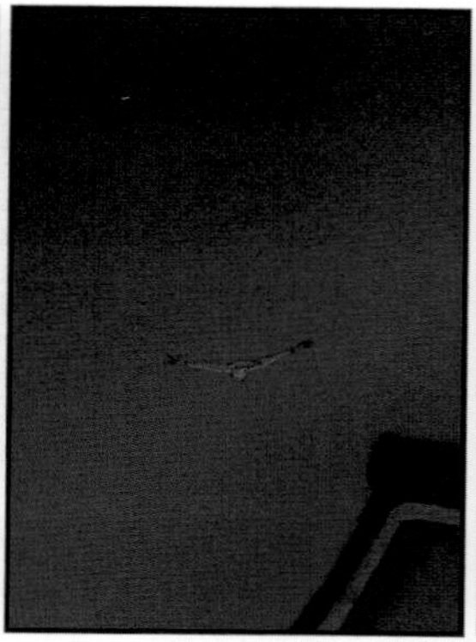
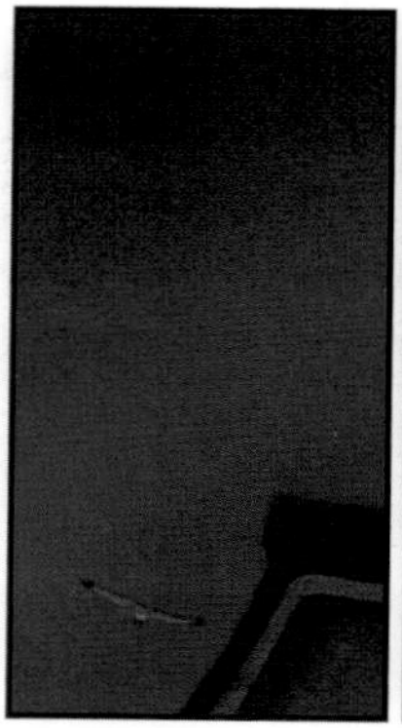
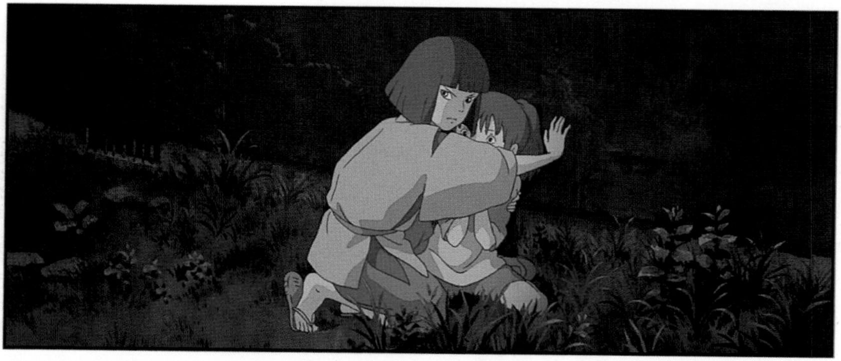
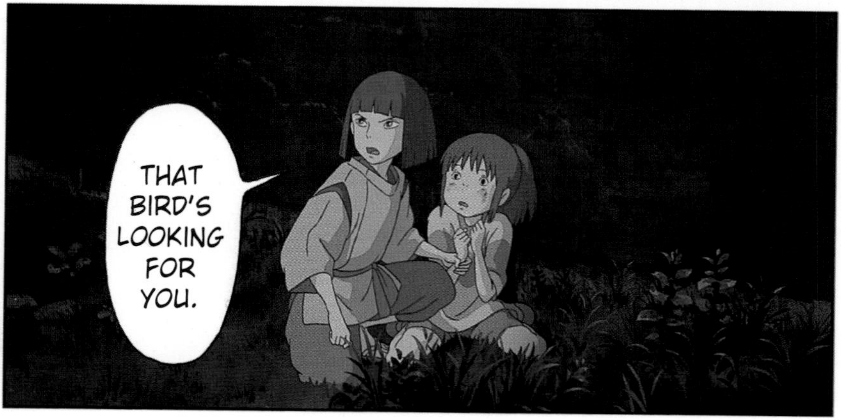
THAT BIRD'S LOOKING FOR YOU.

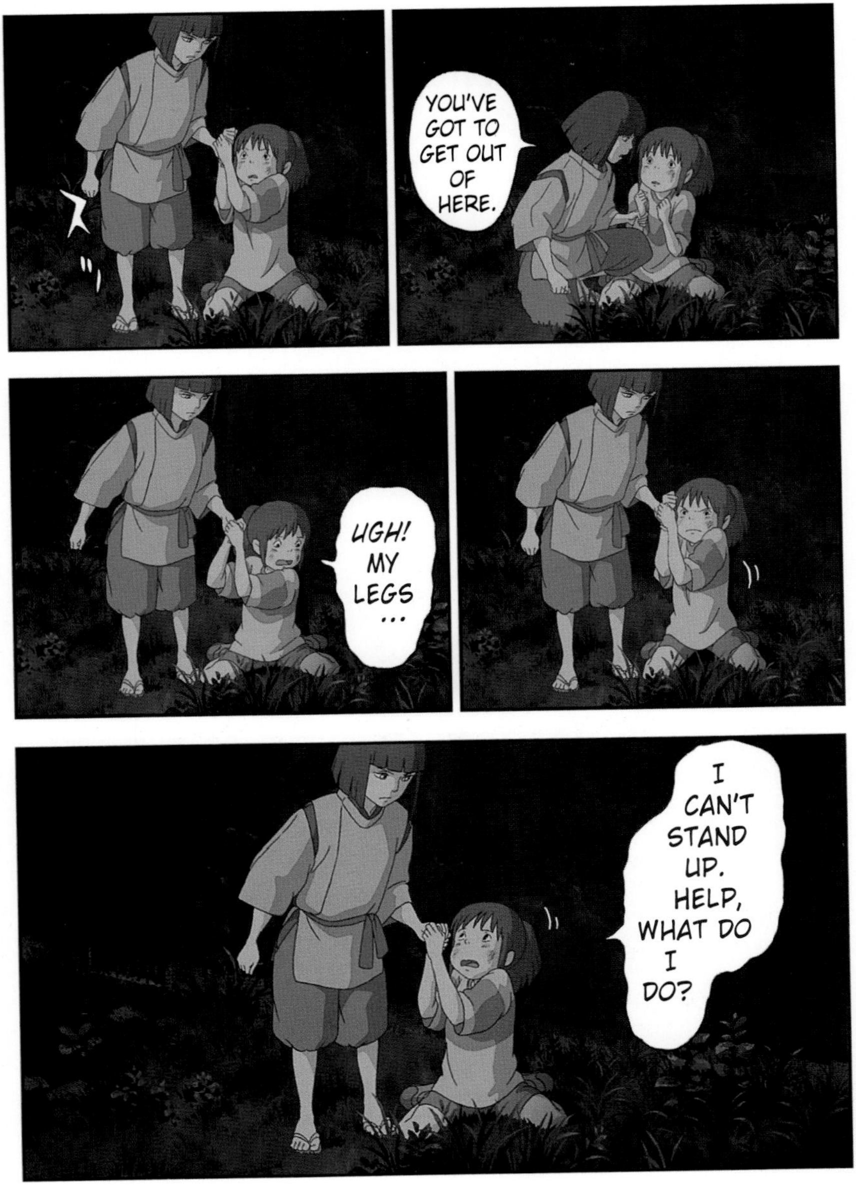
YOU'VE GOT TO GET OUT OF HERE.
UGH! MY LEGS...
I CAN'T STAND UP. HELP, WHAT DO I DO?

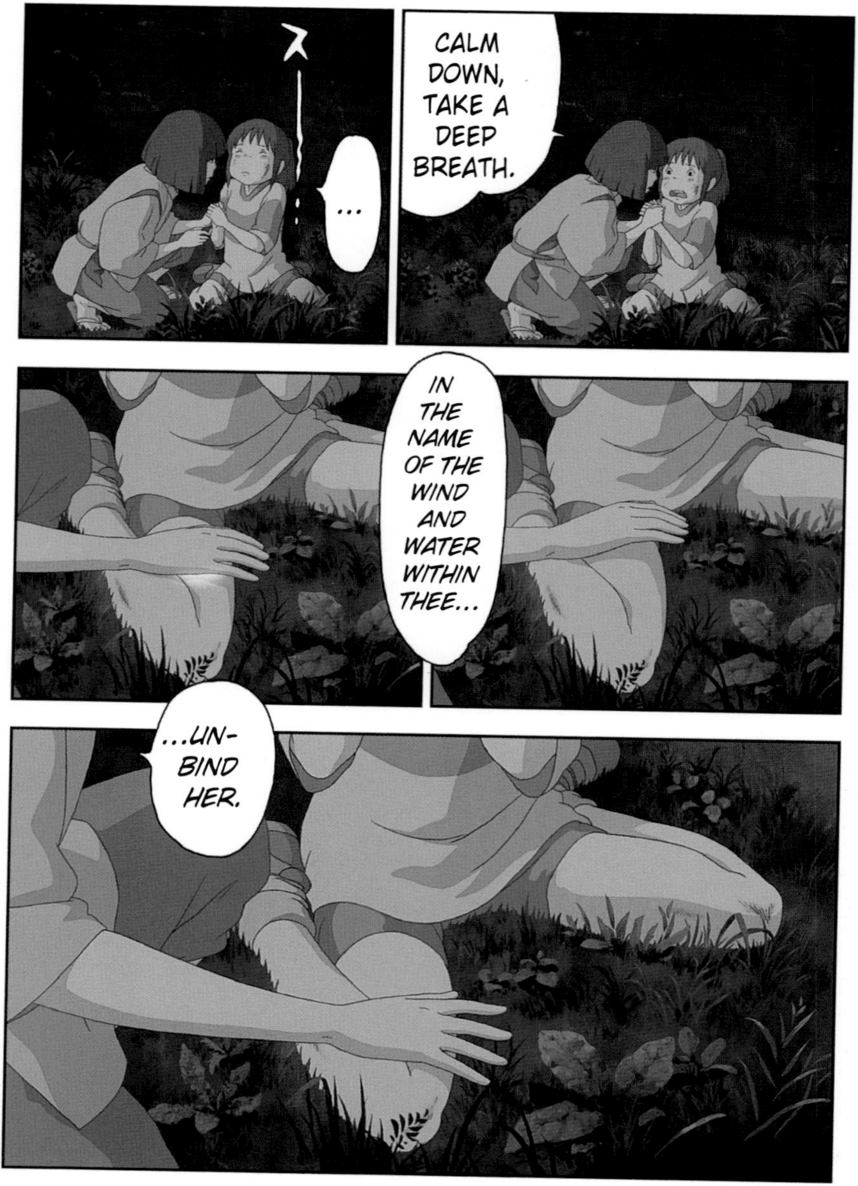
CALM DOWN, TAKE A DEEP BREATH.
ス
...
IN THE NAME OF THE WIND AND WATER WITHIN THEE...
...UN-BIND HER.

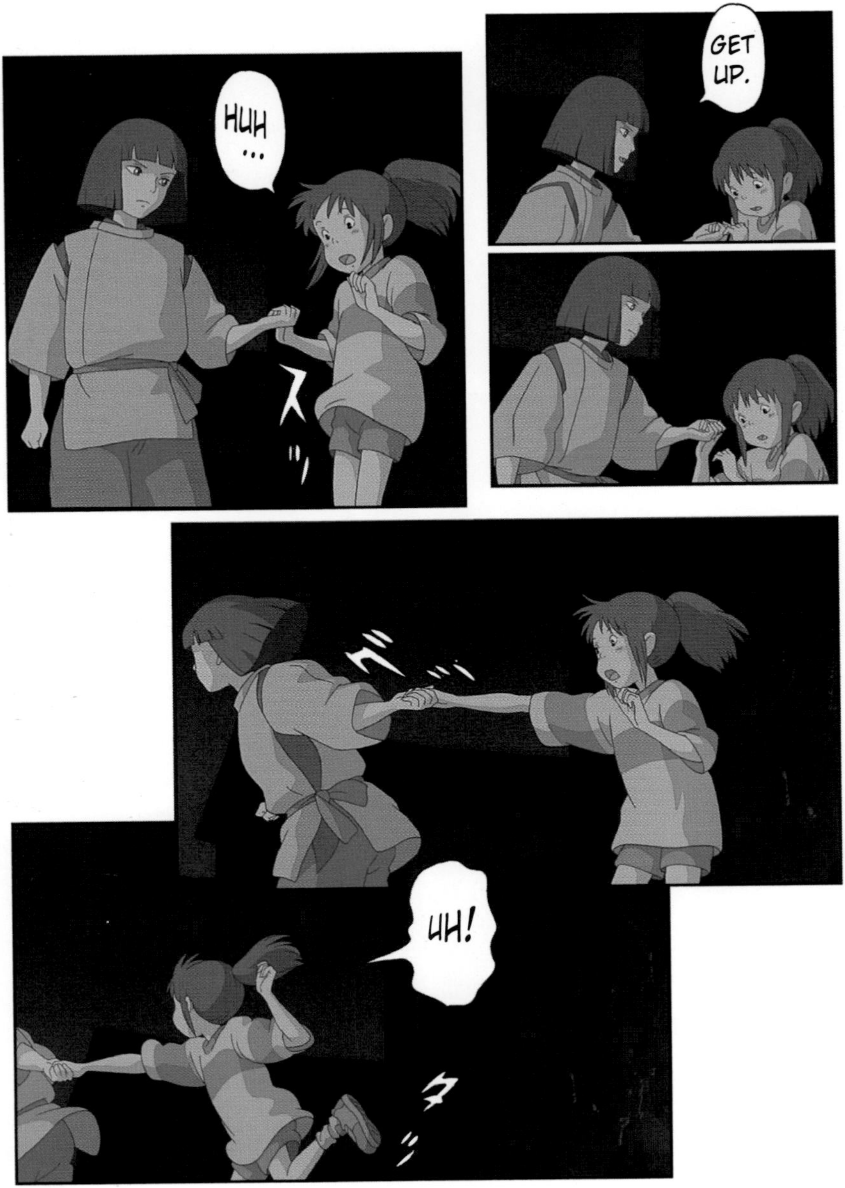
GET UP.
HUH ...
UH!

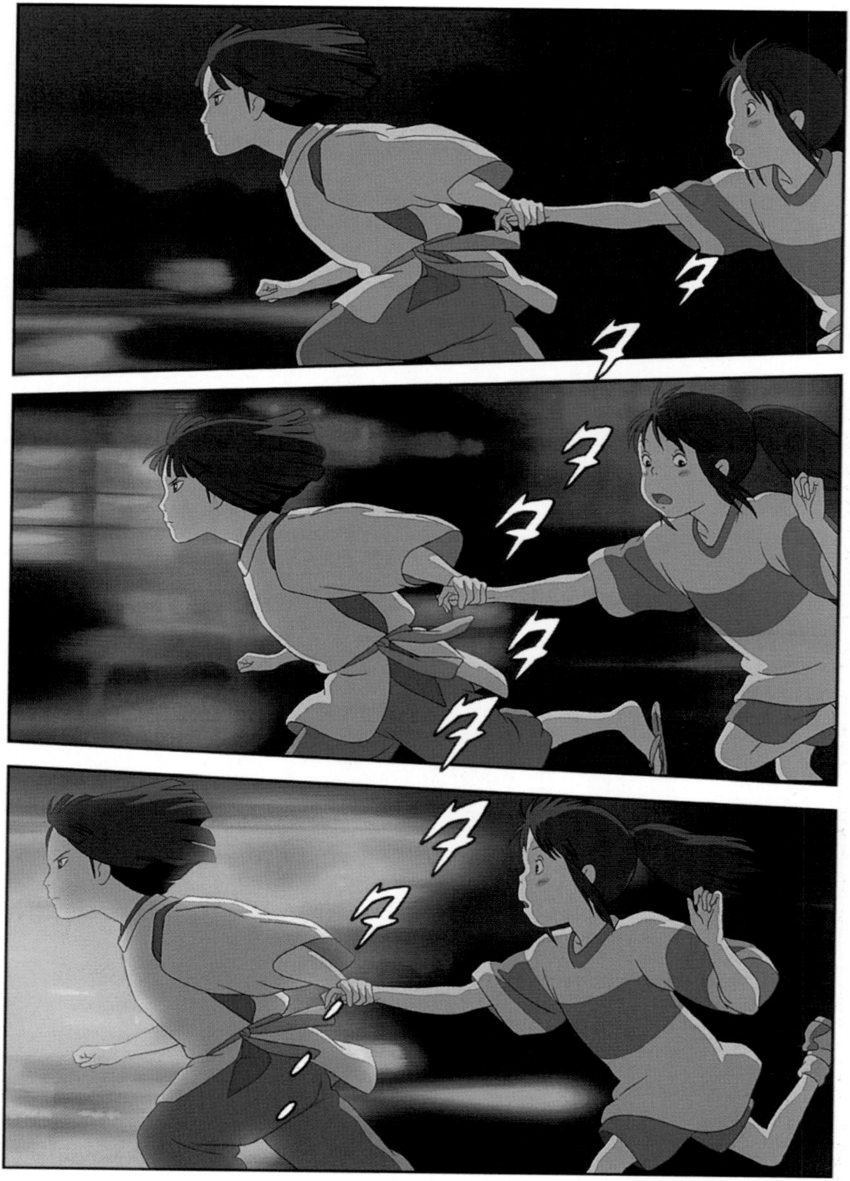
タ
タ
タ
タ
タ
タ
タ
タ

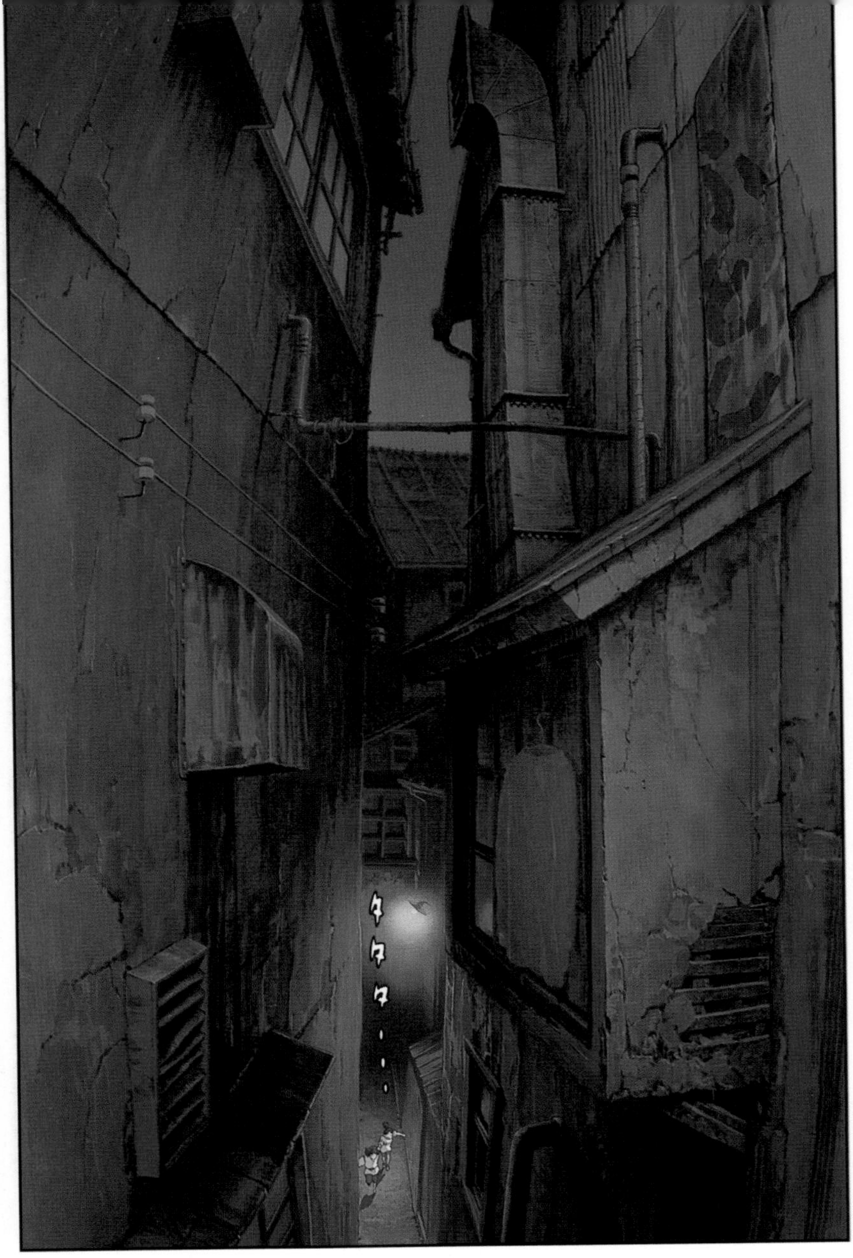
タタタ...

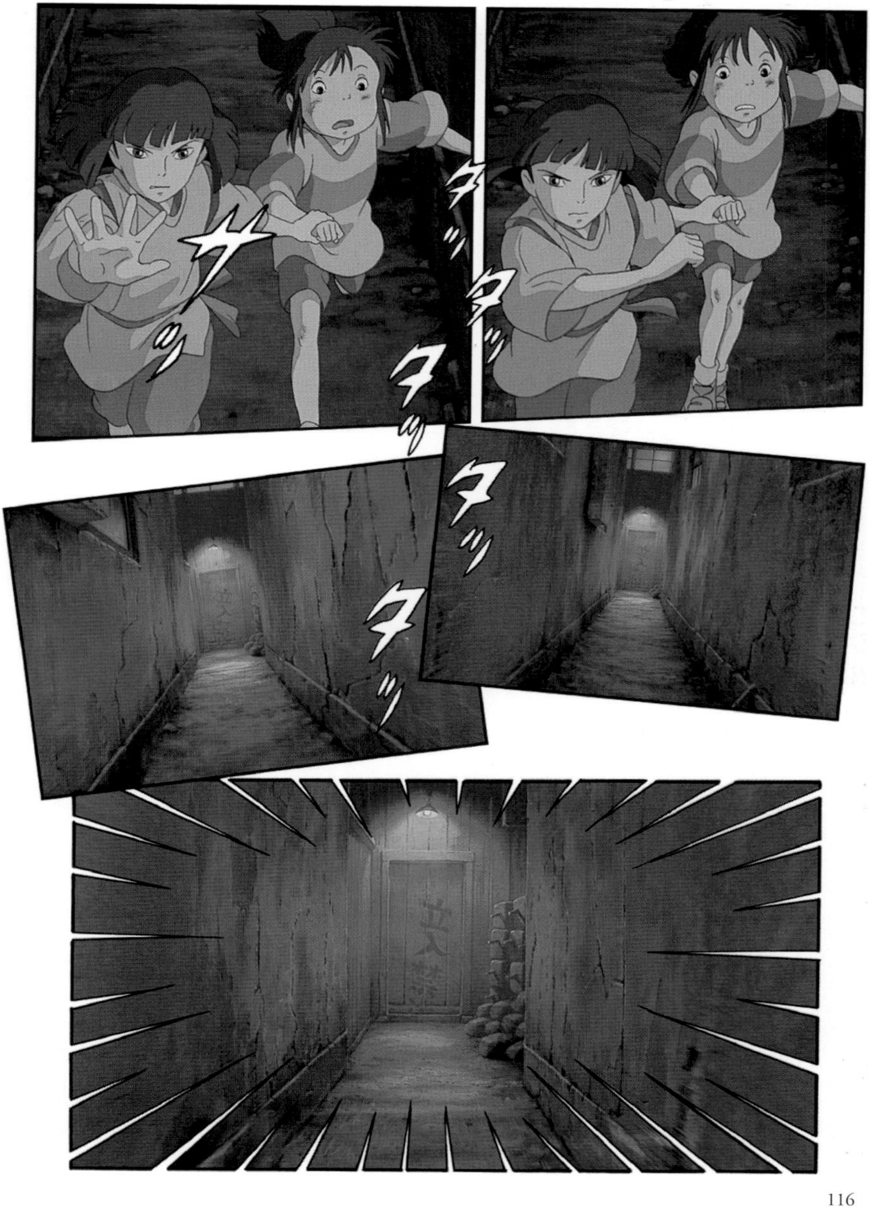
サッ
タッ
タッ
タッ
タッ
タッ

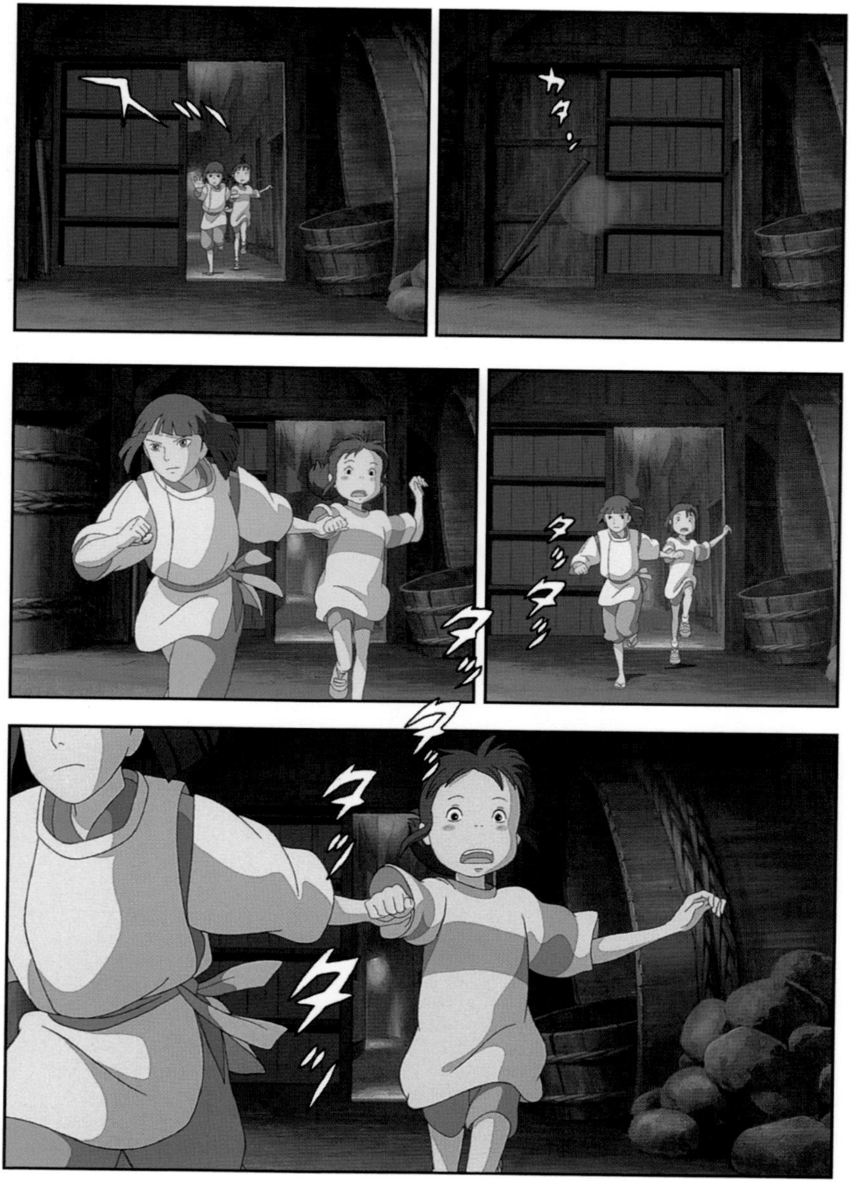
カタッ
スッ
タッタッ
タッ
タッ
タッ
タッ

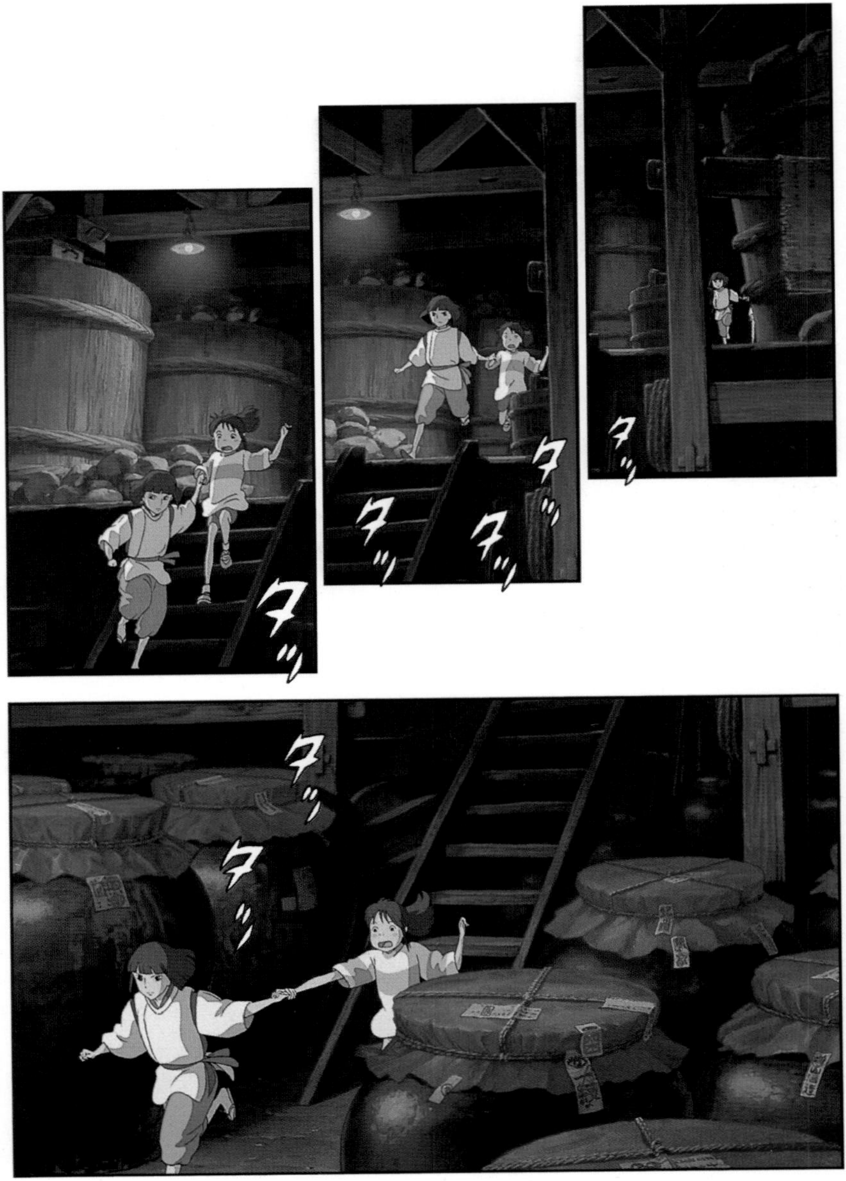
タッ
タッ
タッ
タッ
タッ
タッ
タッ

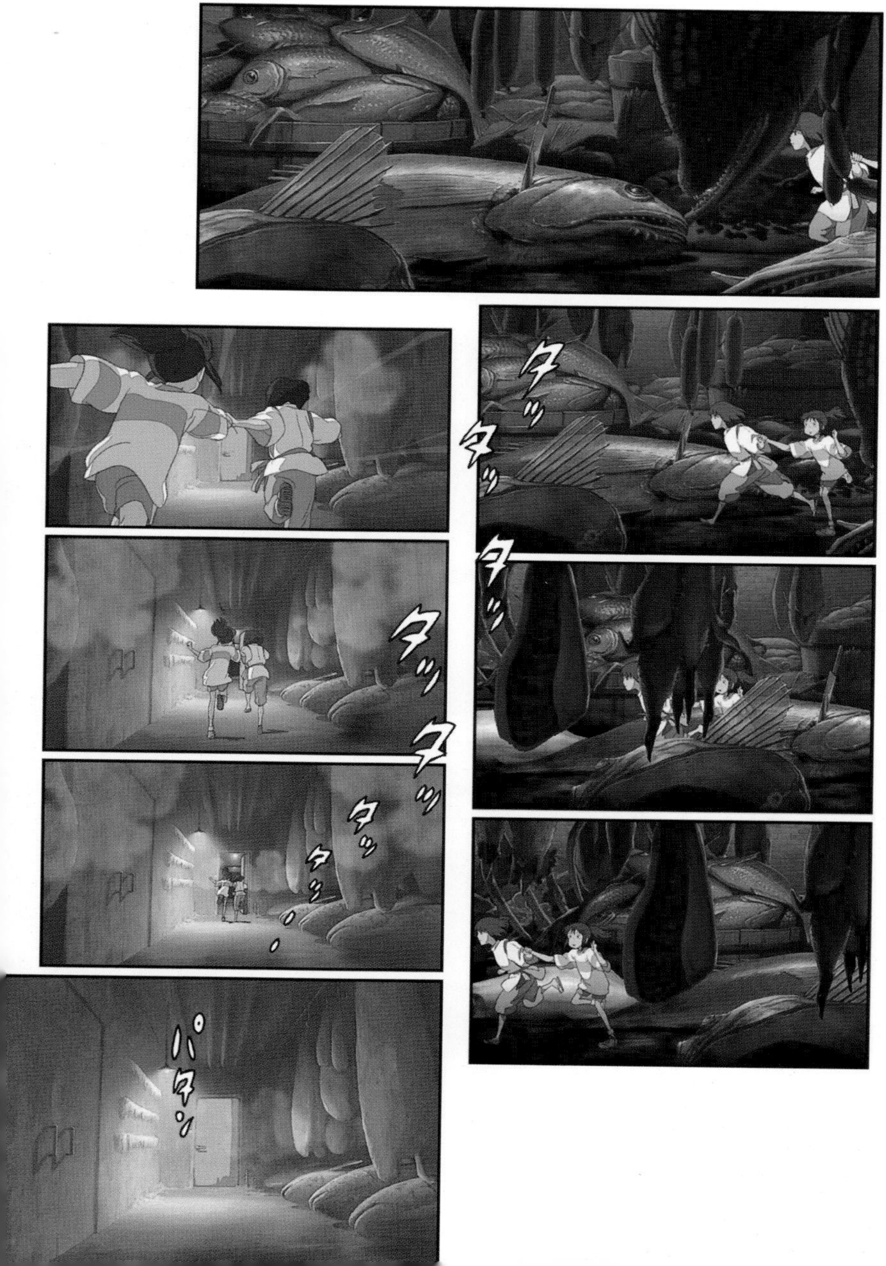
タッ
タッ
タッ
タッ
タッ
タッ
タッ…
パタン

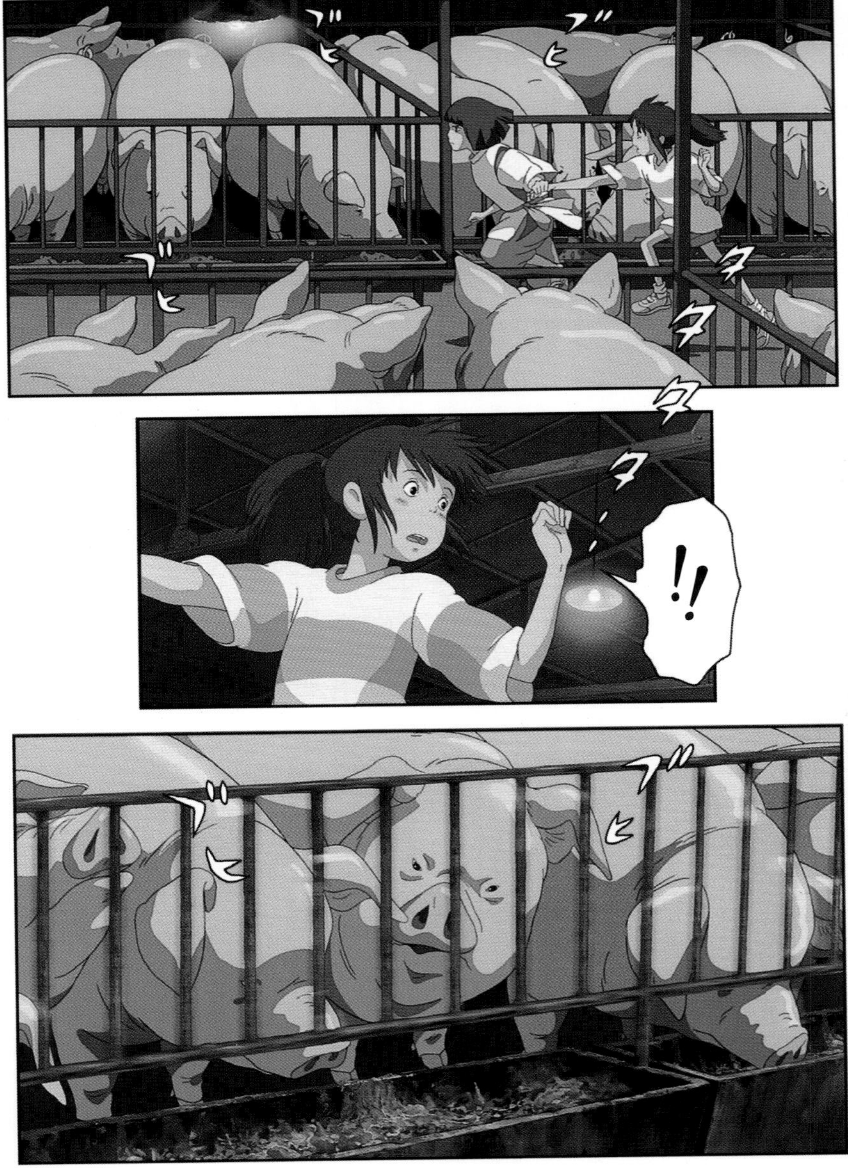
ブヒ
ブヒ
タタタタ
ブヒ
タタ…
!!
ブヒ
ブヒ

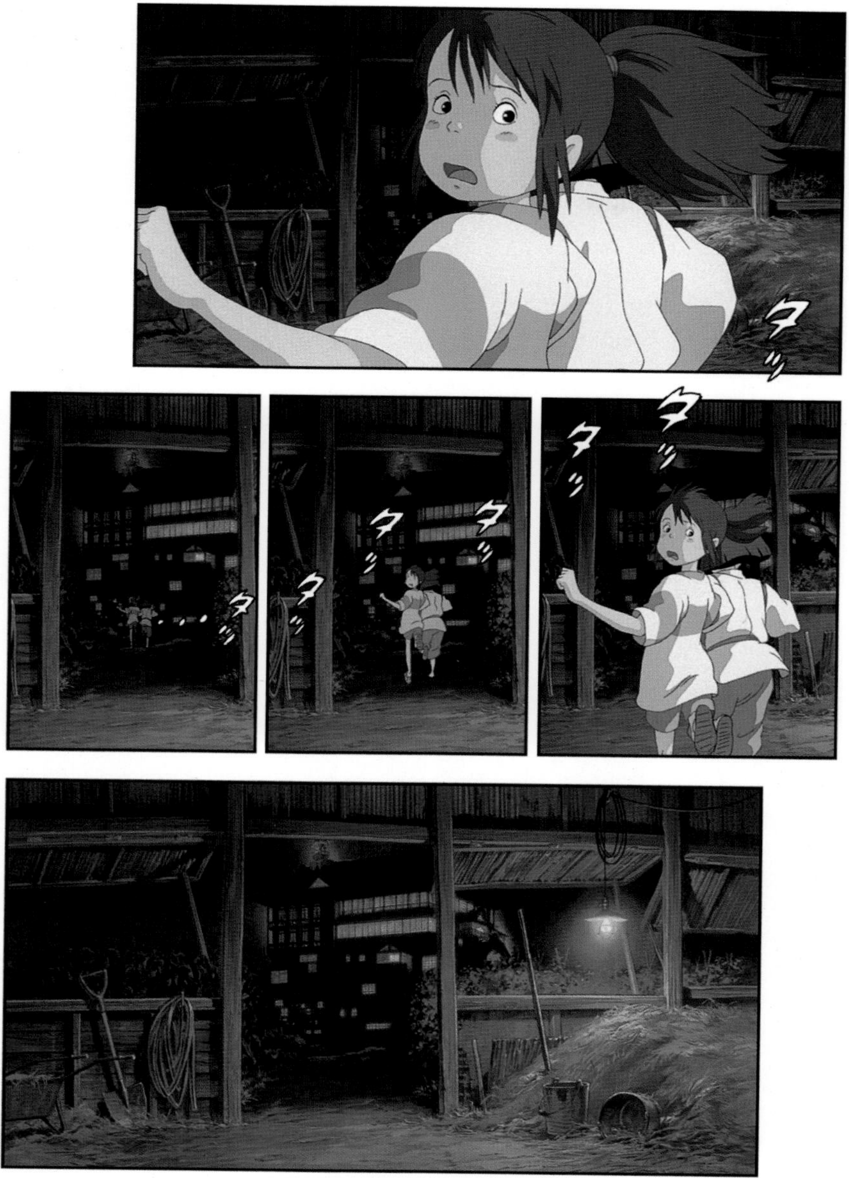
タッ
タッ
タッ
タッ
タッ
タッ
タッ

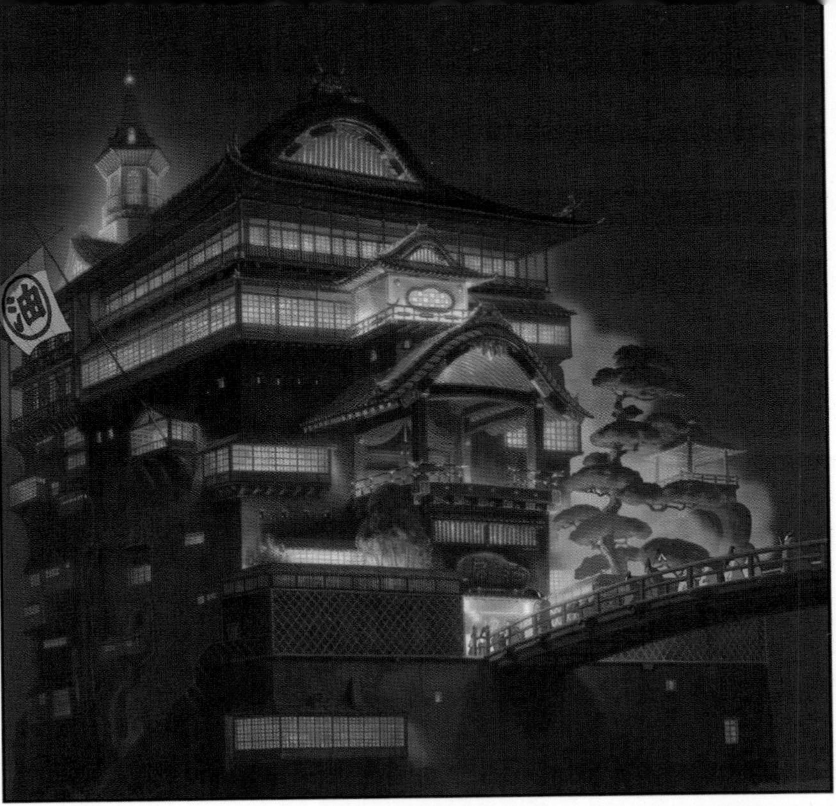

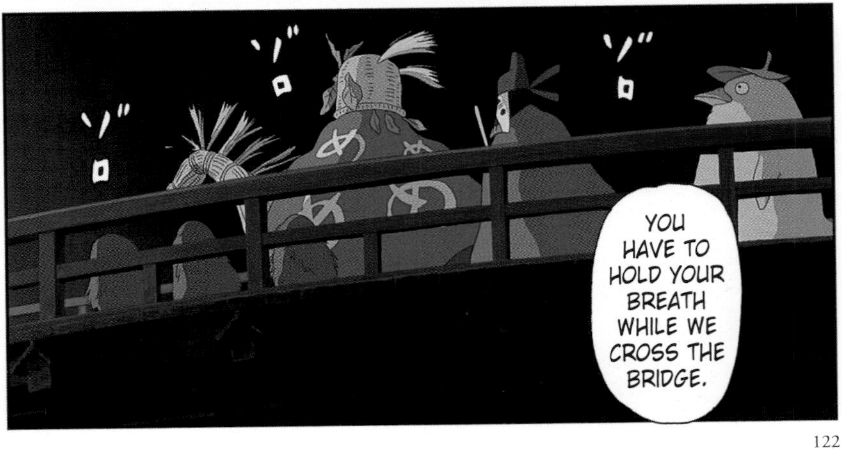
YOU HAVE TO HOLD YOUR BREATH WHILE WE CROSS THE BRIDGE.

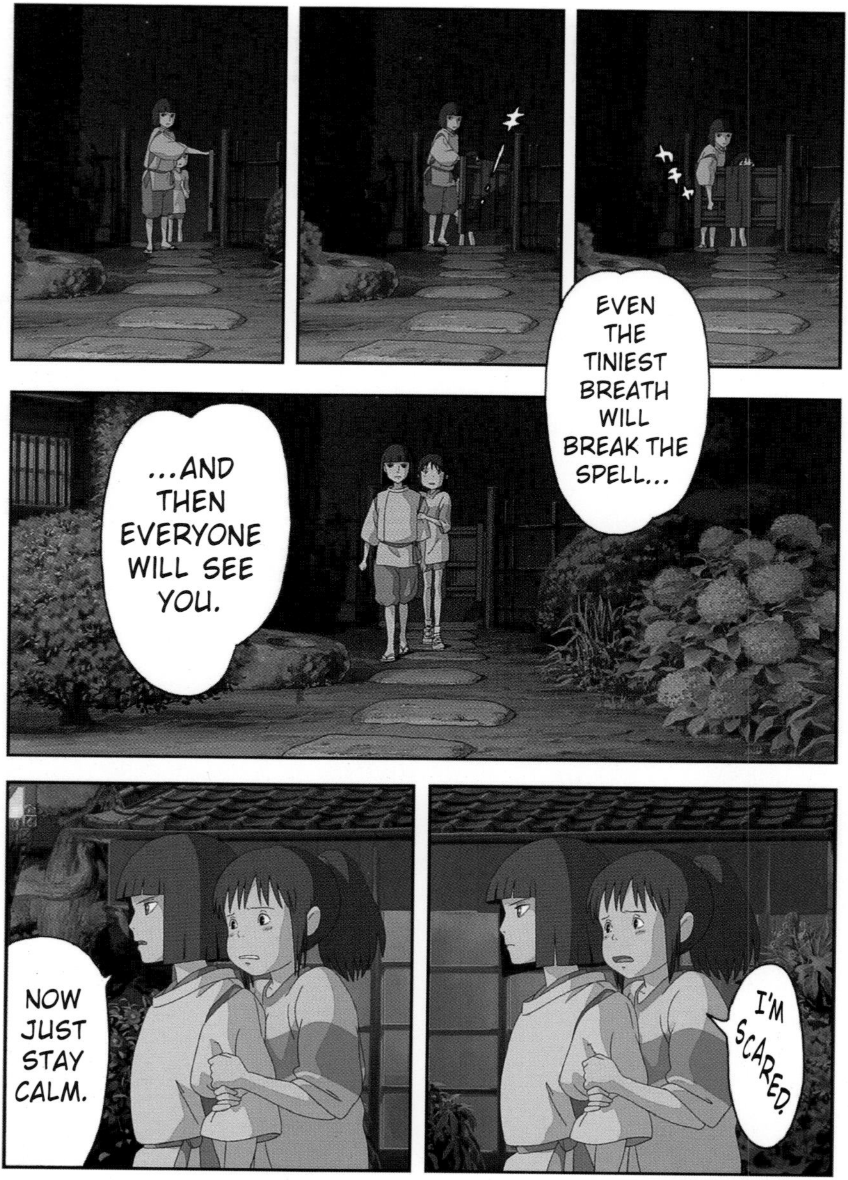
EVEN THE TINIEST BREATH WILL BREAK THE SPELL...
...AND THEN EVERYONE WILL SEE YOU.
I'M SCARED.
NOW JUST STAY CALM.

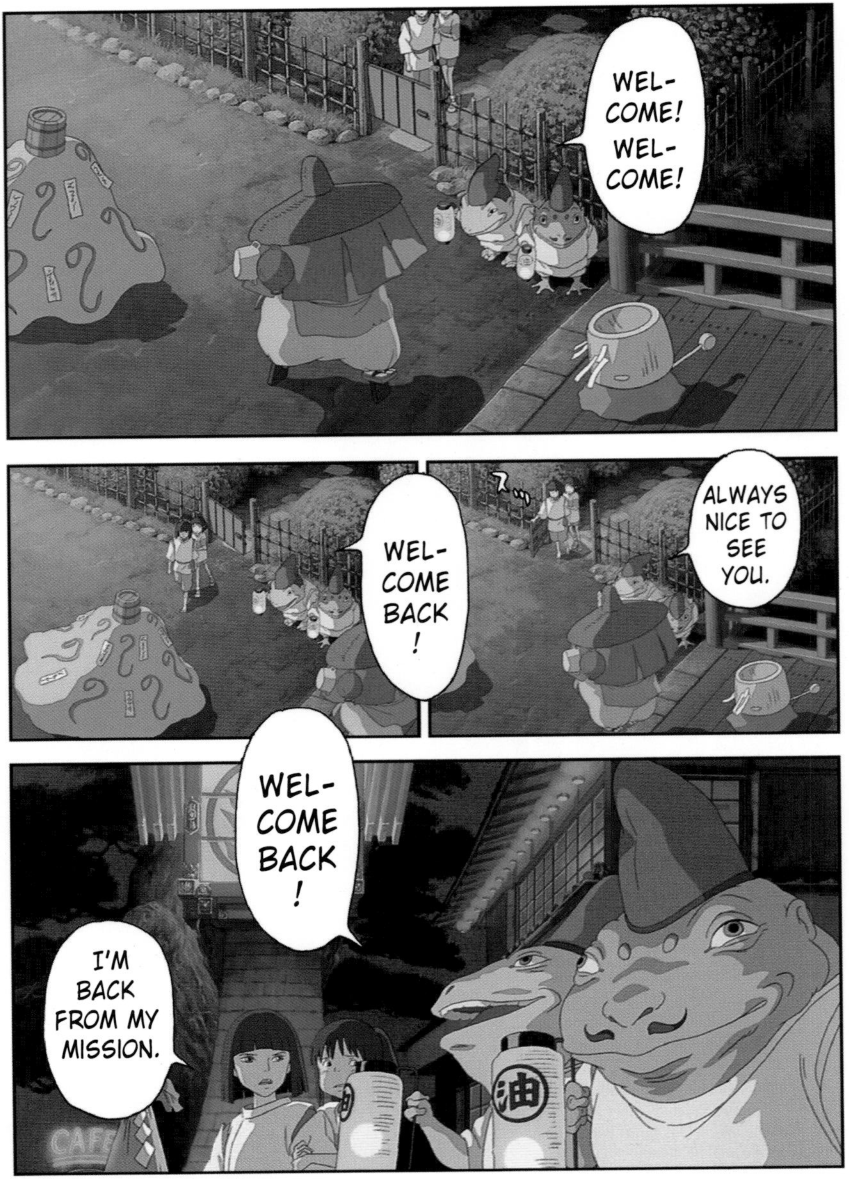
WEL-
COME!
WEL-
COME!
ス…
ALWAYS
NICE TO
SEE
YOU.
WEL-
COME
BACK
!
WEL-
COME
BACK
!
I'M
BACK
FROM MY
MISSION.
油
油
CAFE

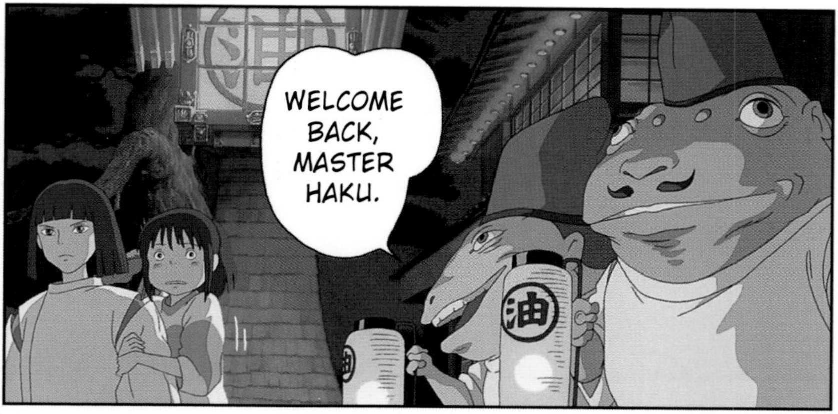
WELCOME BACK, MASTER HAKU.

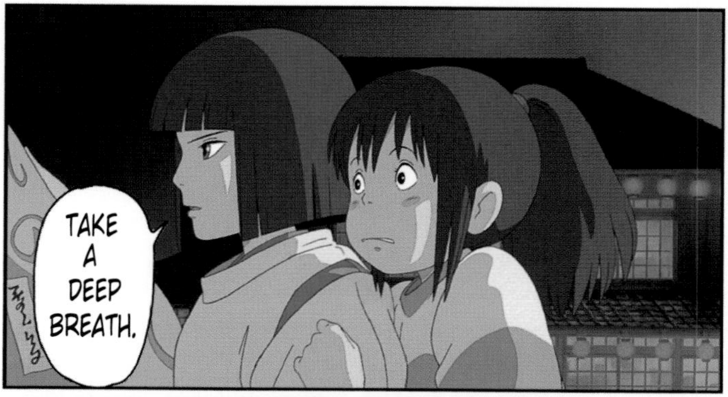
TAKE A DEEP BREATH.

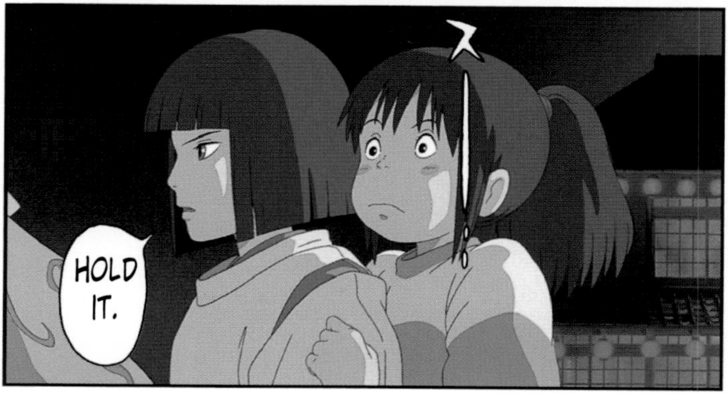
ス
HOLD IT.

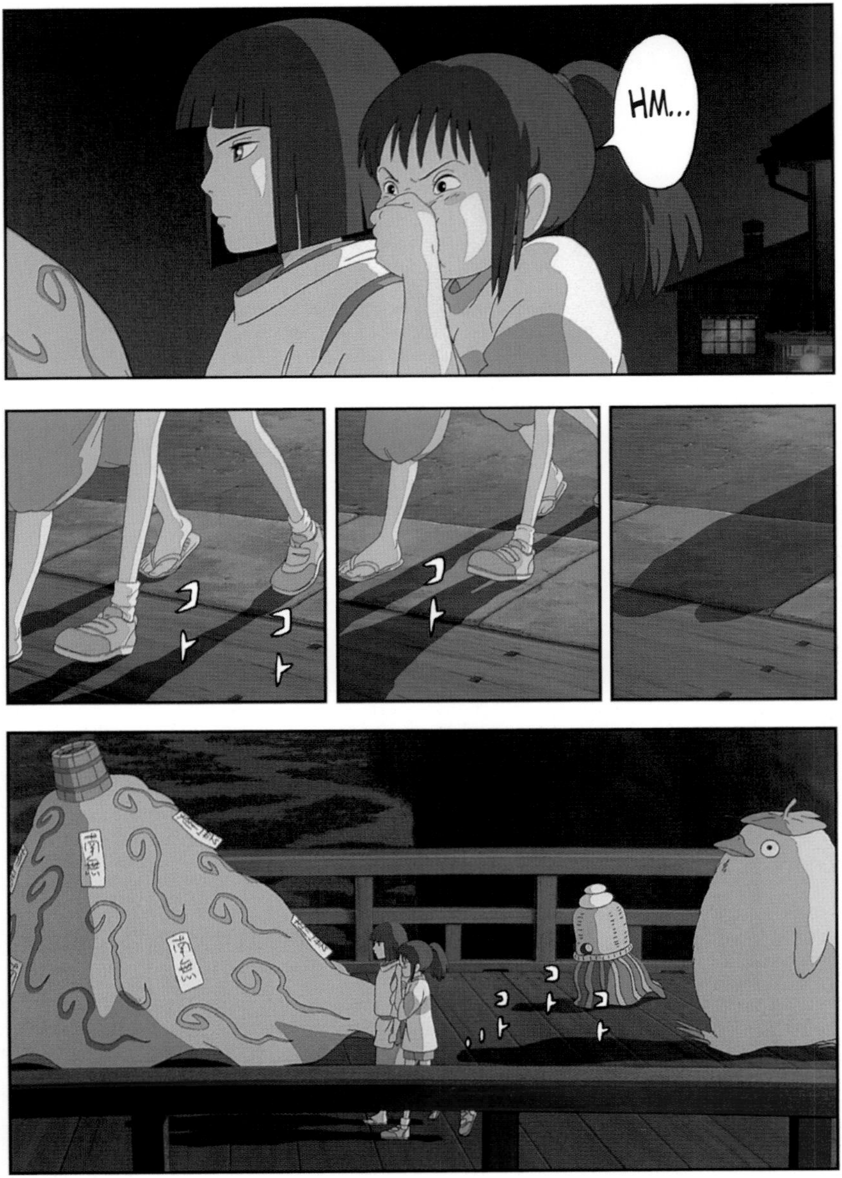
HM...
コト
コト
コト
コト
コト
コト

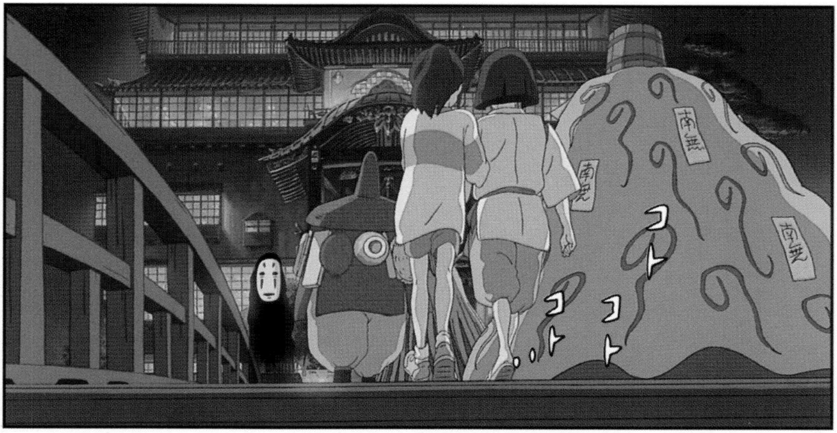
南無
南無
南無
コト
コト
コト
…

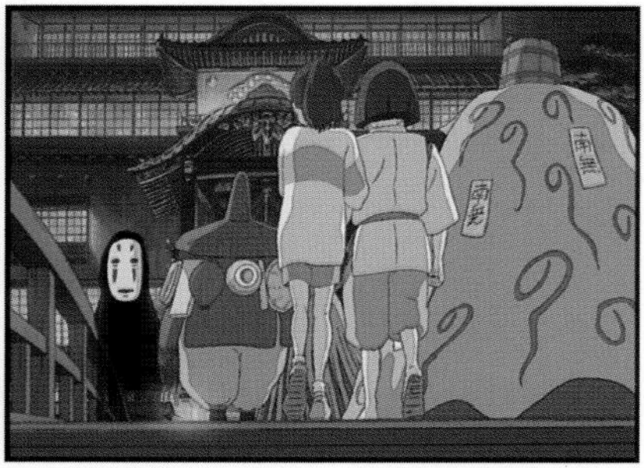
南無
南無

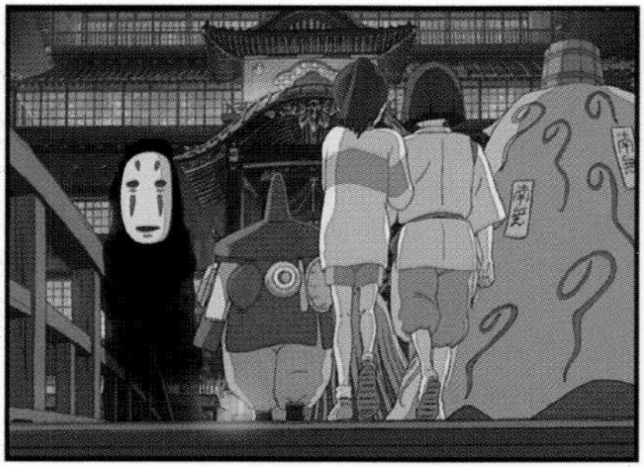
南無
南無

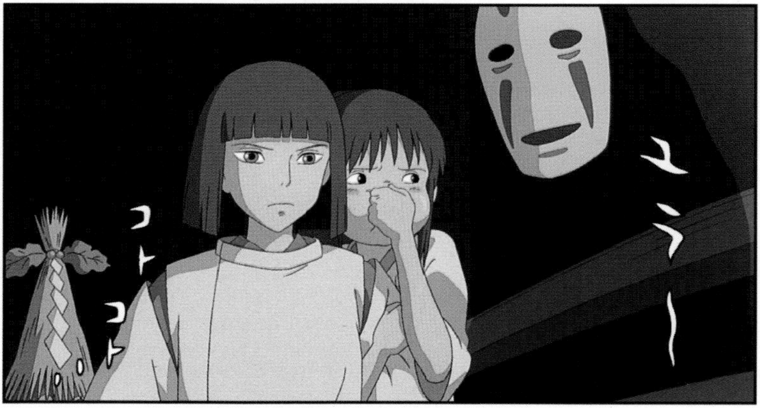
スゥー
コト
コト

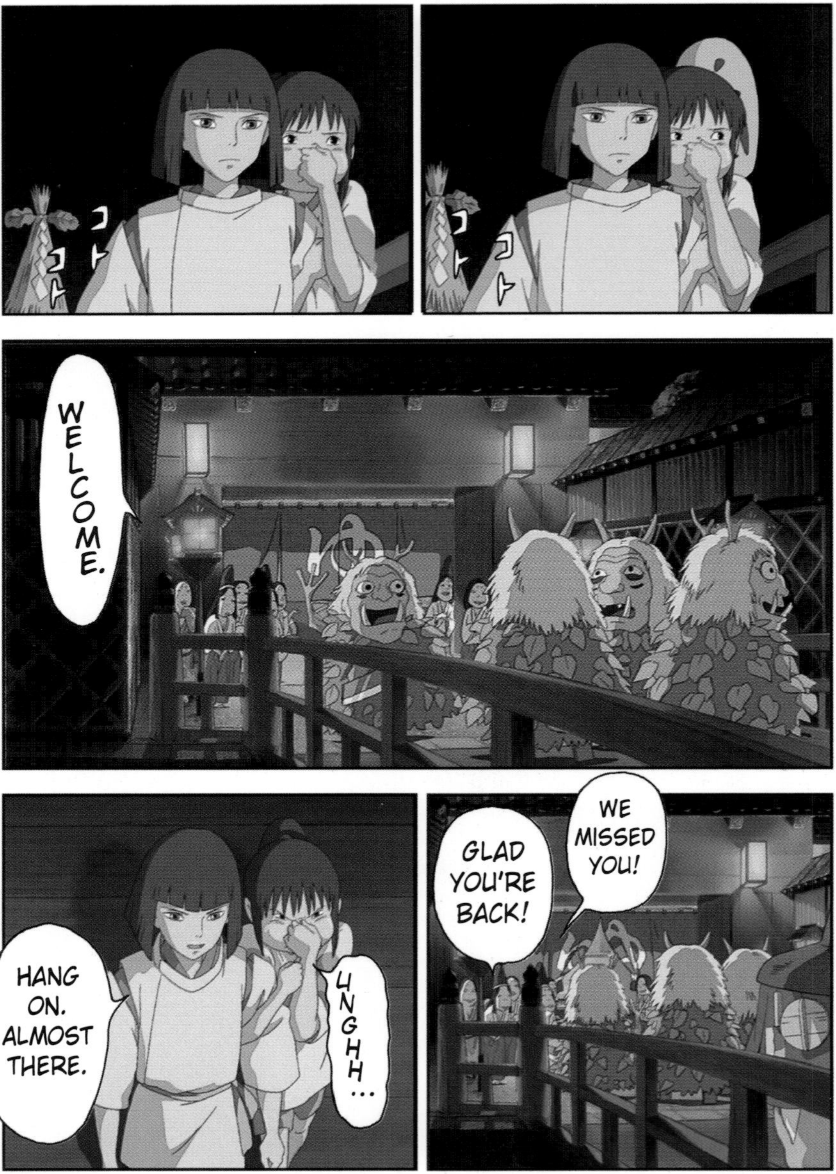
コト コト
コト コト
WELCOME.
HANG ON. ALMOST THERE.
UNGHH...
GLAD YOU'RE BACK!
WE MISSED YOU!

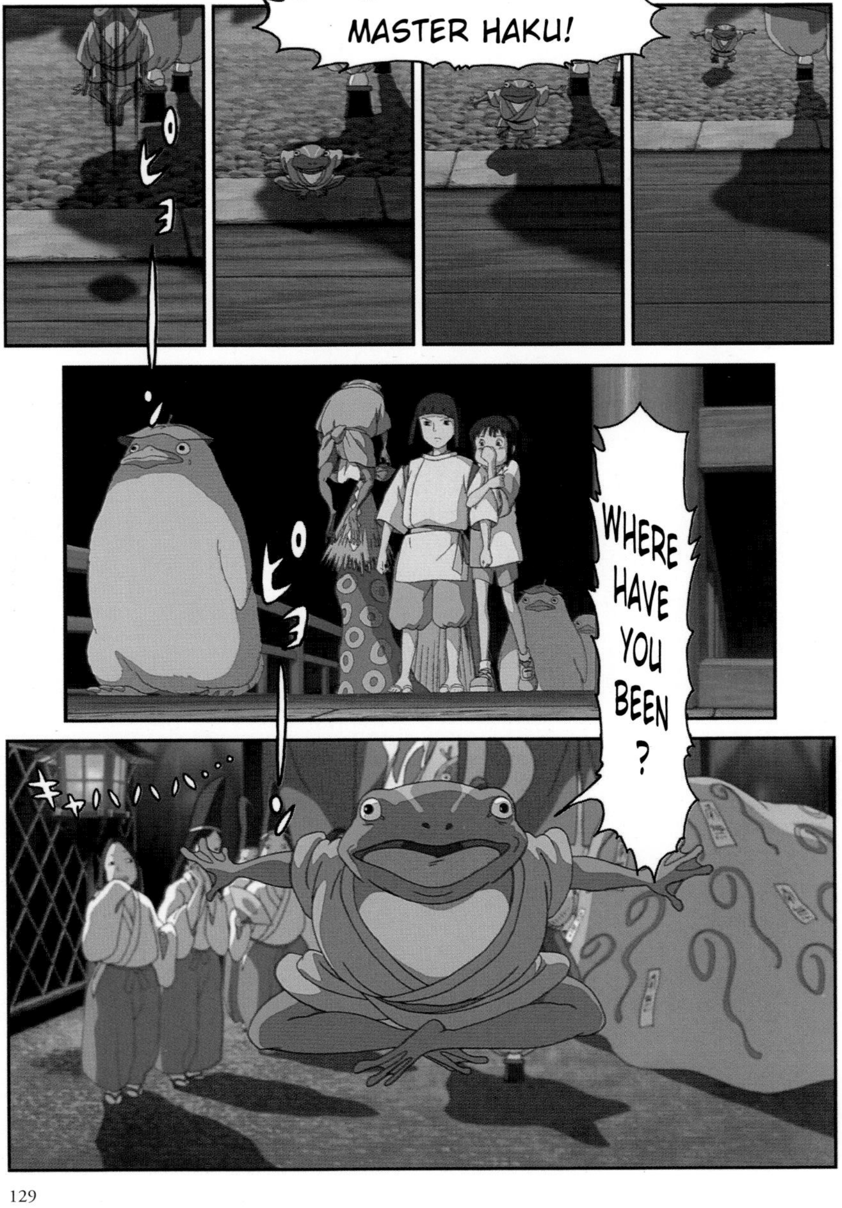
MASTER HAKU!
ピョ
WHERE HAVE YOU BEEN?
ピョ
キャ

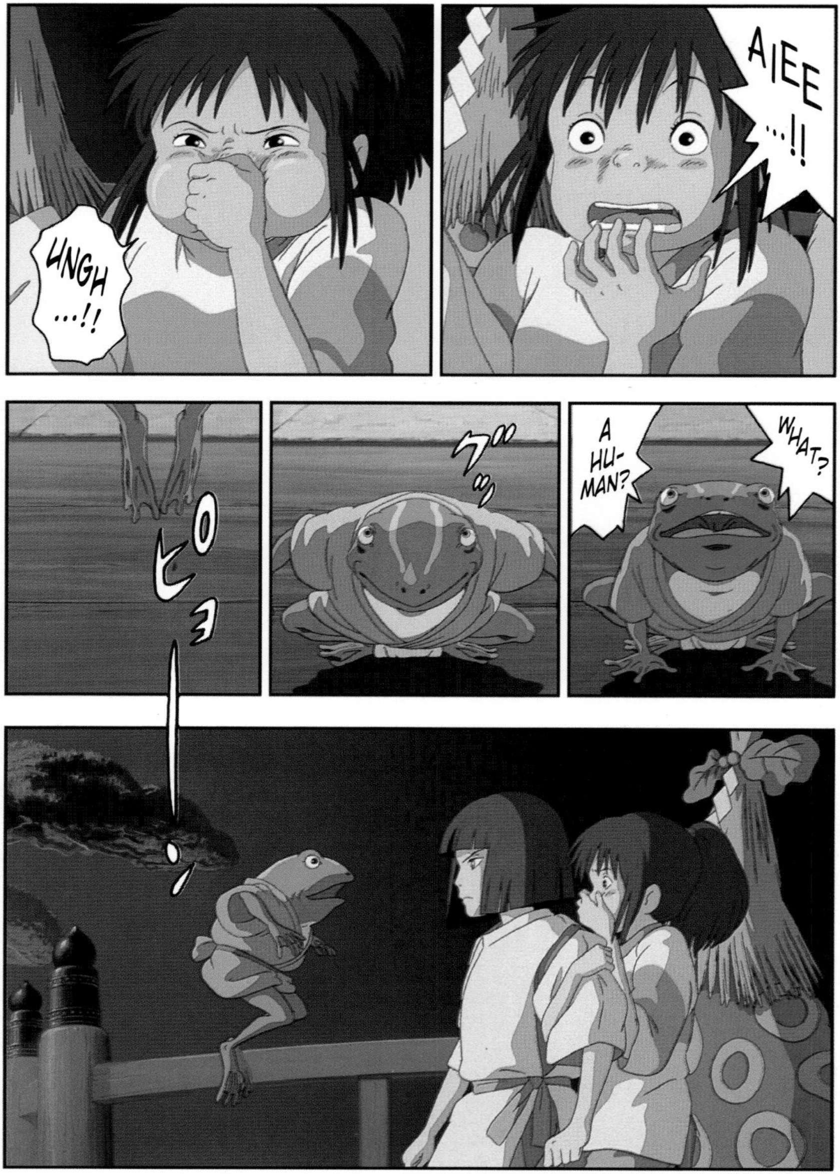
AIEE ...!!
UNGH ...!!
WHAT?
A HU-MAN?
グッ
ピョーン

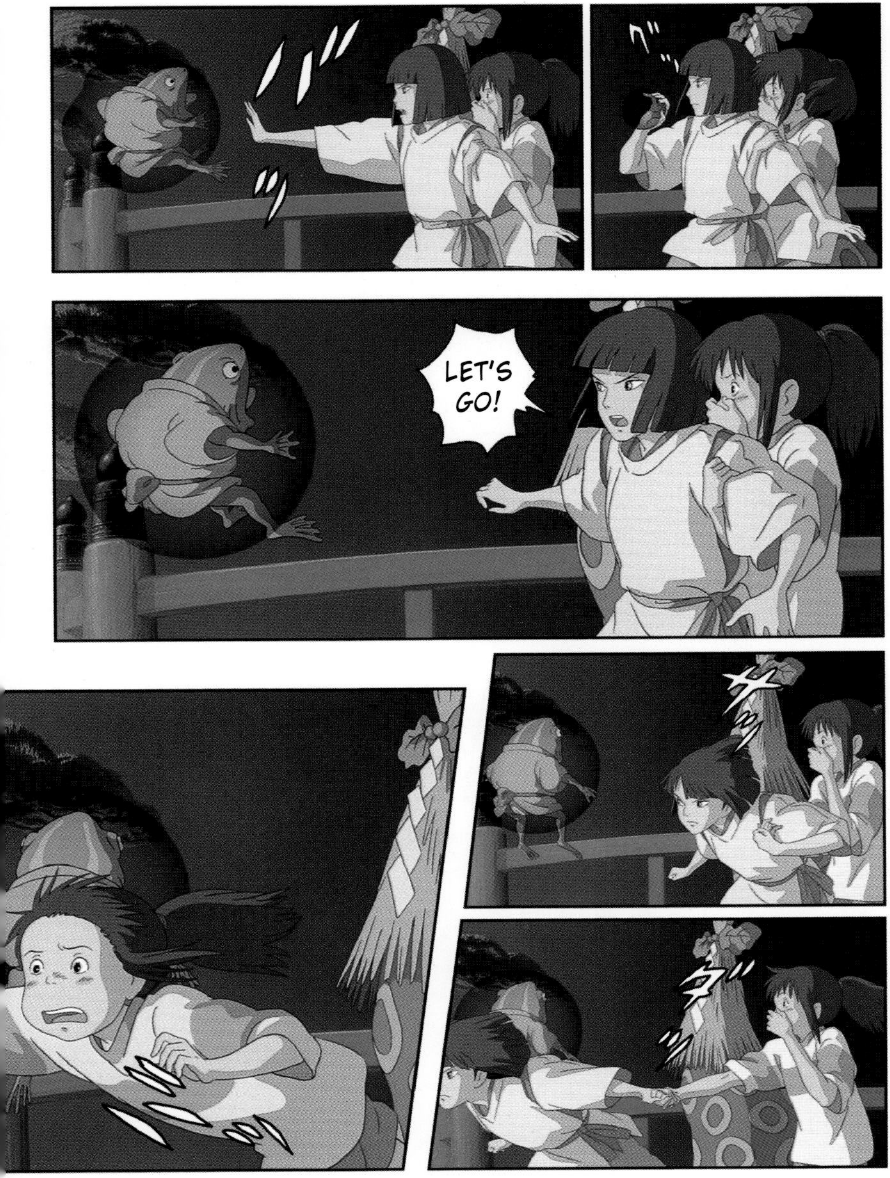
LET'S GO!

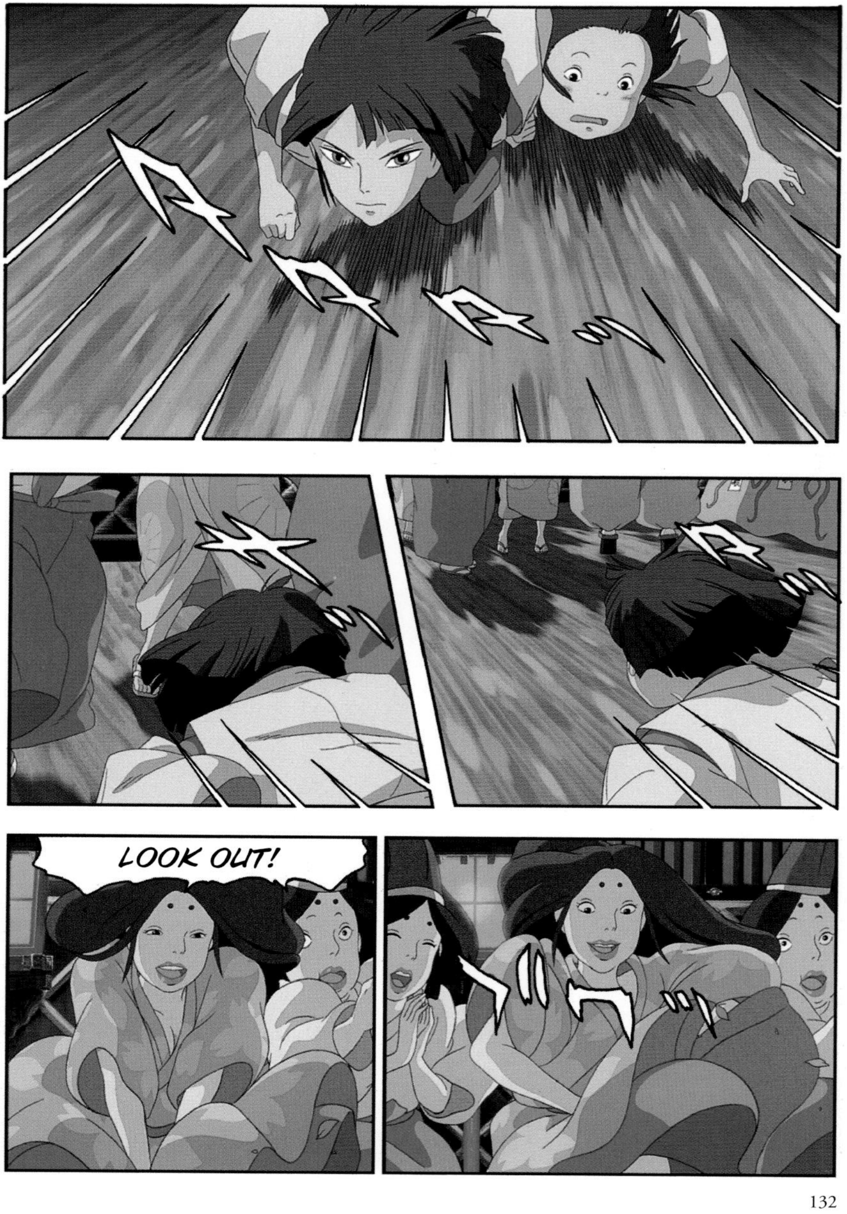
LOOK OUT!

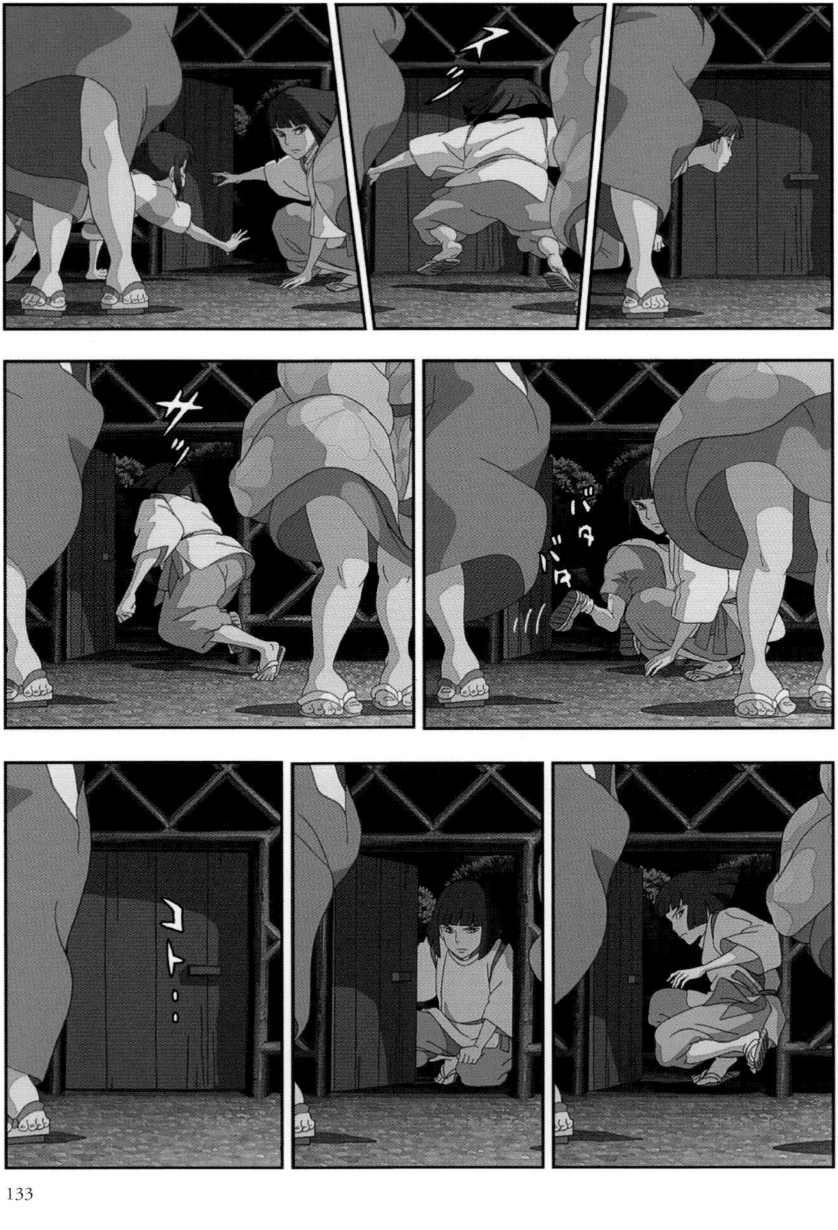
スッ
バタバタ
ザッ
コト…

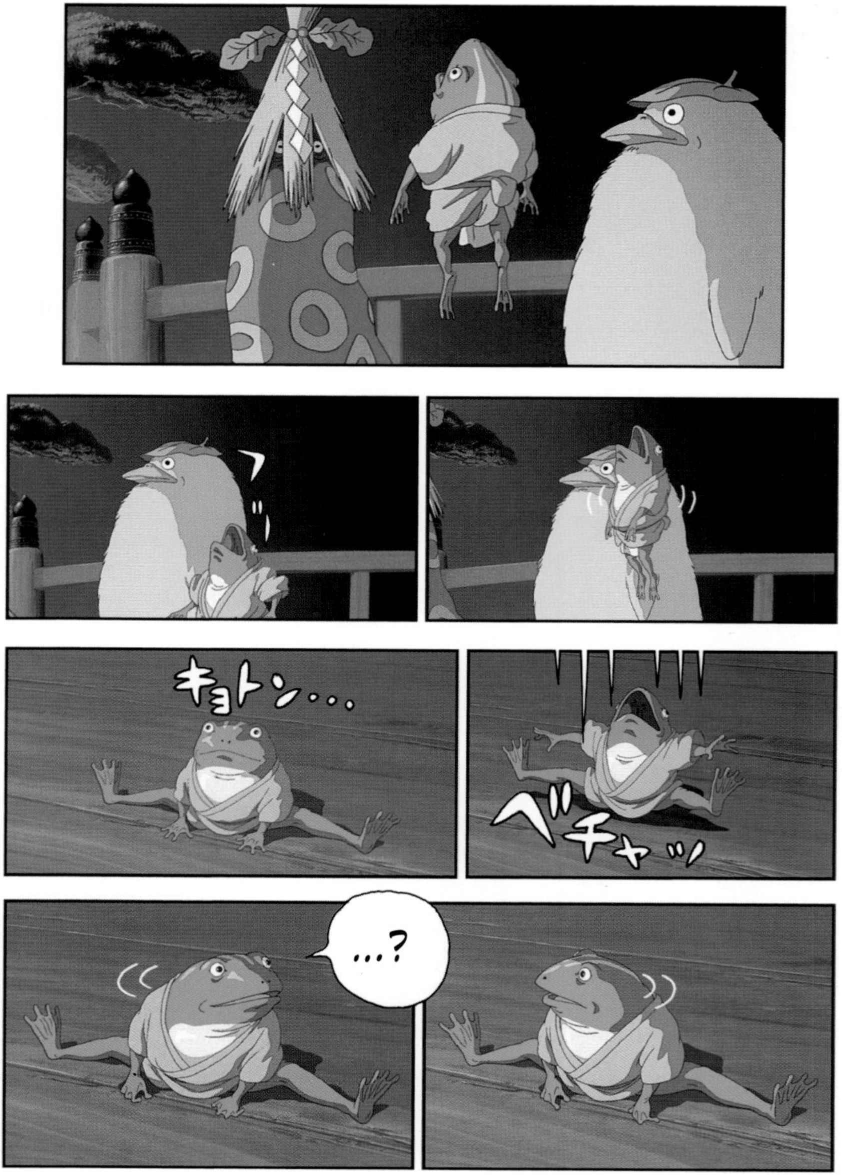
キョトン…
ベチャッ!
…?

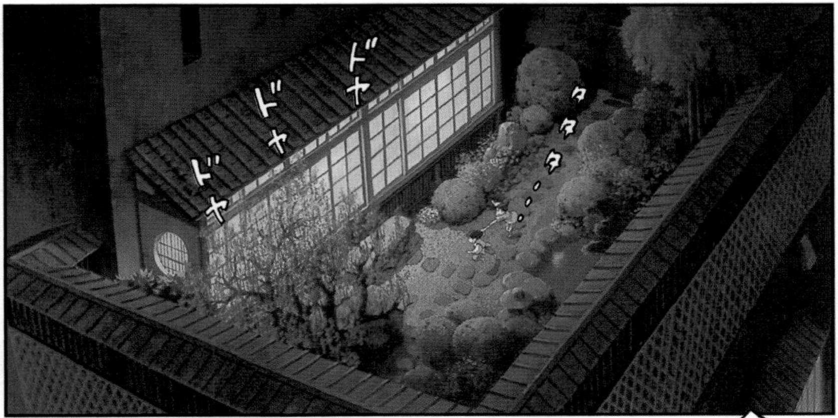
タタタ…
ドヤ
ドヤ
ドヤ

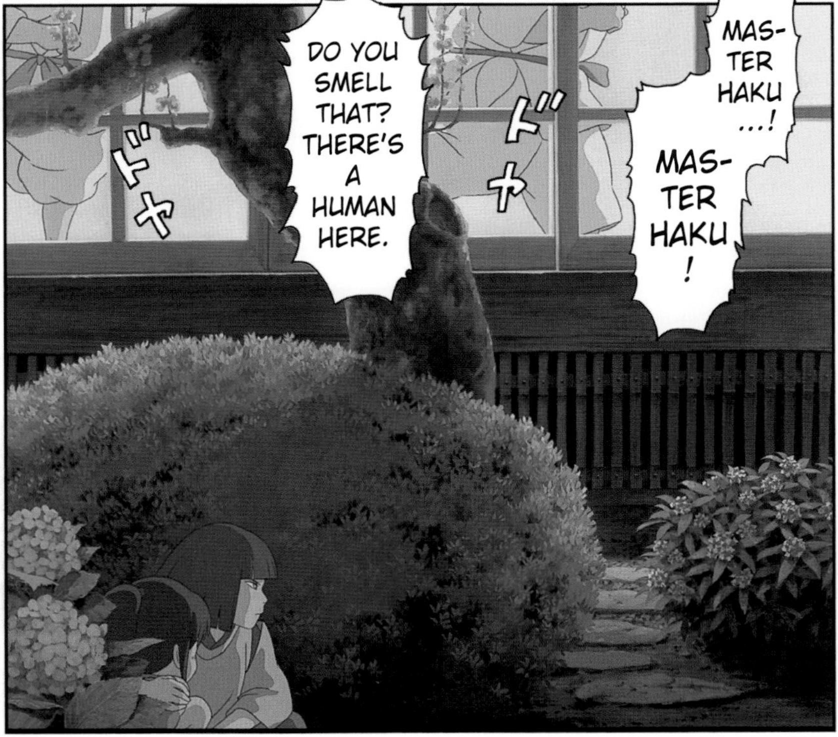
MAS-TER HAKU ...!
MAS-TER HAKU !
ドヤ
DO YOU SMELL THAT? THERE'S A HUMAN HERE.
ドヤ

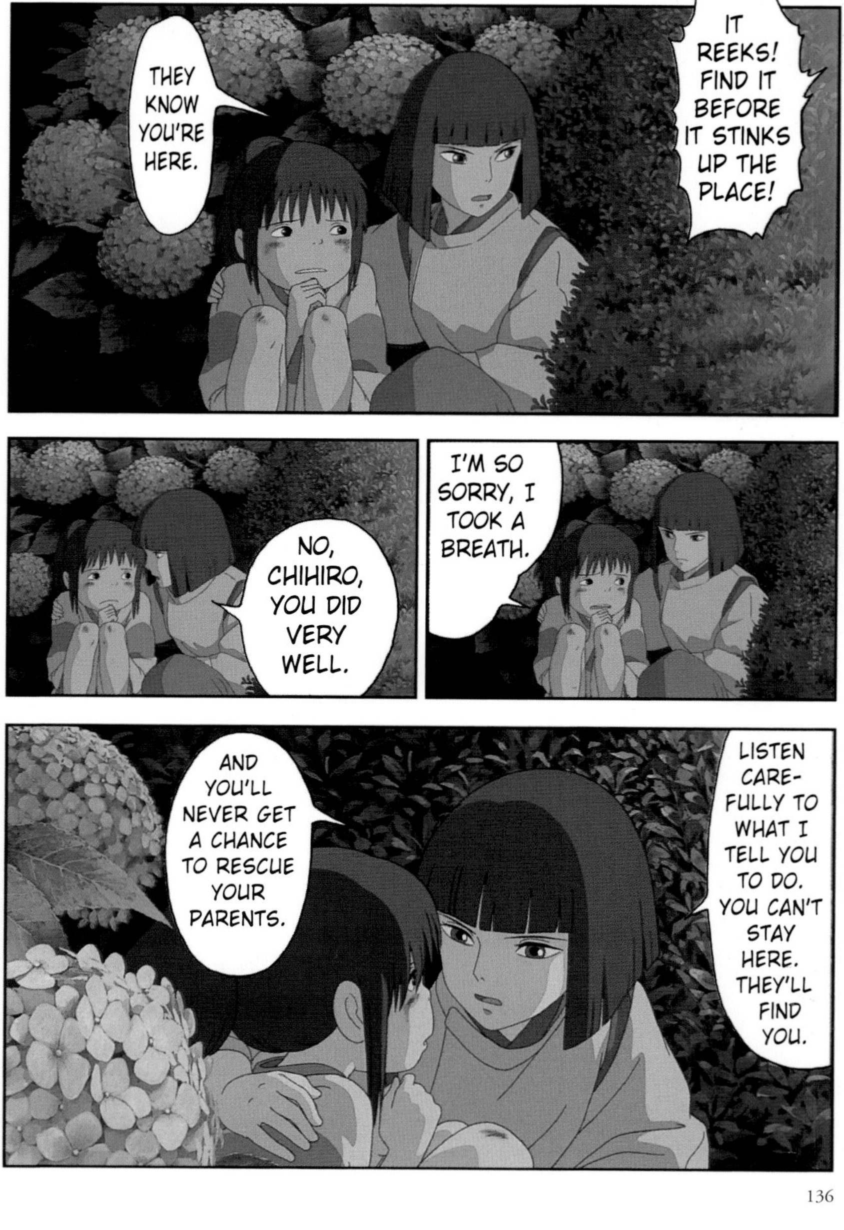
IT REEKS! FIND IT BEFORE IT STINKS UP THE PLACE!
THEY KNOW YOU'RE HERE.
I'M SO SORRY, I TOOK A BREATH.
NO, CHIHIRO, YOU DID VERY WELL.
LISTEN CARE-FULLY TO WHAT I TELL YOU TO DO. YOU CAN'T STAY HERE. THEY'LL FIND YOU.
AND YOU'LL NEVER GET A CHANCE TO RESCUE YOUR PARENTS.

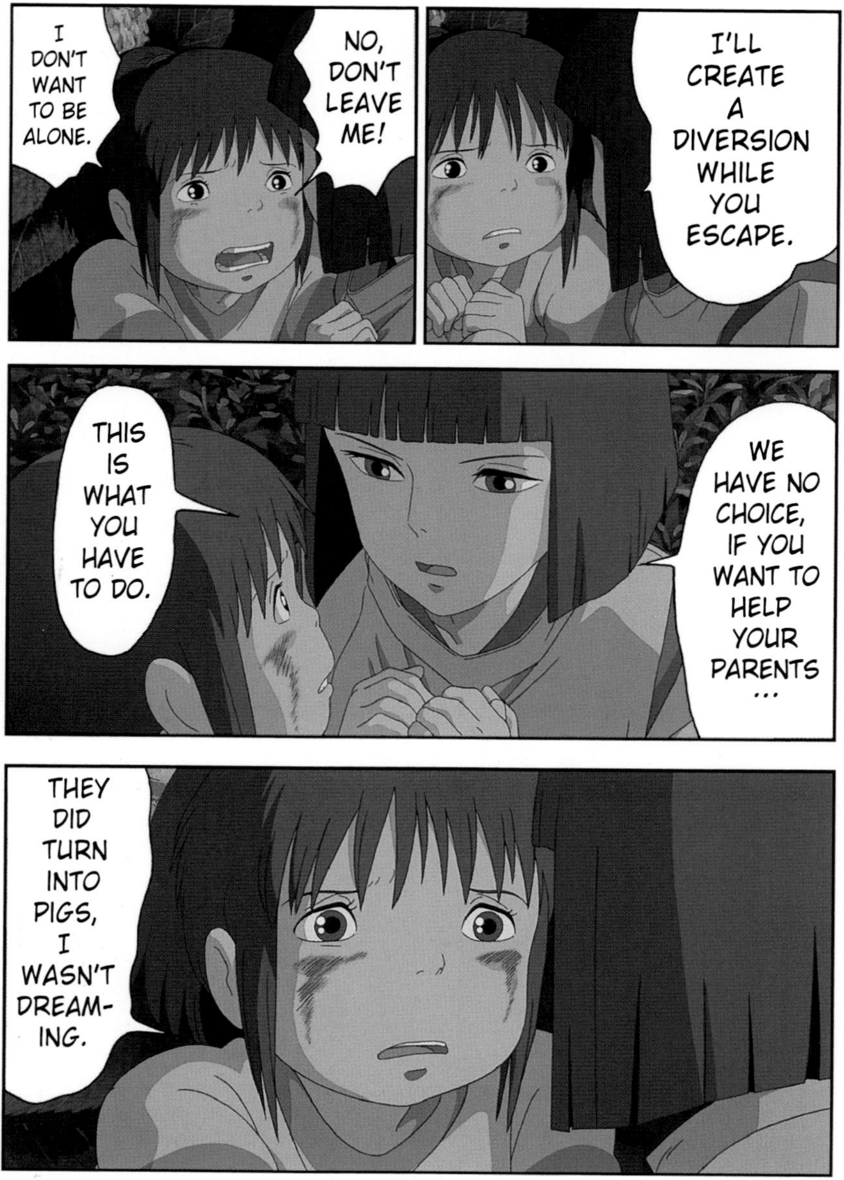
I'LL CREATE A DIVERSION WHILE YOU ESCAPE.
NO, DON'T LEAVE ME!
I DON'T WANT TO BE ALONE.
WE HAVE NO CHOICE, IF YOU WANT TO HELP YOUR PARENTS...
THIS IS WHAT YOU HAVE TO DO.
THEY DID TURN INTO PIGS, I WASN'T DREAMING.

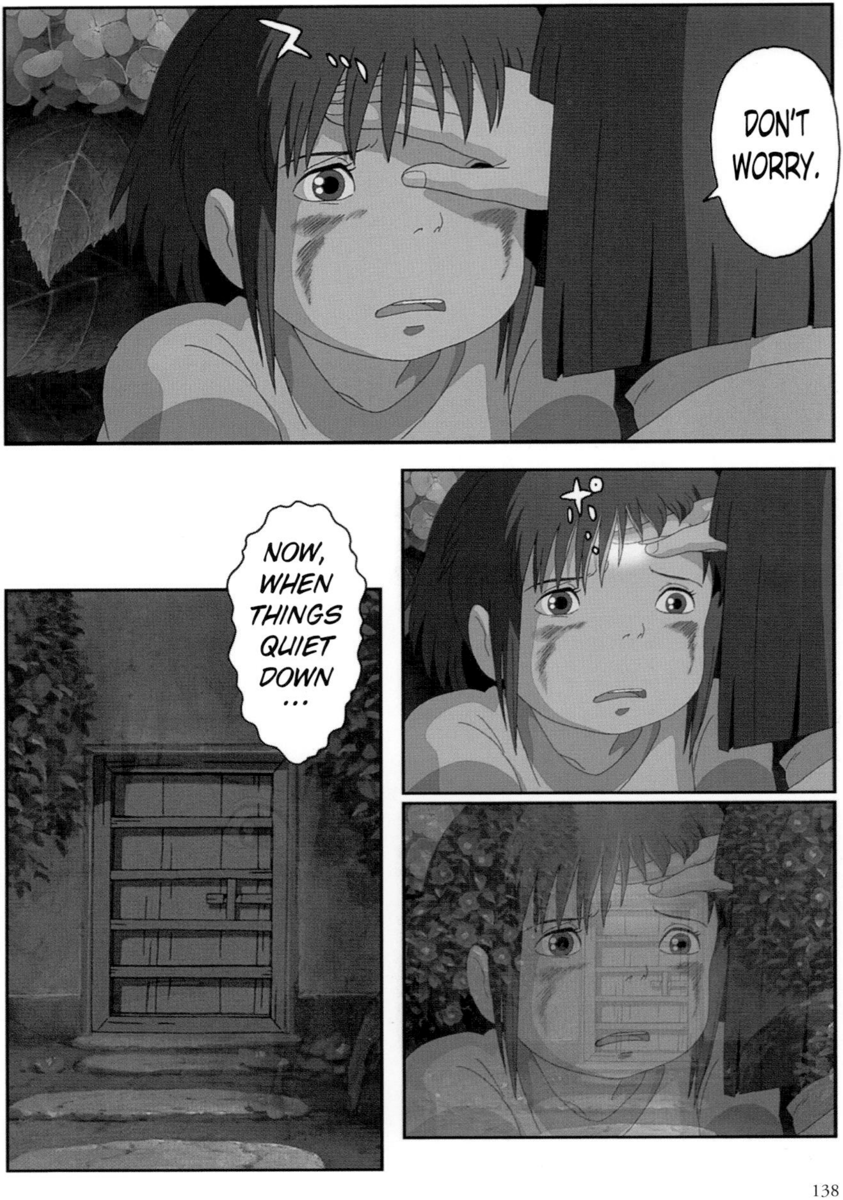
DON'T WORRY.
NOW, WHEN THINGS QUIET DOWN...

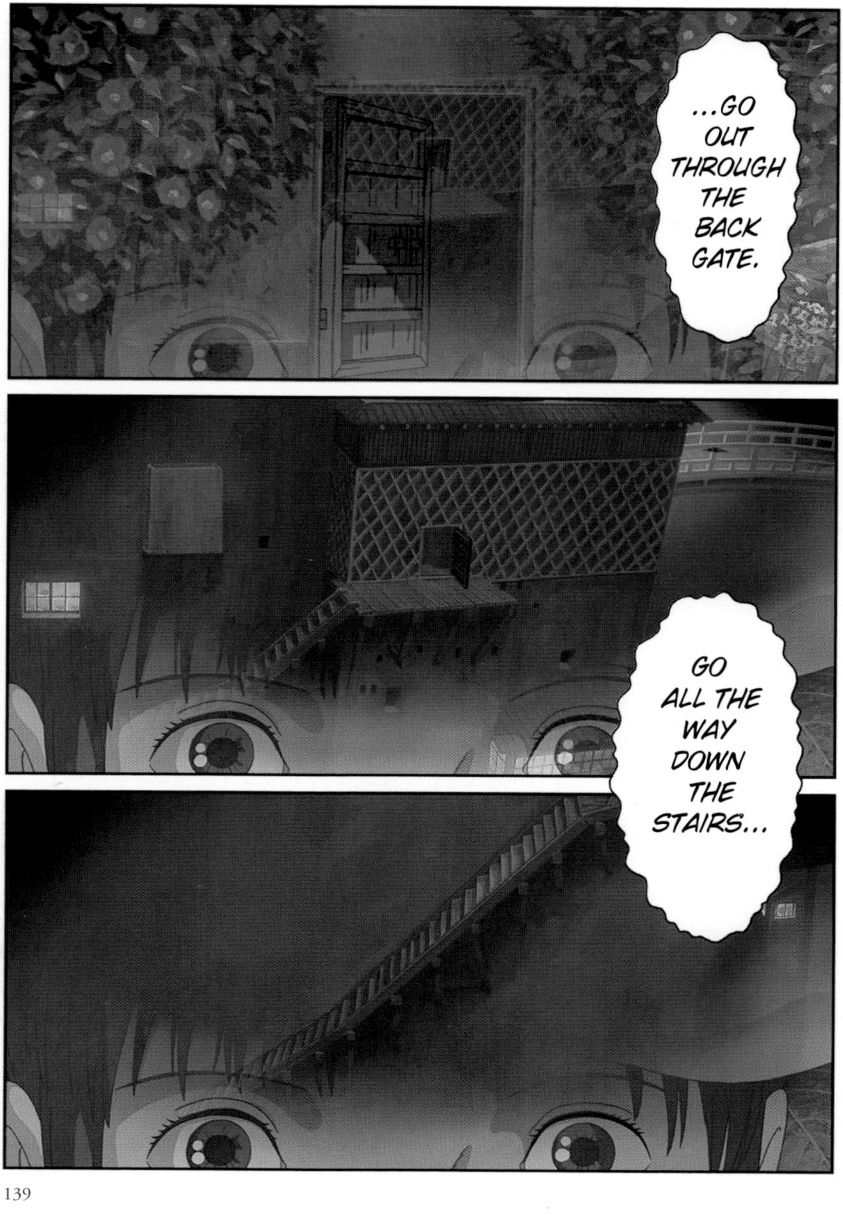
...GO OUT THROUGH THE BACK GATE.
GO ALL THE WAY DOWN THE STAIRS...

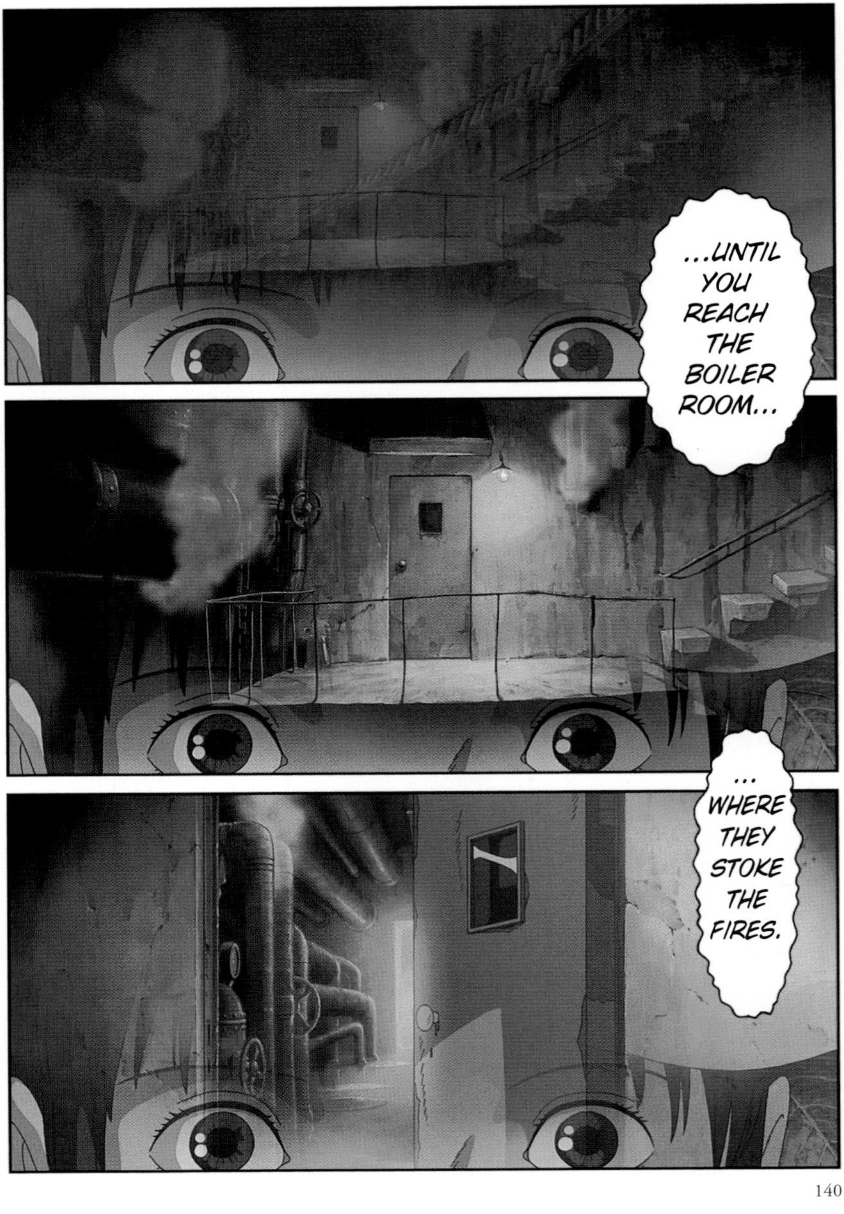
...UNTIL YOU REACH THE BOILER ROOM...
... WHERE THEY STOKE THE FIRES.

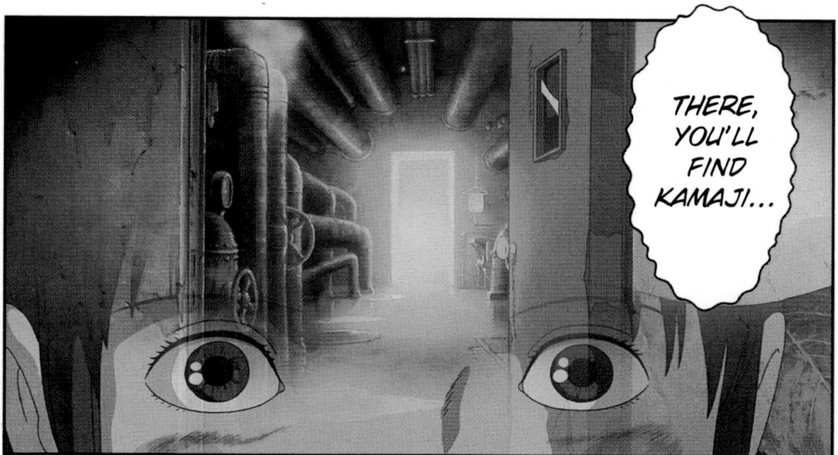
THERE, YOU'LL FIND KAMAJI...
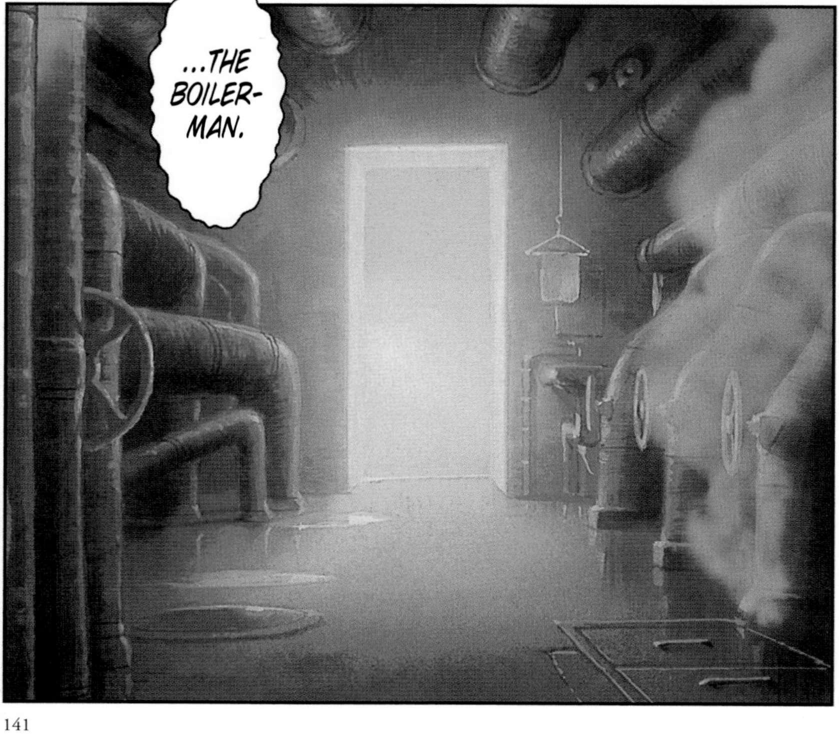
...THE BOILER-MAN.

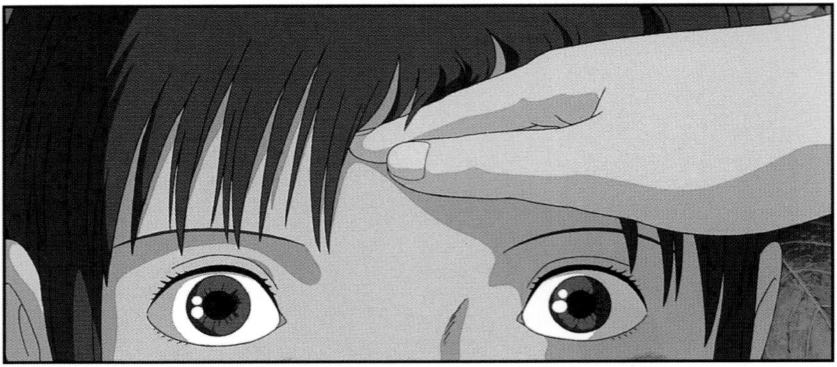

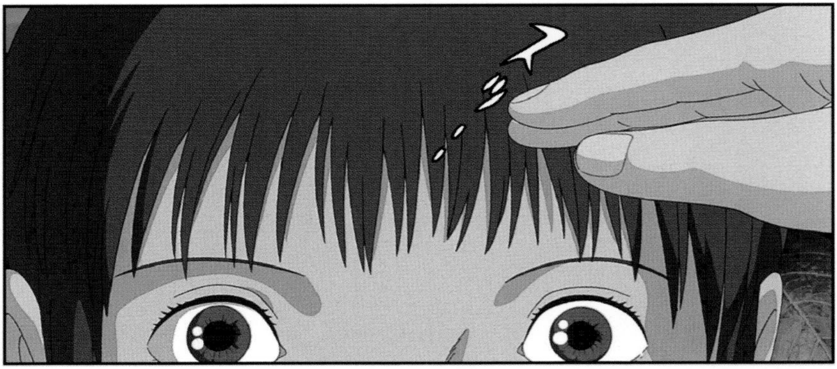

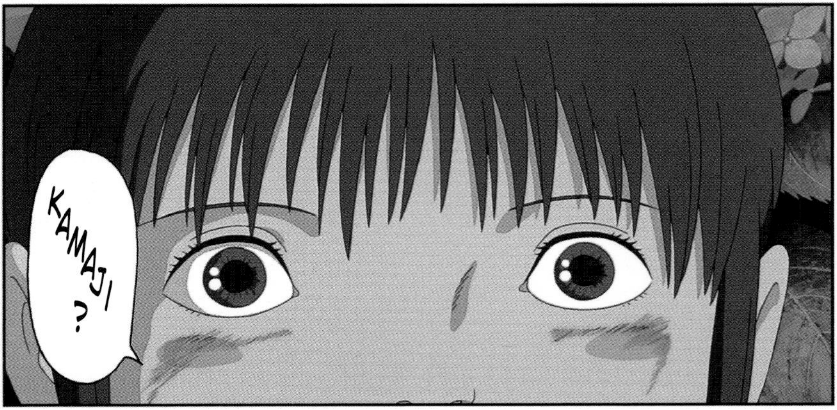
KAMAJI?

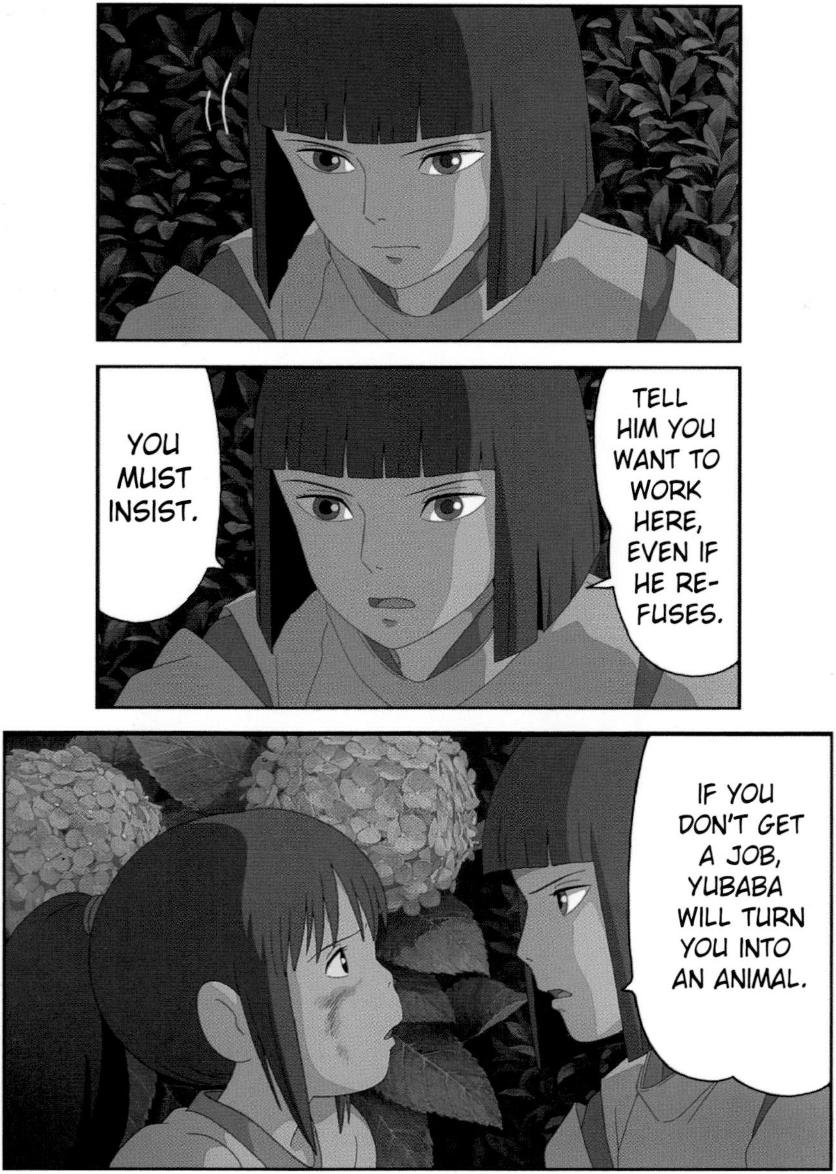
TELL HIM YOU WANT TO WORK HERE, EVEN IF HE RE-FUSES.
YOU MUST INSIST.
IF YOU DON'T GET A JOB, YUBABA WILL TURN YOU INTO AN ANIMAL.

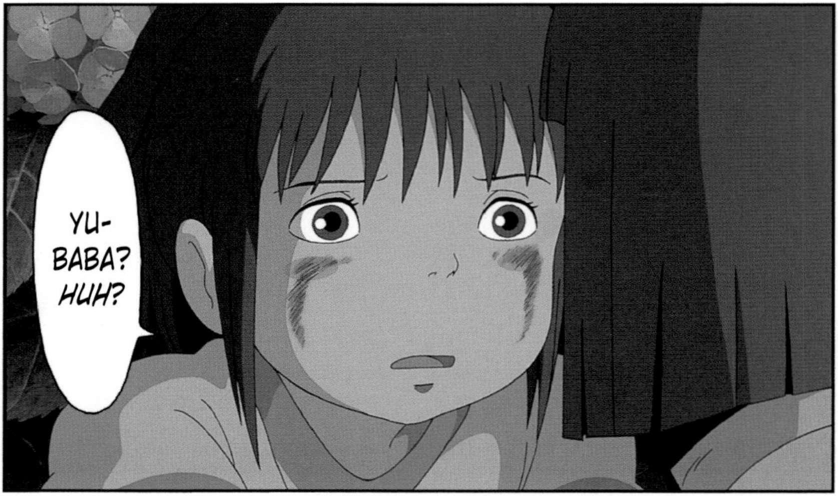
YU-
BABA?
HUH?
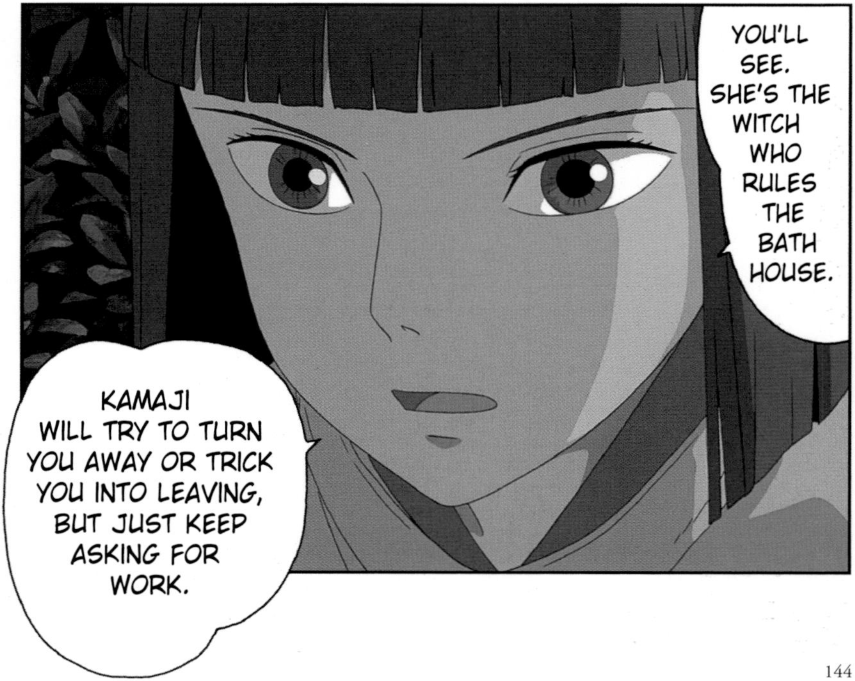
YOU'LL SEE. SHE'S THE WITCH WHO RULES THE BATH HOUSE.
KAMAJI WILL TRY TO TURN YOU AWAY OR TRICK YOU INTO LEAVING, BUT JUST KEEP ASKING FOR WORK.

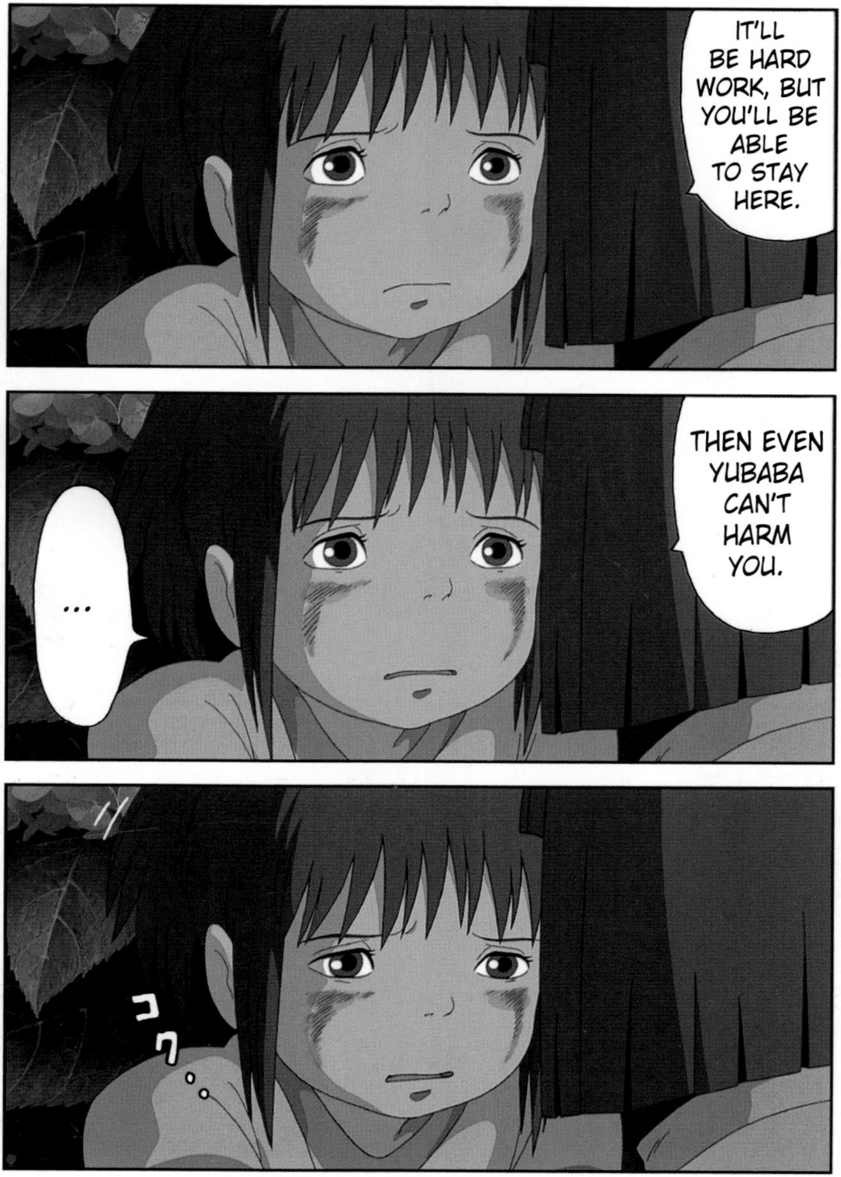
IT'LL BE HARD WORK, BUT YOU'LL BE ABLE TO STAY HERE.
THEN EVEN YUBABA CAN'T HARM YOU.
...
コク

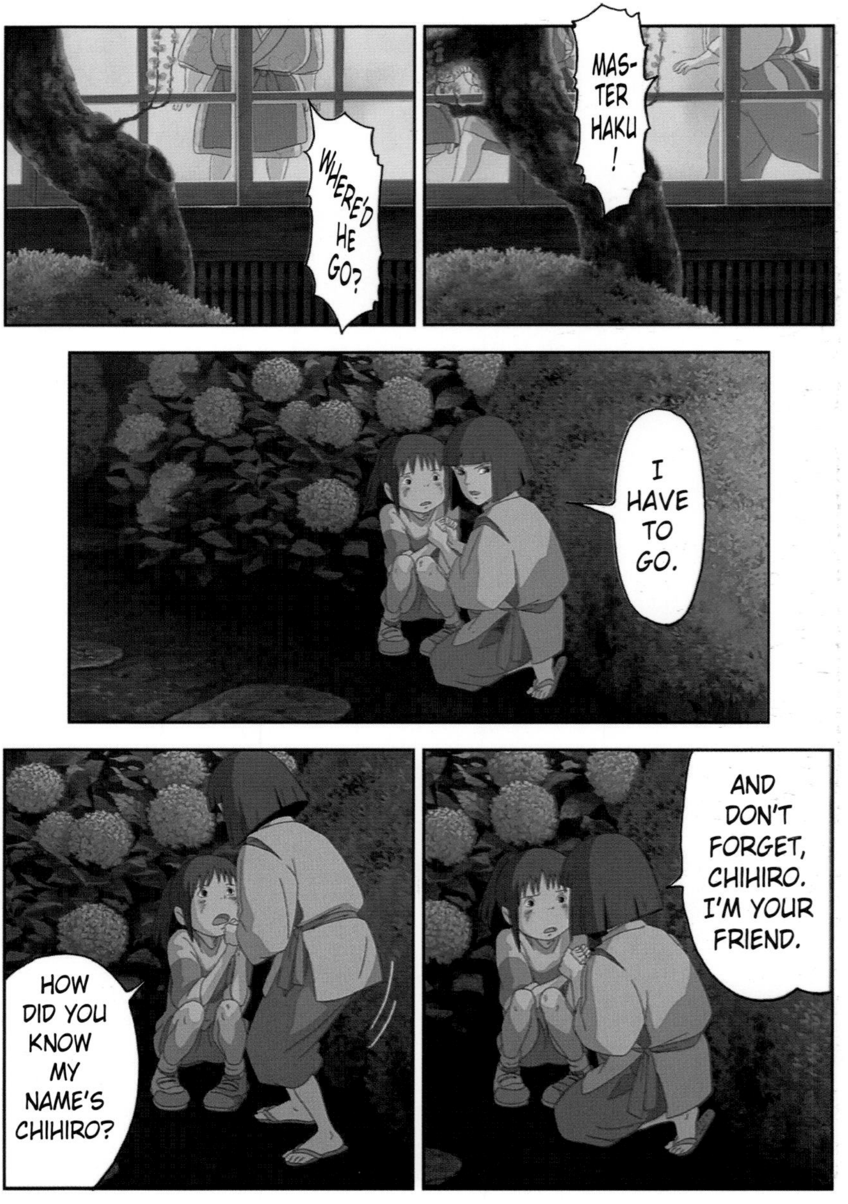

WHERE'D HE GO?
MAS-TER HAKU!
I HAVE TO GO.
HOW DID YOU KNOW MY NAME'S CHIHIRO?
AND DON'T FORGET, CHIHIRO. I'M YOUR FRIEND.

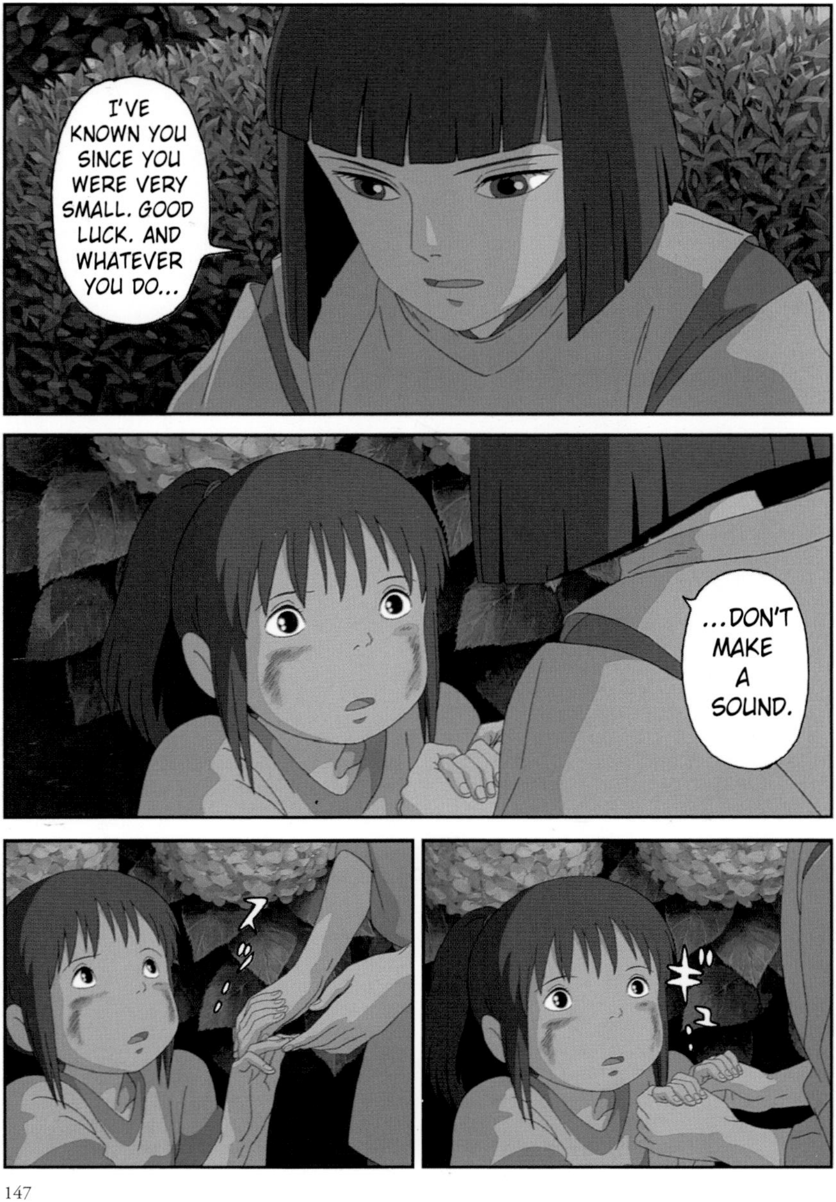
I'VE KNOWN YOU SINCE YOU WERE VERY SMALL. GOOD LUCK. AND WHATEVER YOU DO...
...DON'T MAKE A SOUND.
ギュ
スッ

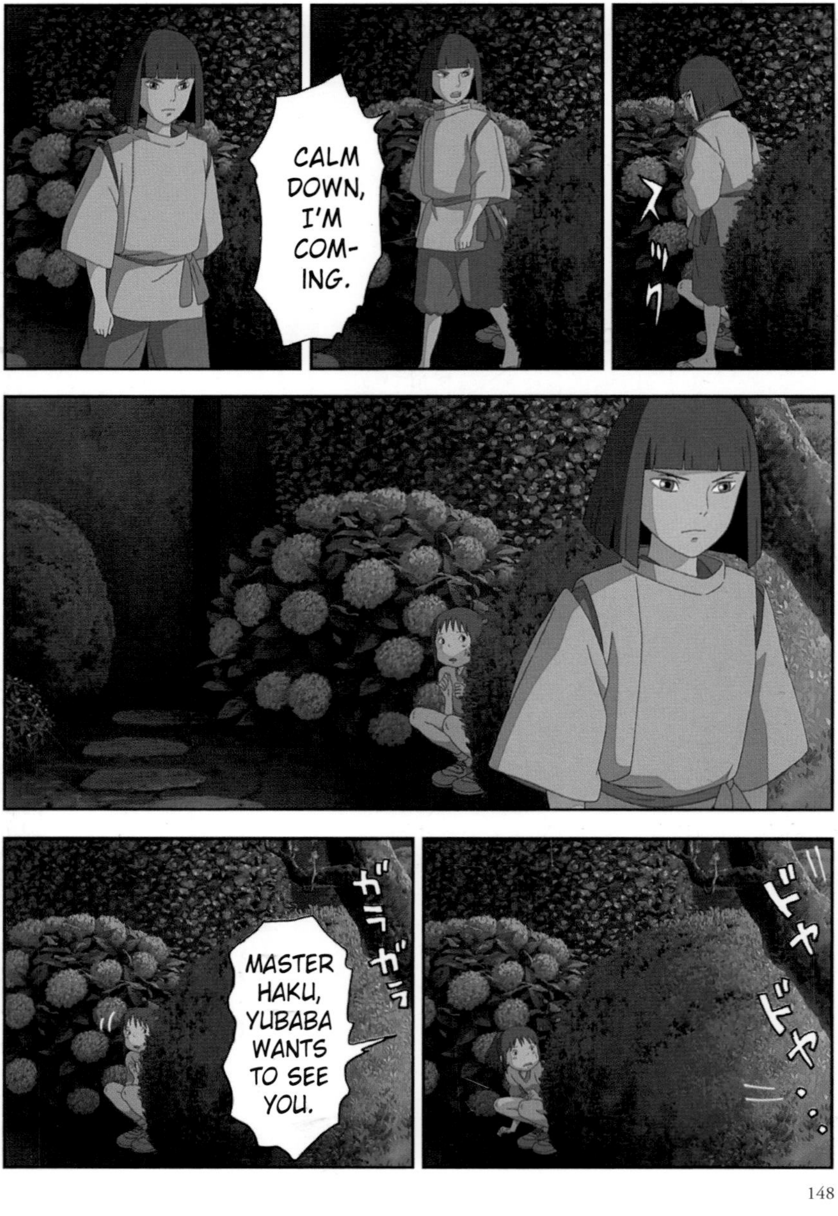
スッ
CALM DOWN, I'M COMING.
ドヤドヤ…
ガラガラ
MASTER HAKU, YUBABA WANTS TO SEE YOU.

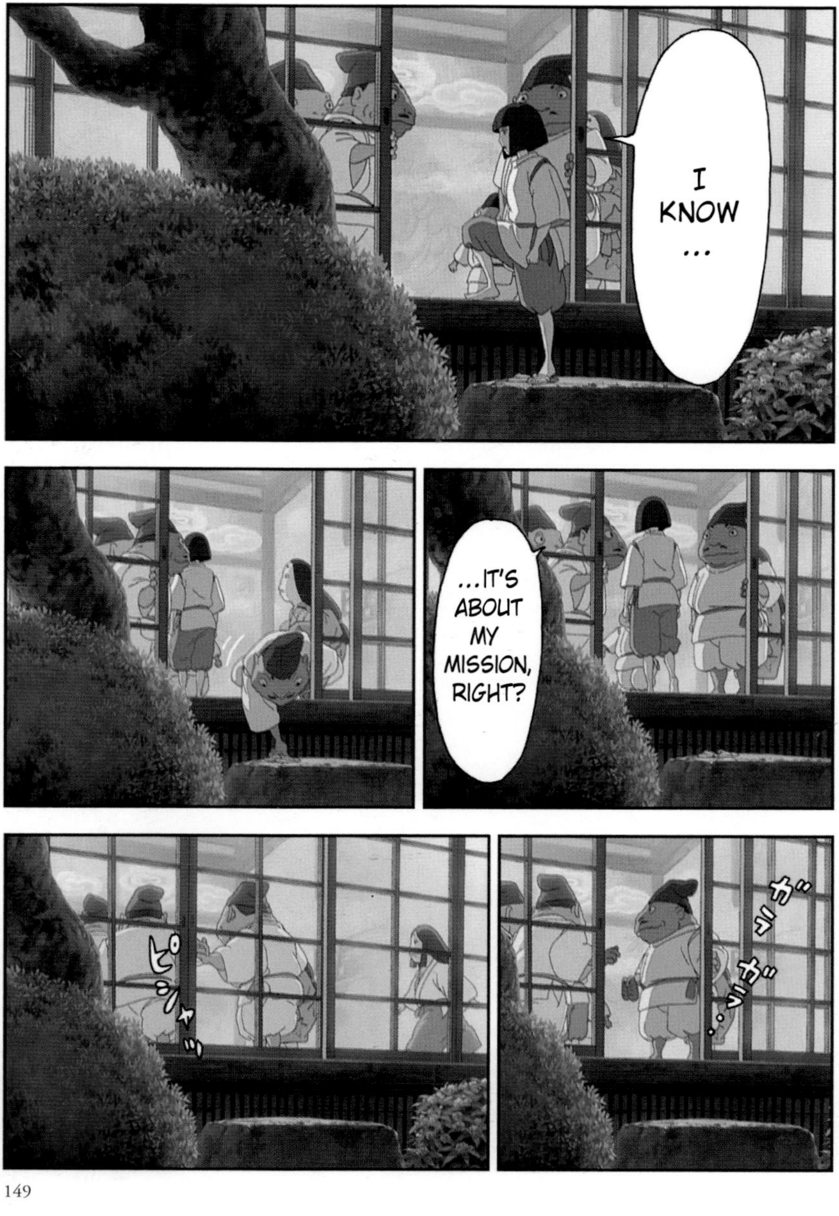
I KNOW ...
...IT'S ABOUT MY MISSION, RIGHT?
ガソガソ‥
ピシャッ

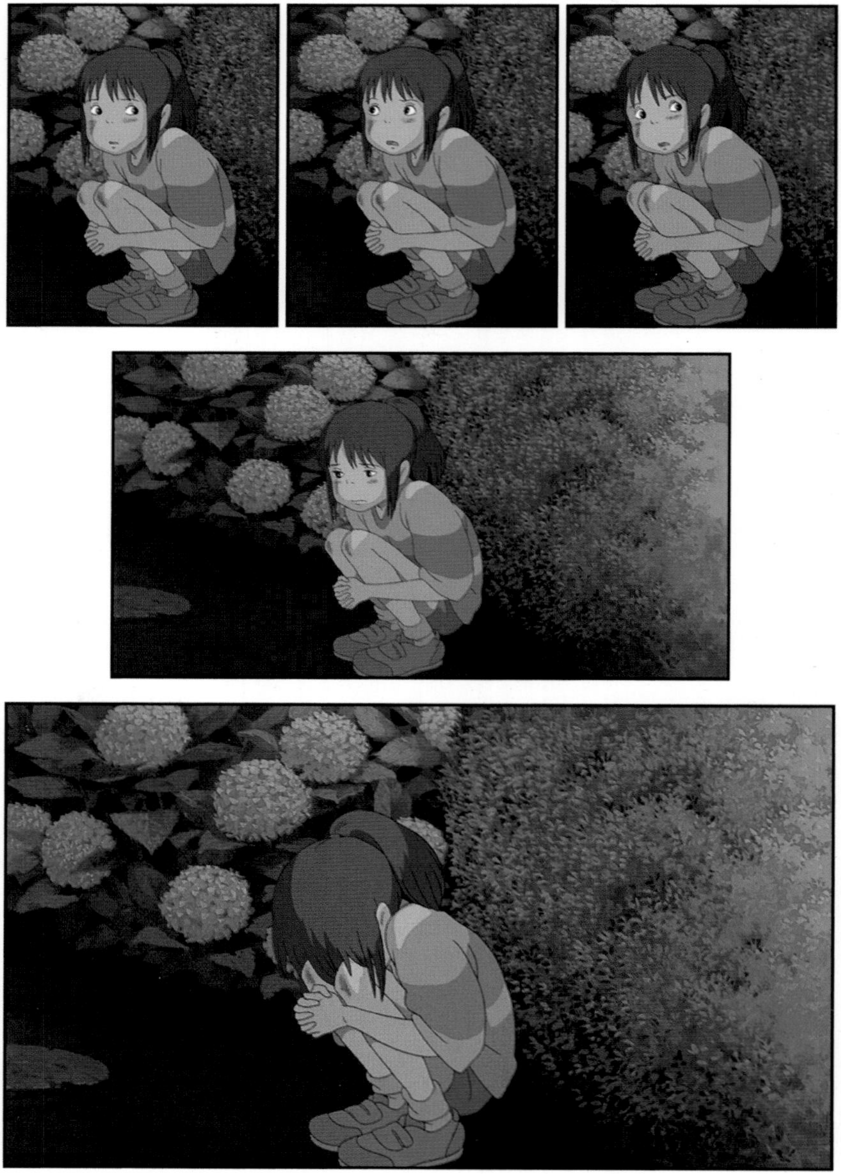

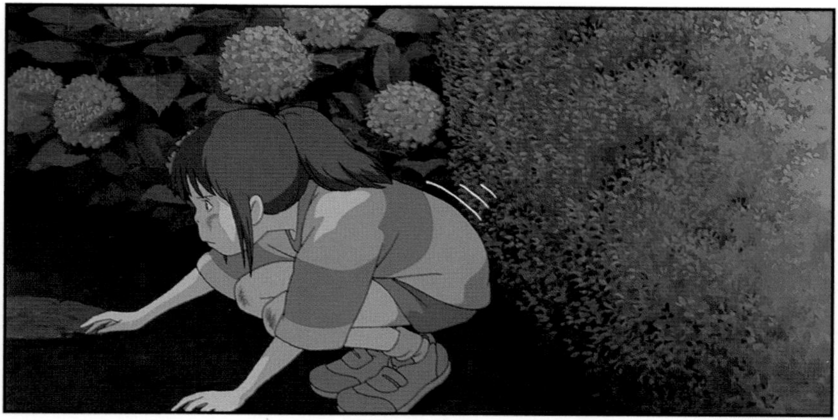
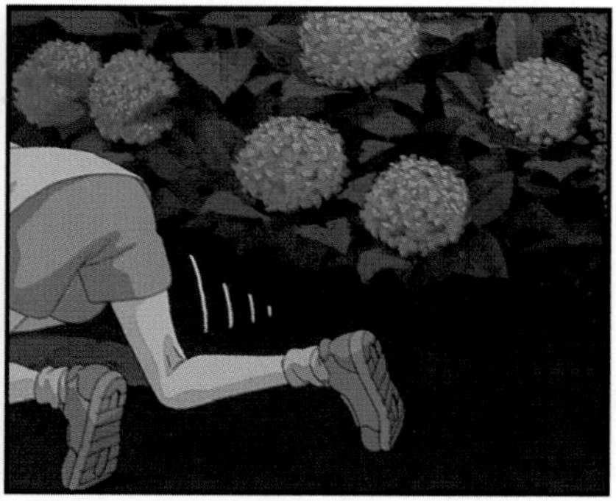
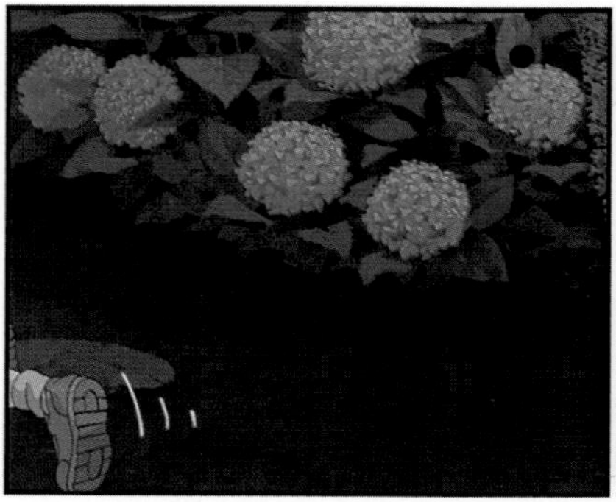
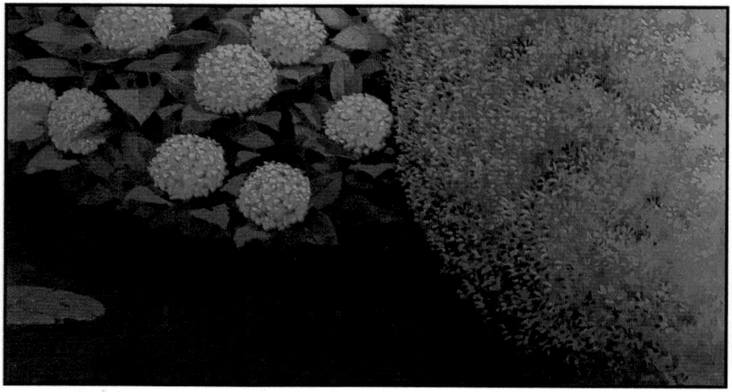

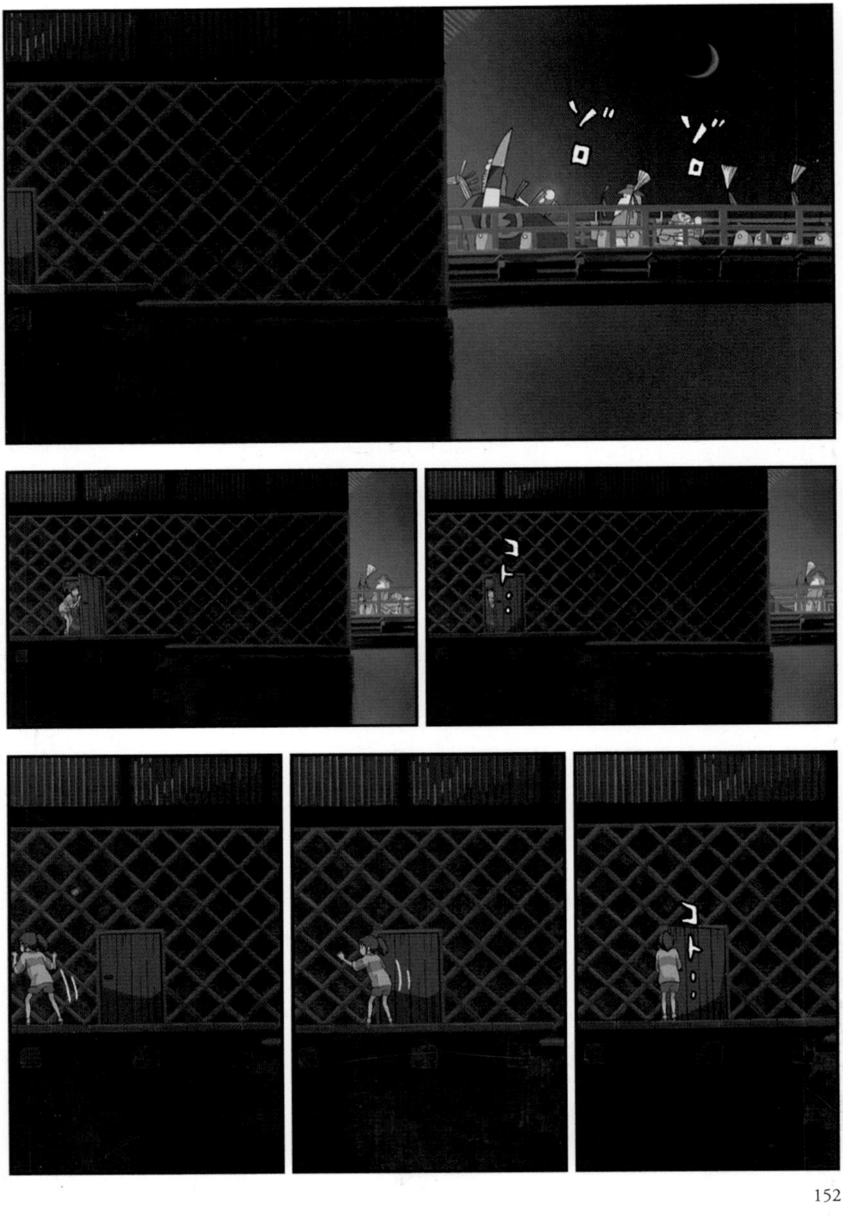
ゾロ
ゾロ
コト・・
コト・・

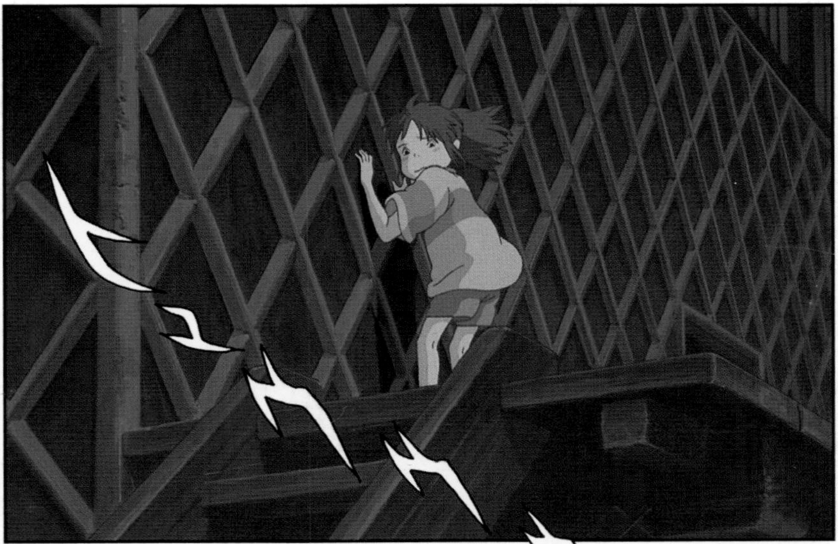
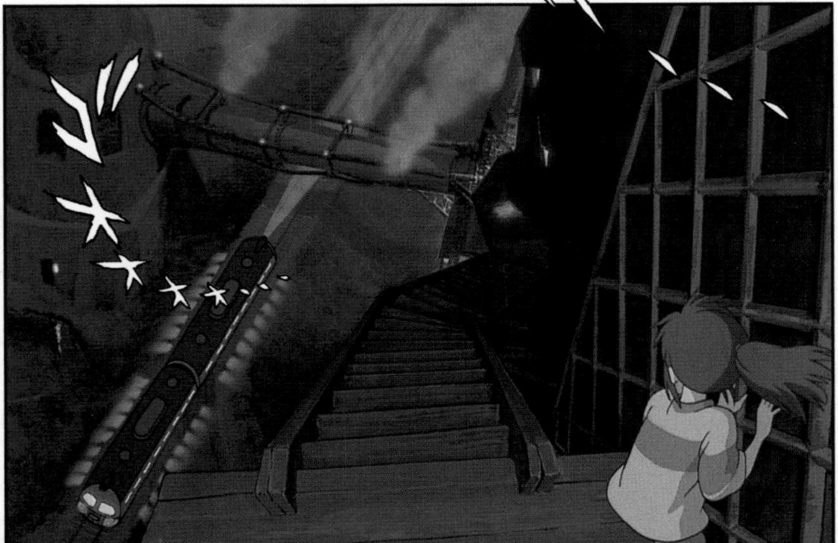
ゴオォォォ

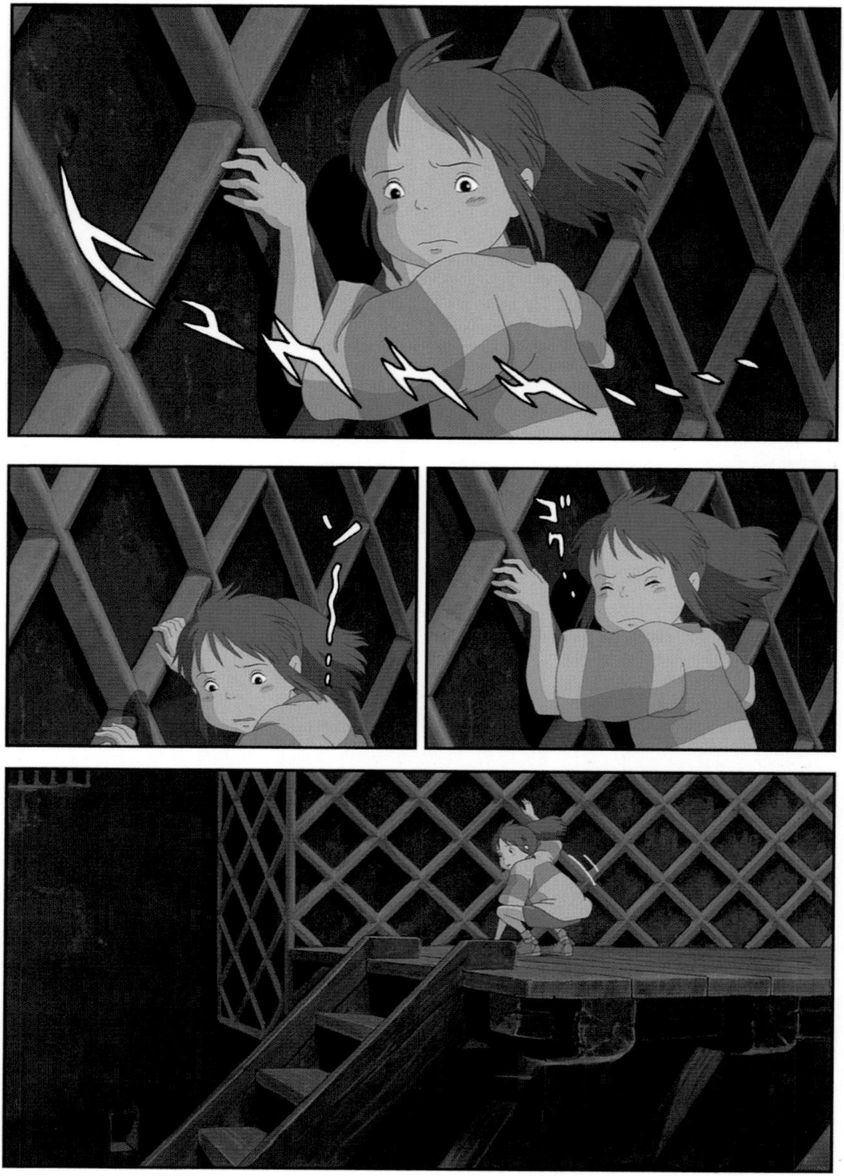
ヒュオオオ……
ゴク・・
ソーー・・・

スッ
AUGH!
ドテ
ドテ

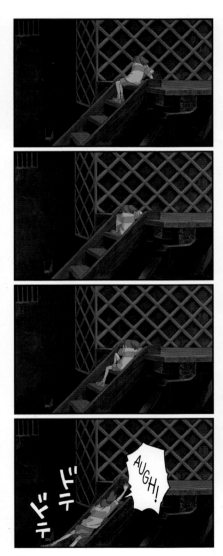

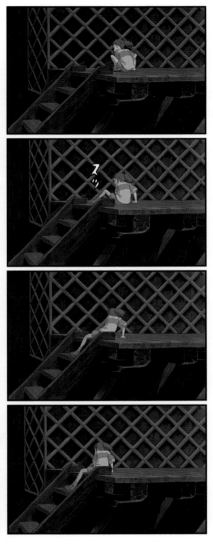

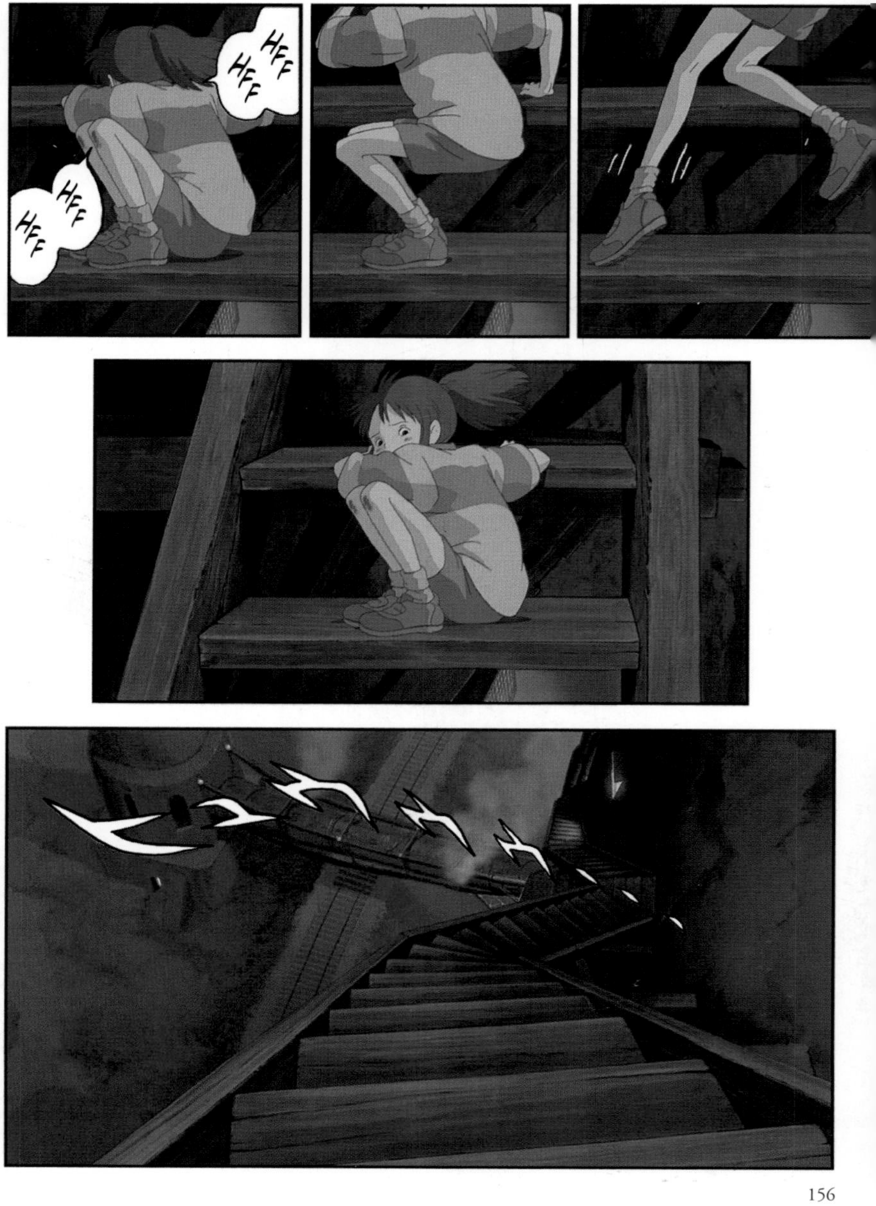
HFF HFF
HFF HFF

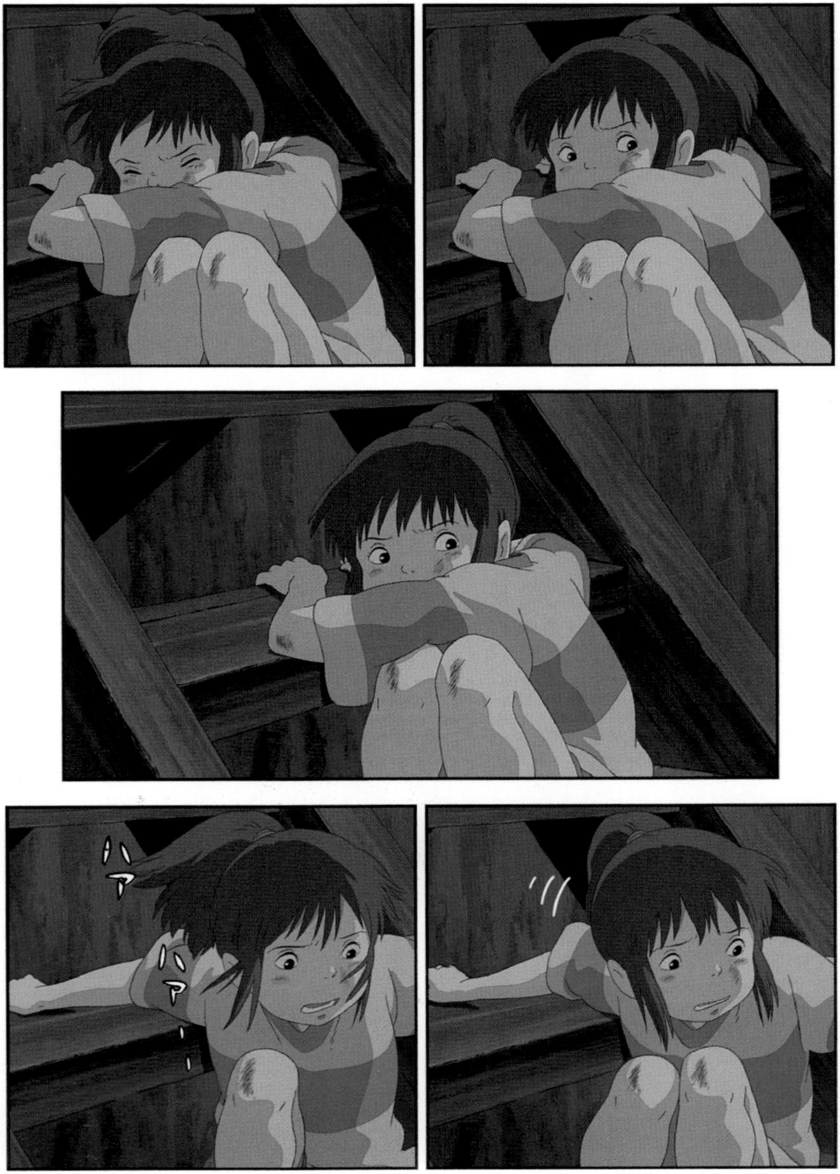
ハァ
ハァ

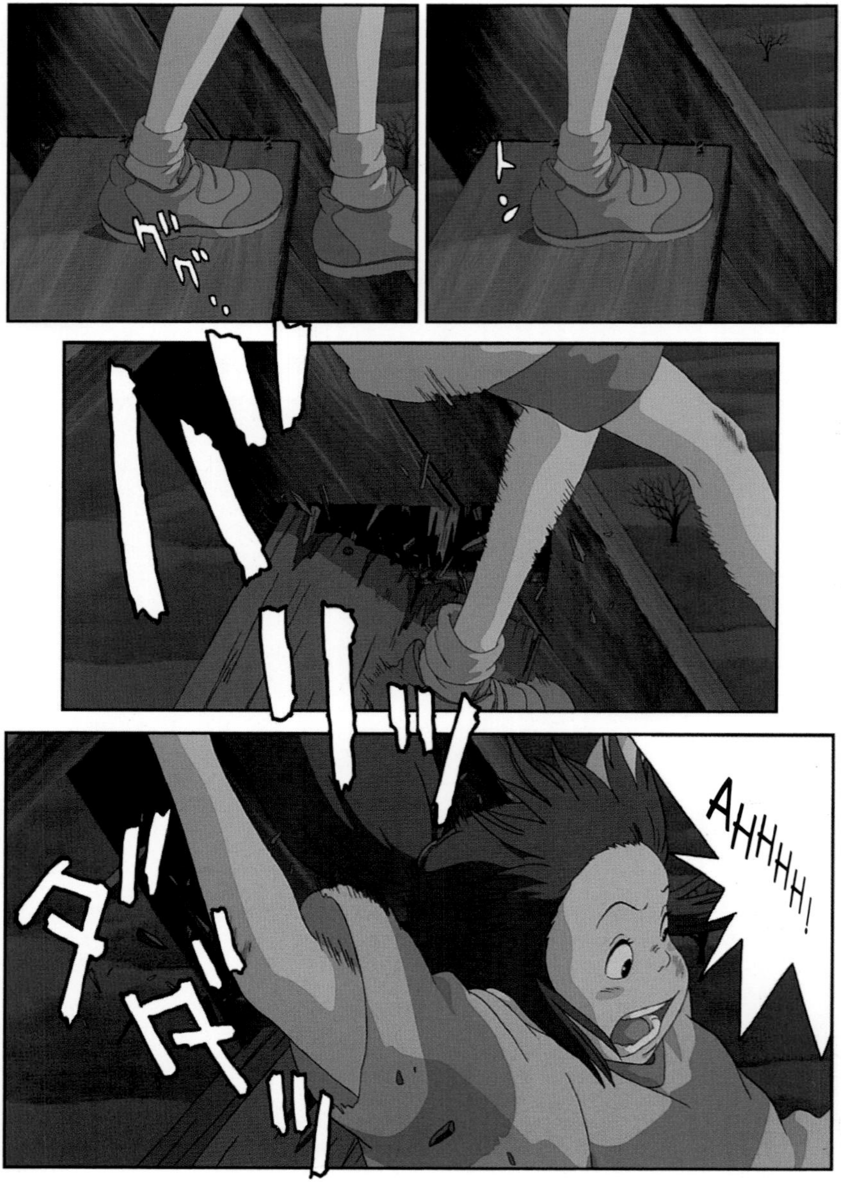
ト..
ググ..
バリーッ
AHHHHH!
ダダッ

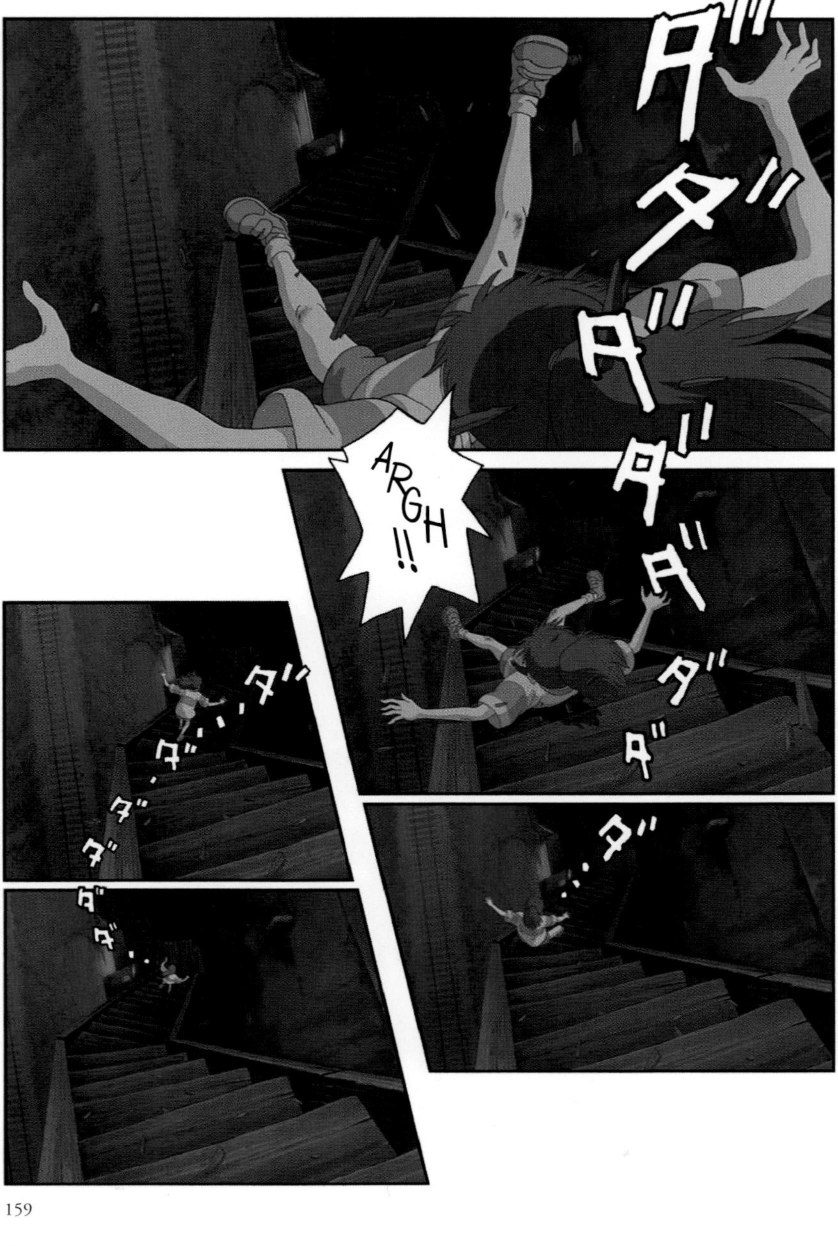
ダダダダダ
ARGH!!
ダダダ
・・ダ
ダ、ダ、ダ、ダ
ダダ・・

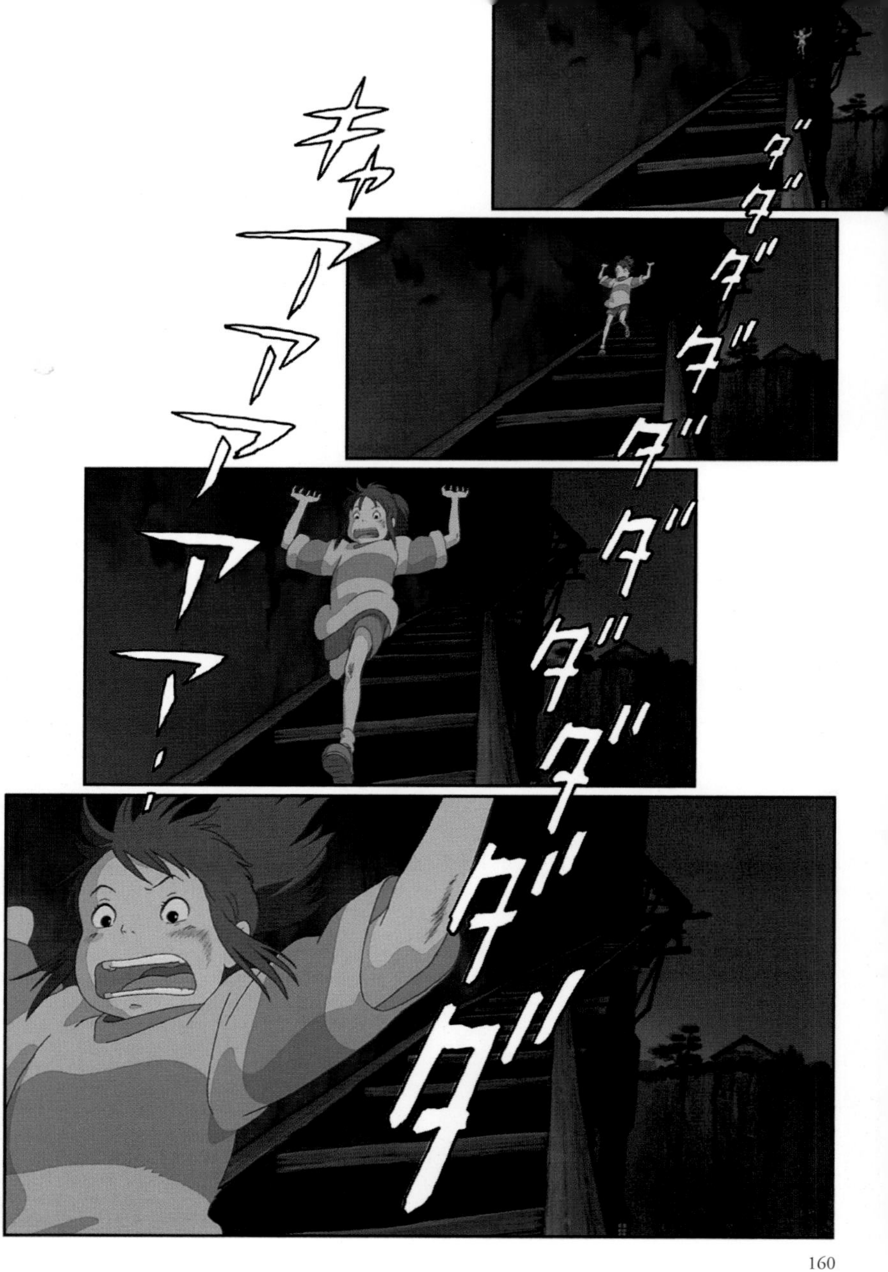
ダダダダダダダダダダ
キャアアアアア!

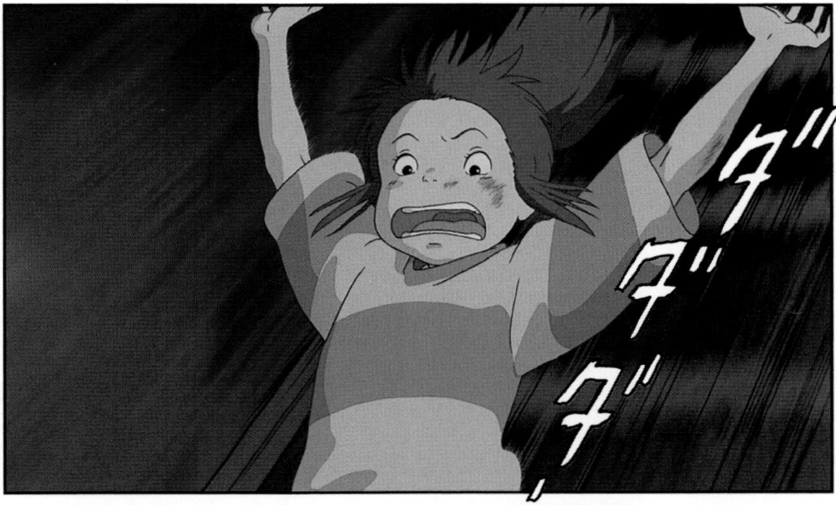
ダッダッダッ
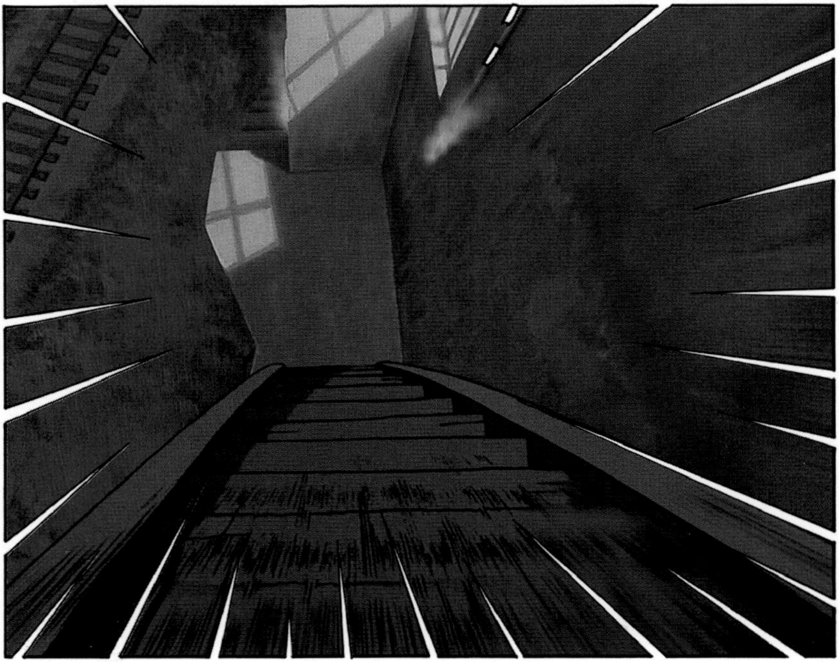

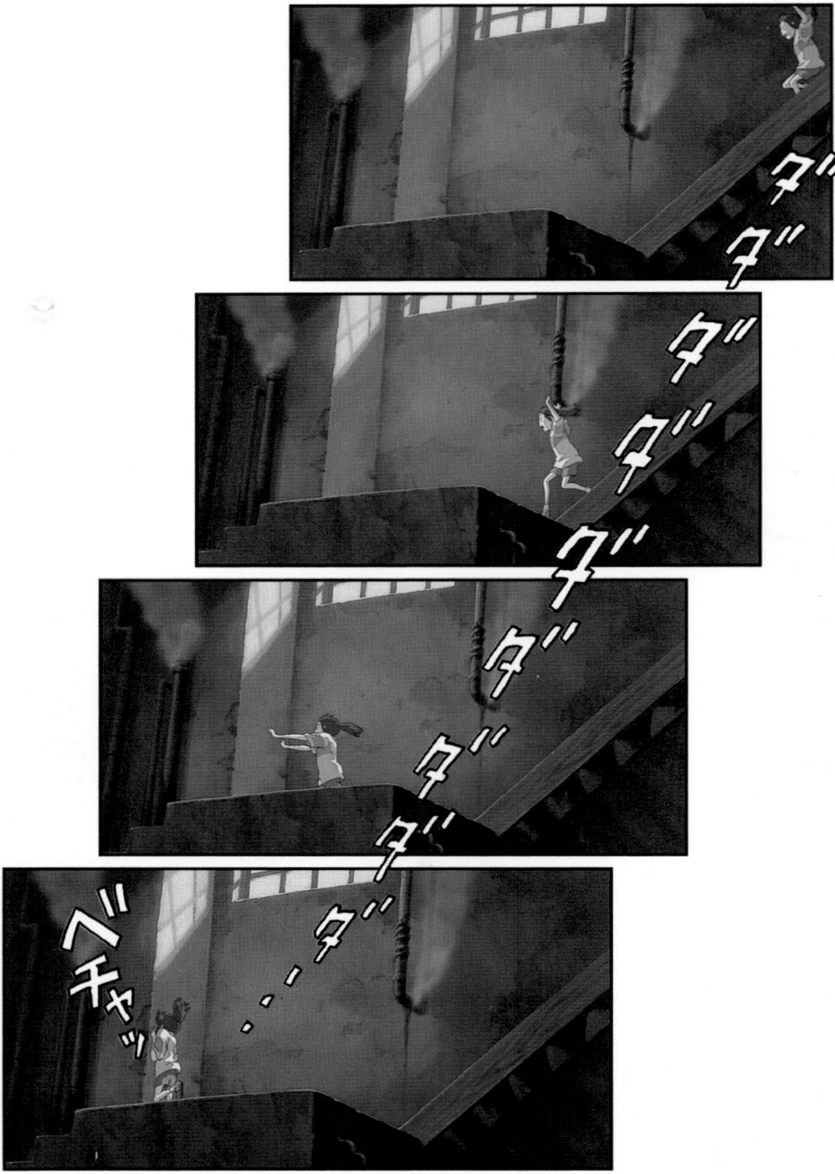
ダダダダダダダダダ…
ベチャッ

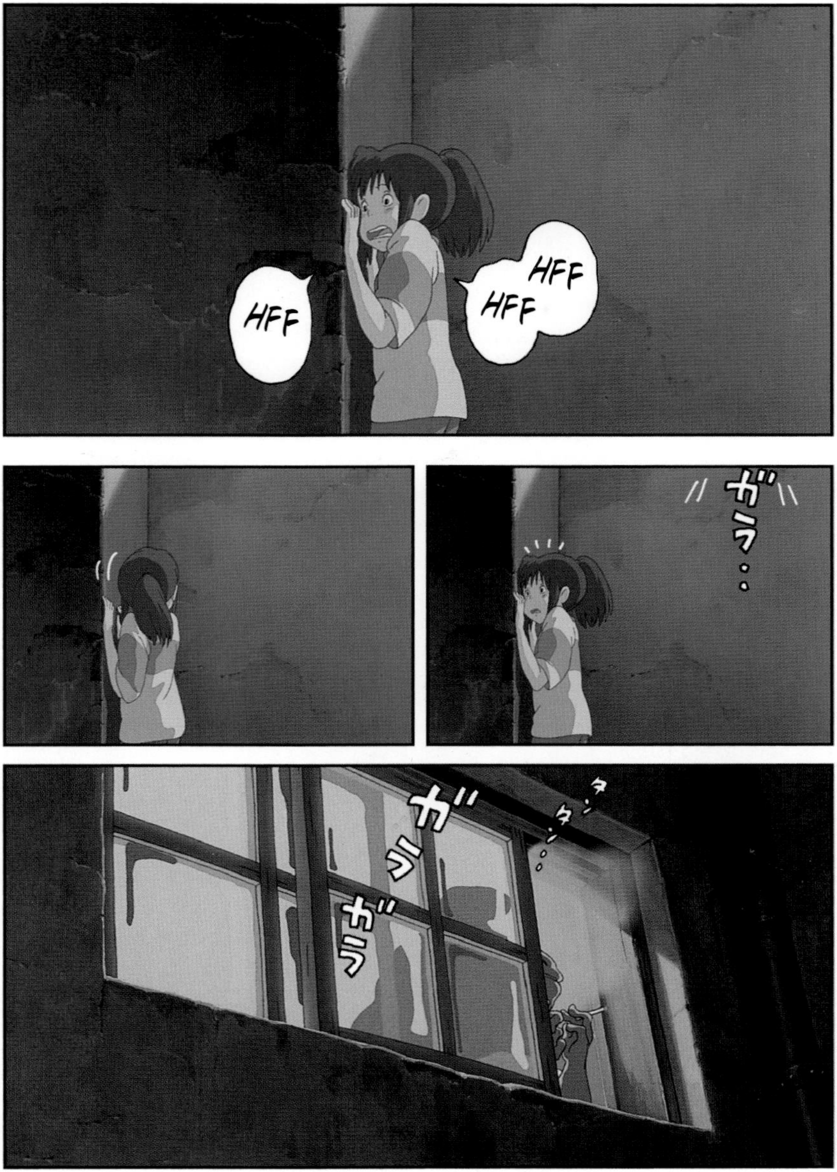
HFF HFF
HFF
ガラ・・
タン タン・・
ガラ
ガラ

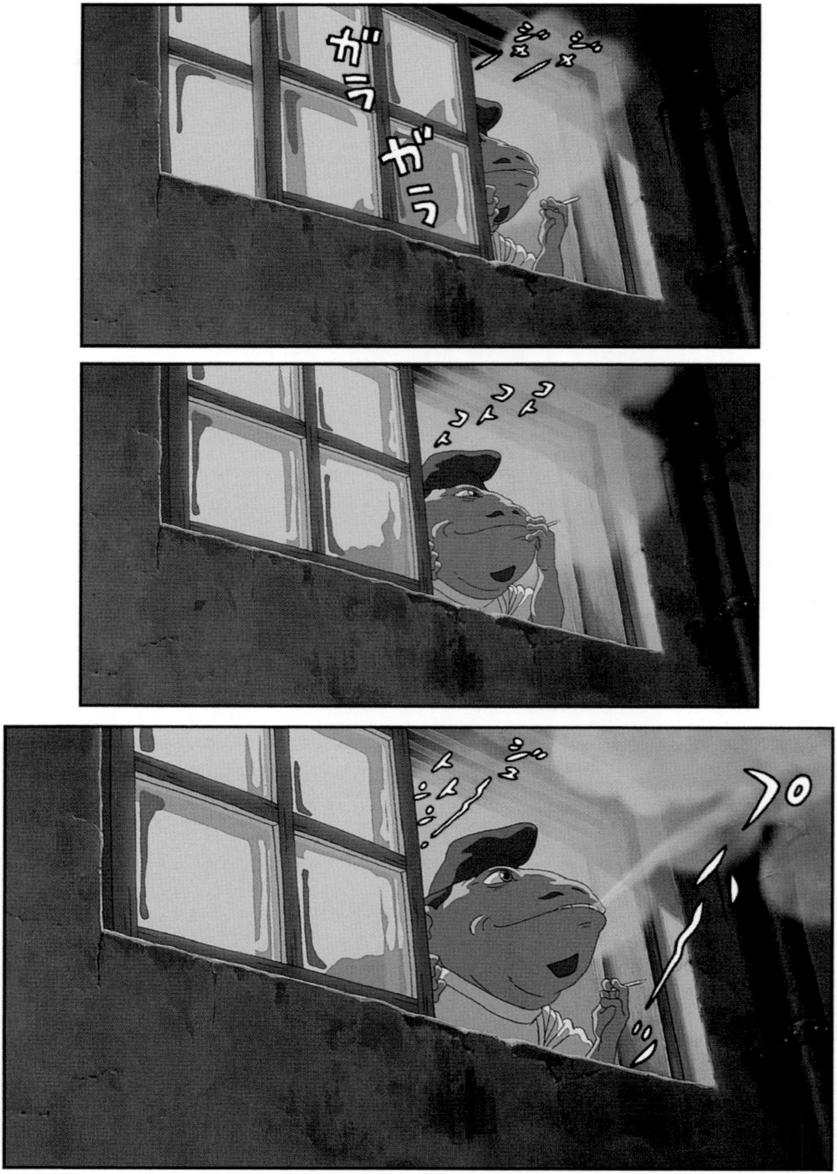
ガラ
ガラ
コトコトコト
プハーッ

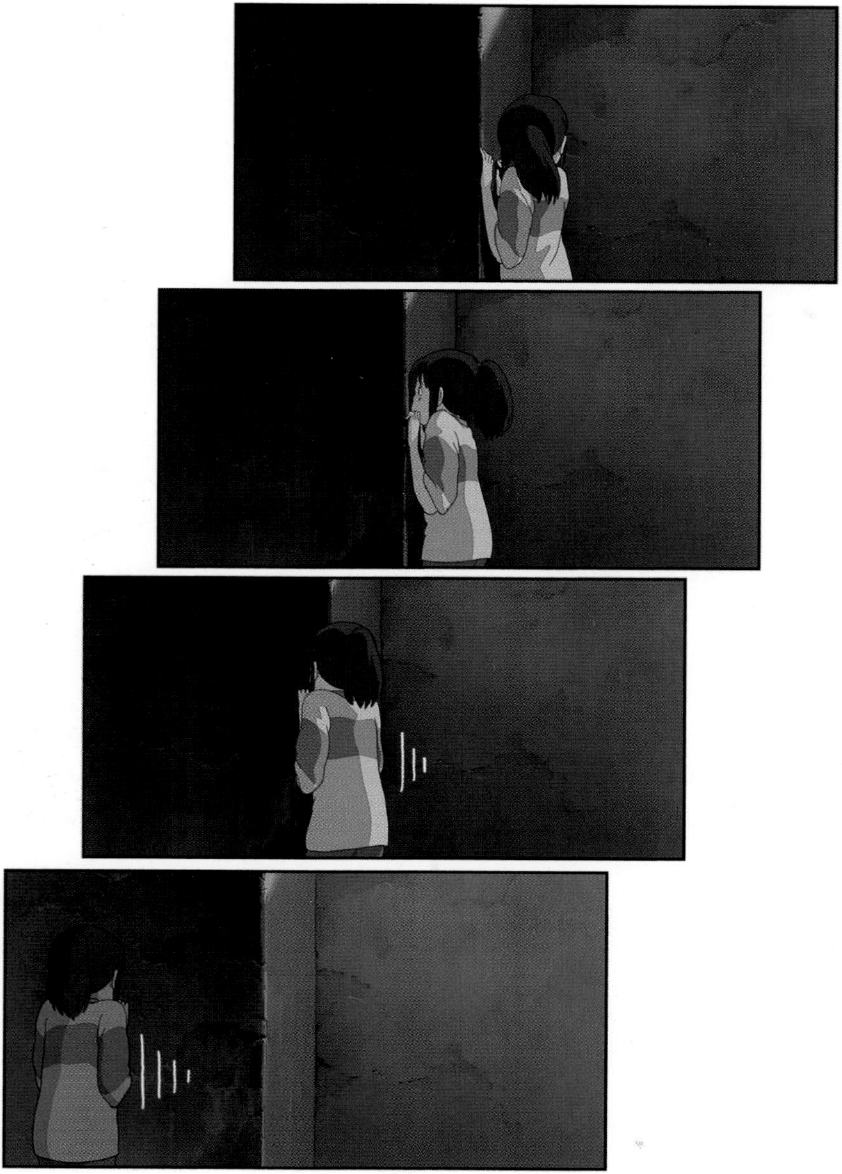

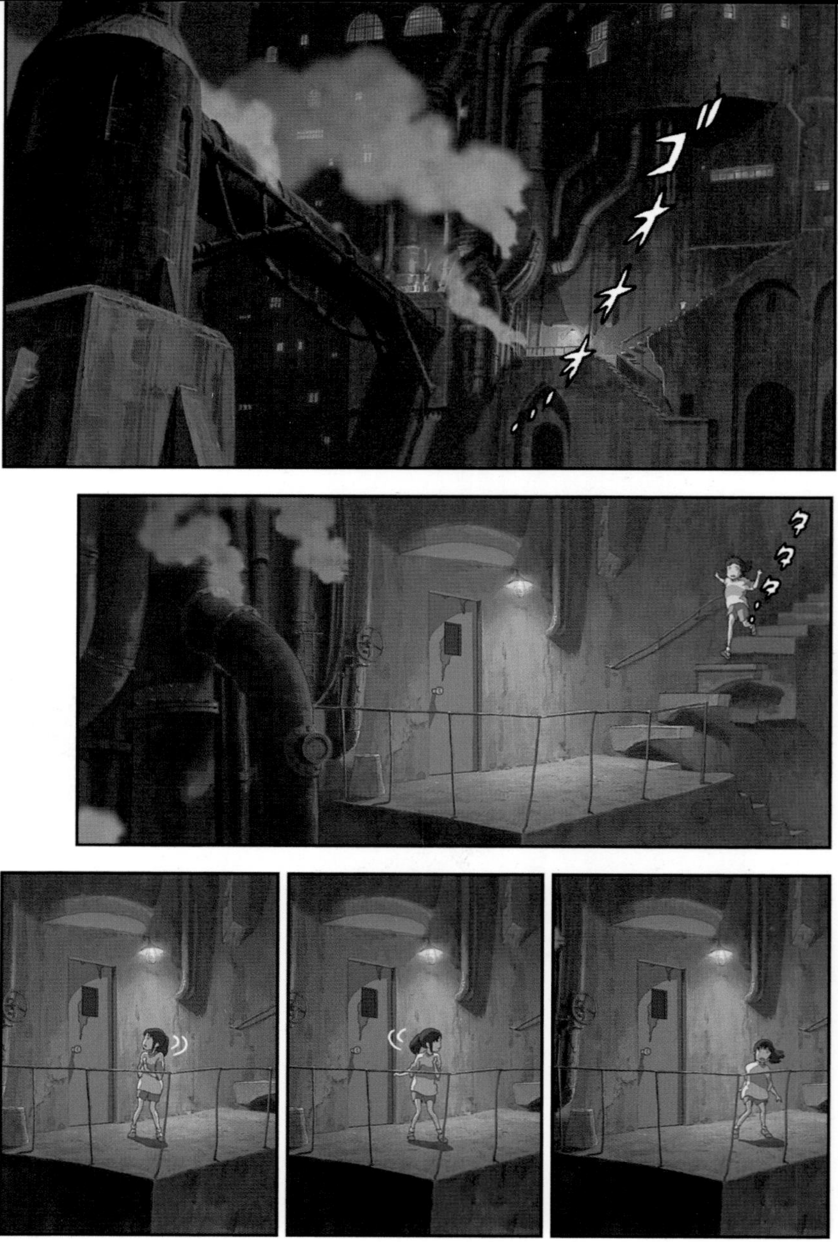
ゴオオオ…
タタタ…

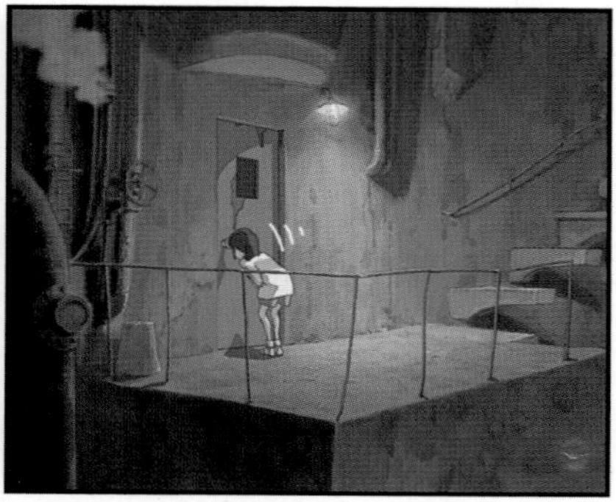

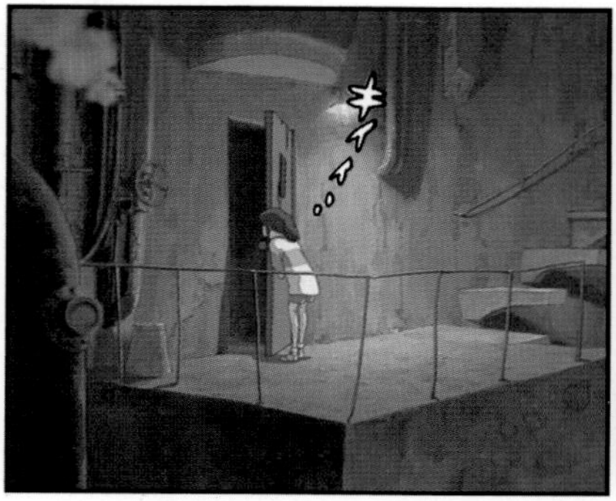

キィィ..

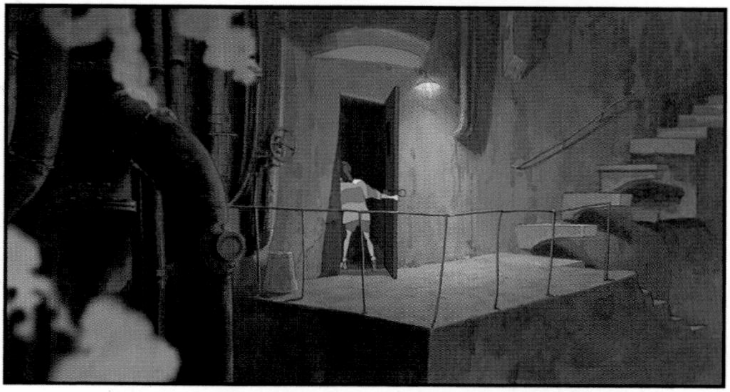

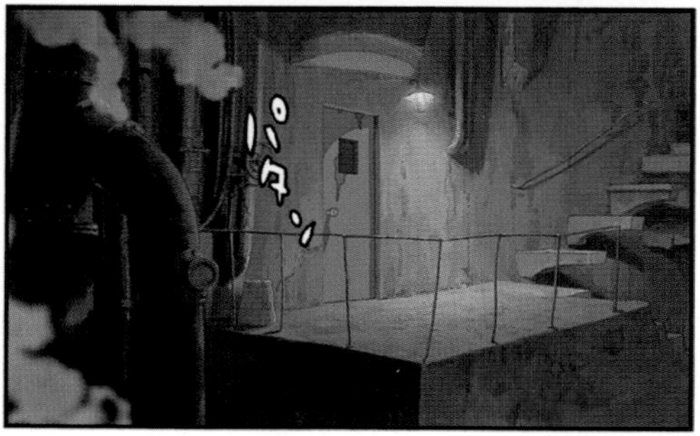

パタ..

TO BE CONTINUED

Your Guide to *Spirited Away* Sound Effects!

To increase your enjoyment of the distinctive Japanese visual style of Spirited Away, we've included a guide to the sound effects used in this manga (comic book) style adaptation of the actual anime (animated) movie. These sound effects are written in the phonetic characters called katakana.

Looking at the very first example, you can see how the sound effects are listed: first, by page and panel number (so 6.1-3 means page 6, going through panels one through three); then, the literally-translated sound spelled out by the katakana (so "FX: BUROROROROOO..." is the sound ブロ ロロロオオ... spells out on page 6, panels 1-3); finally, how this sound effect might have been spelled out, or what it stands for, in English (so [vroooom] is how we might spell out this particular sound, a car engine-you'll be interested to see the different way Japanese describe the sound of things!).

If there are different sound FX in the same panel, an extra number will be added to the index to show them apart; for an example, see 25.2.1 vs. 25.2.2. Remember all numbers are given in the original Japanese reading order: right-to-left.

You'll sometime see a small "tsu" at the end of a sound FX, which looks like this: ツ. This isn't part of the sound itself; it's just a way of showing that the sound is the kind that ends suddenly, rather than the kind that fades out: fades tend to be indicated by two or three dots. You'll also see a mark like a long dash: − . This means that the sound lasts for a while. Sometimes instead of the long dash, extras of the same vowel are used instead; it's the artist's choice. Note that the − and the ツ can be combined!

One last note: the vowels in katakana should be pronounced as they are in Japanese. In Japanese, "A" is ah, "I" is ee, "U" is ooh, "E" is eh, and "O" is oh. Try putting these effects into your style of speaking!

6.1-3	FX:	BUROROROROOO... [vroooom]
8.3-5	FX:	BUROROROOOO... [vrooooom]
8.5	FX:	BEE... ["yuk!"]
10.1	FX:	GABA [fwish]
10.3-5	FX:	BUROROROOOO... [vrooooom]
12.3	FX:	BUWA [fwoosh]
13.1-10	FX:	BUROROROROOOO... [vrooooom]
16.2-4	FX:	BUROROROOO... [vrooooom]
19.1-2	FX:	BUOROROROOO... [vrooooom]

20.1-2	FX:	BUOOOO... [vrooooom]
20.3-4	FX:	BUROROROOOO... [vrooooom]
21.3	FX:	BUROROOO... [vrooooom]
21.4-6	FX:	BUOOOO [vrooooom]
22.1-5	FX:	BUROROROOOOO [vrooooom]
22.1-2	FX:	GATA GATA [thump thump]
22.3	FX:	GATA [thump]
22.3-4	FX:	DOTE [whud]
22.4-5	FX:	GATA [thump]
22.5	FX:	GATA [thump]
23.1-3	FX:	GATA GATA GATA [thumps]
23.4	FX:	GATA GATA GATA [thumps]

24.1	FX:	GATA GATA [thump thump]
24.3	FX:	ZA ZAAAAAA [fsssssssh]
25.1-4	FX:	BUROROOOOO [vrooooom]
25.2.1	FX:	BASHA [plish]
25.2.2	FX:	DOGO [fwoosh]
25.3.1	FX:	BASHA [plish]
25.3.2	FX:	DOGA [fwoosh]
25.4	FX:	GATA GATA GATA [thumps]
26.1-4	FX:	BUOOOOOO [vrooooom]
26.1-2	FX:	BASHI [fwak]
26.2	FX:	BASHI [fwak]
26.3	FX:	BASHI [fwak]
26.4	FX:	BASHI [fwak]
28.3	FX:	DA [foop]
28.4-5	FX:	KIIIIIII [screech]
30.1	FX:	GACHA [chak]
30.3	FX:	BATAN [chnk]
31.1	FX:	GACHA [chak]
31.3	FX:	BATAN [chnk]
31.4	FX:	GASA... [fshh]
31.6	FX:	TA TA TA... [tmp tmp tmp]
32.4	FX:	OOOOO... [fwooooo]
33.1	FX:	KASA... KASA... [fip fip]
33.2	FX:	HYUUU [fweee]
35.3	FX:	DA [tmp]
35.4	FX:	TA TA [tmp tmp]
36.2	FX:	CHIRA ["sound" of a glance]
36.4	FX:	ZOOOO [shiver]
38.1	FX:	CHIRA ["sound" of a glance]
38.2	FX:	DA [tmp]
38.3	FX:	TA TA TA... [tmp tmp tmp]
38.4	FX:	TA TA... [tmp tmp]
38.5	FX:	GU [tug]
39.3	FX:	KATSUN KOTSUN [tok tok]
39.4	FX:	KATSUN KOTSUN [tok tok]
39.5	FX:	KATSUN KOTSUN [tok tok]
41.3.1	FX:	GOOOOO [rrrrrrrrrr]
41.3.2	FX:	GOTON GOTON [klaketta klaketta]
41.4.1	FX:	GOTON [klaketta]
41.4.2	FX:	POTA... POTA... [plip plip]
43.1	FX:	KOTSU KOTSU [tok tok]
43.5	FX:	HYUUUU... [fweeeee]
47.6	FX:	GOOOOO... [whirrrr]
48.1	FX:	OOOOO... [whrrrrr]
48.2	FX:	ZOKU [shiver]
48.3	FX:	BA [fip]
48.4	FX:	TA TA [tmp tmp]
49.1	FX:	TA TA TA... [tmp tmp tmp]

50.3	FX:	SUTA [tup]
51.3	FX:	KUN KUN [sniff sniff]
52.2	FX:	SU [fsh]
52.4	FX:	SU [fsh]
53.2	FX:	BA [fup]
53.4	FX:	TA [tmp]
53.5	FX:	TA TA TA [tmp tmp tmp]
54.3	FX:	KYORO KYORO [hmph hmph]
55.2	FX:	TA TA TA... [tmp tmp tmp]
56.4	FX:	DA [tmp]
56.5	FX:	TA TA TA... [tmp tmp tmp]
61.3	FX:	HYOI... [fwip]
61.4	FX:	BARI... [krunch]
61.5.1	FX:	KOTON [tok]
61.5.2	FX:	MOGU MOGU [chew chew]
62.1	FX:	SU [fsh]
62.2	FX:	PAKU... [mnch]
62.6.1	FX:	PAKU [mnch]
62.6.2	FX:	MOGU [chew]
63.1	FX:	HAGU... [glmp]
63.2	FX:	PAKU [mnch]
63.3	FX:	BA [fip]
63.4	FX:	MOGU MOGU [chew chew]
63.5	FX:	MORI MORI [glmp glmp]
63.6	FX:	PAKU [mnch]
64.1	FX:	KYORO KYORO [fwip fwip]
64.3.1	FX:	PAKU PAKU [mnch mnch]
64.3.2	FX:	BAKU BAKU [glmp glmp]
64.5	FX:	PUI [hmph]
66.3	FX:	CHIRA ["sound" of a glance]
71.3-4	FX:	OOOOO... [whrrrrrr]
71.5	FX:	GOOOOOO [rrrrrrr]
72.2	FX:	DA [tmp]
72.4	FX:	TA [tmp]
74.5	FX:	PO [sound of lamp lit]
75.2	FX:	SA [fsh]
75.3	FX:	TA TA [tmp tmp]
75.5	FX:	TA TA TA [tmp tmp tmp]
76.1.1	FX:	SA [fsh]
76.1.2	FX:	TA TA... [tmp tmp]
76.2.1	FX:	BA [fwoosh]
76.2.2	FX:	TA... [tmp]
76.4	FX:	FU [fwoo]
77.1-2	FX:	TA TA TA... [tmp tmp tmp]
77.3	FX:	JI JI... [buzz buzz]
78.1	FX:	GOSHI GOSHI [rub rub]
78.3	FX:	TA [tmp]
78.4	FX:	TA TA TA... [tmp tmp tmp]

79.2	FX:	TA [tmp]
79.5	FX:	GUI... [tug]
80.1ʹ	FX:	KUCHA KUCHA... [munch munch]
81.1	FX:	SA [startled sound]
81.3	FX:	GON [thmp]
81.4	FX:	GARA... [clack]
81.5.1	FX:	GARA [clack]
81.5.2	FX:	GUSHA [crash]
81.5.3	FX:	GARA [clatter]
82.2	FX:	PISHI PISHI [fwak fwak]
82.3	FX:	FU... [fwip]
83.1	FX:	BUN [fwish]
83.2	FX:	PISHI [fwak]
83.3	FX:	PISHI [whack]
83.4	FX:	GURA... ["tilting" sound]
84.1.1	FX:	ZUZUUUN [whump]
84.1.2	FX:	GARA [clack]
84.2	FX:	GARA... [clatter]
85.2	FX:	ZUZU... [whumm]
85.3	FX:	BA [fwoosh]
85.4	FX:	BUHI BUHI [oink oink]
86.1	FX:	TA TA TA... [tmp tmp tmp]
88.3	FX:	DA [tmp]
88.4.1	FX:	HAA HAA HAA [huff huff huff]
88.4.2	FX:	TA TA TA [tmp tmp tmp]
89.1	FX:	HAA HAA [huff huff]
90.2	FX:	TA TA TA [tmp tmp tmp]
90.3	FX:	TA TA TA... [tmp tmp tmp]
91.1.1	FX:	CHYORO CHYORO... [plish plish]
91.1.2	FX:	TA TA TA... [tmp tmp tmp]
91.2	FX:	TA [tmp]
91.3	FX:	TA TA TA [tmp tmp tmp]
91.4	FX:	BASHA [splash]
91.5	FX:	DOBON [fwosh]
92.1	FX:	BASHA [splash]
92.2	FX:	BASHA [splash]
92.3	FX:	ZABA ZABA [pshh pshh]
92.4	FX:	ZABA... [pshh]
94.2	FX:	GON GON [thok thok]
94.3	FX:	CHIRA ["sound" of a glance]
95.3	FX:	SU... [fsh]
97.2	FX:	SA [fsh]
97.4-5	FX:	ZUZUUUUN... [fwoshh]
97.5	FX:	PATAN PATAN BATAN... [plip plip plip]
98.1	FX:	YURA... [fwom]
98.1-7	FX:	ZAWA ZAWA ZAWA ZAWA ZAWA ZAWA... [vmm vmm vmm vmm vmm vmm]
99.3.1	FX:	DA [tmp]
99.3.2	FX:	ZAWA ZAWA [vmm vmm]
99.4.1	FX:	HAA HAA [hff hff]
99.4.2	FX:	TA TA... [tmp tmp]
99.5	FX:	DOTA... [whud]
99.6	FX:	TA TA... [tmp tmp]
100.1	FX:	TA TA TA... [tmp tmp tmp]
100.4	FX:	TA TA TA... [tmp tmp tmp]
101.1	FX:	KASA [fwich]
101.4	FX:	SO... [fmp]
103.3	FX:	BA [fwish]
105.3	FX:	UGU UGU... [ungh ungh]
105.4	FX:	GOKUN [gulp]
108.3	FX:	SA [fsh]
111.2	FX:	SU [fsh]
112.2	FX:	SUUUU... [fwooo]
113.3	FX:	SU [fip]
113.4	FX:	GU [tug]
113.5	FX:	TA [tmp]
114.1-3	FX:	TA TA TA TA TA TA TA TA... [tmp tmp tmp tmp tmp tmp tmp tmp]
115.1	FX:	TA TA TA... [tmp tmp tmp]
116.1-4	FX:	TA TA TA TA TA [tmp tmp tmp tmp tmp]
116.2	FX:	SA [fsh]
117.1	FX:	KATAN [chak]
117.2	FX:	SU [foop]
117.3-5	FX:	TA TA TA TA TA TA [tmp tmp tmp tmp tmp tmp]
118.1-4	FX:	TA TA TA TA TA TA TA [tmp tmp tmp tmp tmp tmp tmp]
119.2-7	FX:	TA TA TA TA TA TA TA... [tmp tmp tmp tmp tmp tmp tmp tmp]
119.8	FX:	PATAN [slam]
120.1-2	FX:	TA TA TA TA... [tmp tmp tmp tmp]
120.1	FX:	BUHI BUHI BUHI [oink oink oink]
120.3	FX:	BUHI BUHI [oink oink]
121.1-4	FX:	TA TA TA TA TA TA... [tmp tmp tmp tmp tmp tmp tmp]
122.2	FX:	ZORO ZORO ZORO [foom foom foom]
123.1	FX:	KACHA [chak]
123.2	FX:	KIII... [creak]